Edward IV

The Sun in Splendour

David Bret

Copyright David Bret 2022

David Bret has asserted his moral right as the Author of this Work in accordance with the Copyright and Patents Act 1988.

All rights reserved. No part of this publication may be reproduced or transmitted in any form or by any means, electronic or manual, including photocopying, recording or any information storage or retrieval system, without the prior permission in writing by David Bret.

A catalogue record for this book is available from the British Library.

ISBN: 9798412574448

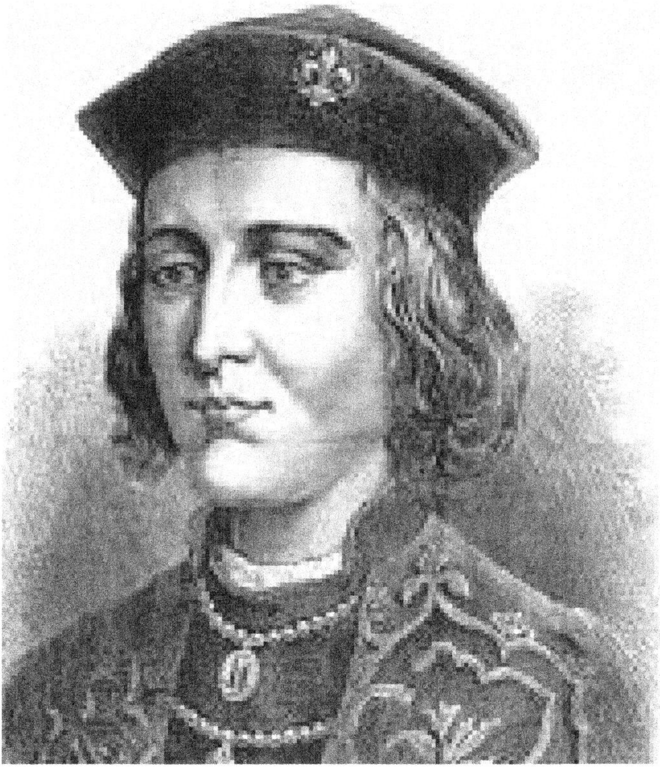

Table of Contents

Lineage: The House of York
        The Nevilles
        The Woodvilles

Preface	8
1: The Rise of Anjou & The Fall of Suffolk: 1443-1454	13
2: St Albans & Its Aftermath: 1455-6	25
3: Blore Heath, John Dynham & The Rout of Ludlow: 1456-9	34
4: Exile In Calais: 1459-60	46
5: The Yorkists' Return & The Battle of Northampton: 1460	58
6: Disaster At Wakefield: 1460	65
7: The Sun In Splendour: Mortimer's Cross & St Albans II: 1461	76
8: Edward IV: Triumph At Towton: 1461	91
9: The Welsh & Northumbria Campaigns: 1461-2	102
10: Edward & Somerset: 1463-4	119
11: Edward & Elizabeth Woodville: 1464	128
12: Edward & The Woodvilles/ Warwick & Charolais: 1465-6	140
13: The Burgundian Alliance: 1466-8	152
14: The Northern Rebellions & Edgecott: 1468-9	170
15: Edward's Apprehension: The Lincolnshire & Exeter Rebellions: 1469-1470	182
16: Edward's Flight & The Re-Adeption of Henry VI: 1470-1	195
17: Edward's Return & The Battle of Barnet: 1471	209

18: The Battle of Tewkesbury & The Death of Henry VI: 1471	221
19: The Second Reign: Rewards, Pardons & Punishments: 1471-4	234
20: The French Invasion: 1474-5	250
21: Edward's Lifestyle & Character/ The Death of Charles of Burgundy: 1475-7	268
22: The Downfall of Clarence: 1477-8	281
23: The Scottish Invasion & The Fading Sun of York: April 1478-April 1482	294
Bibliography	313
Index	328

Illustrations:

Henry VI
Margaret of Anjou
Blore Heath
Mortimer's Cross
Edward IV as a young man
Towton
Elizabeth Woodville
Charles the Bold, Duke of Burgundy
Margaret of York
Antoine, Bastard of Burgundy
Edward IV in later life
Margaret of Anjou
Anne Neville and her husbands
Louis XI of France
Edward's tomb at Windsor

The House of York

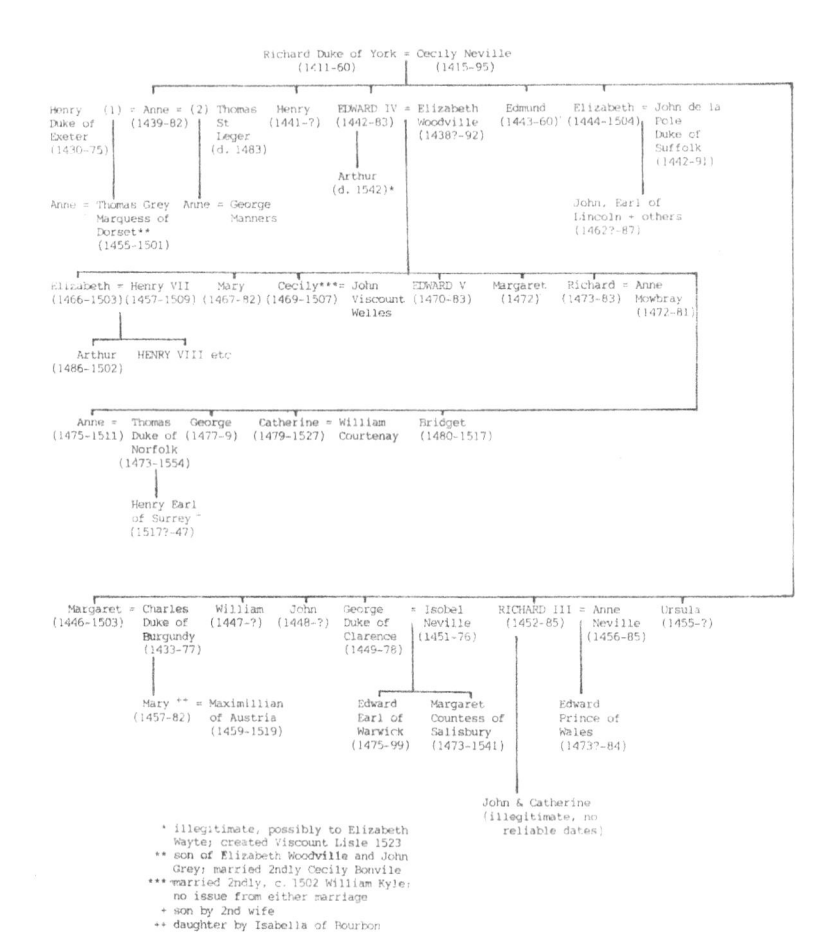

```
                              Richard Duke of York = Cecily Neville
                                    (1411-60)         (1415-95)
┌──────────────────┬──────────────┬──────────────┬──────────────────────┐
Henry   (1) = Anne = (2) Thomas  Henry   EDWARD IV = Elizabeth   Edmund      Elizabeth = John de la
Duke of      (1439-82)   St      (1441-?) (1442-83)  Woodville   (1443-60)   (1444-1504)  Pole
Exeter                   Leger                      (1438?-92)                            Duke of
(1430-75)               (d. 1483)                                                         Suffolk
                                         Arthur                                           (1442-91)
                                         (d. 1542)*
Anne = Thomas Grey  Anne = George                                          John, Earl of
       Marquess of         Manners                                         Lincoln + others
       Dorset**                                                            (1462?-87)
       (1455-1501)
┌──────────┬──────────┬──────────┬──────────┬──────────┬──────────┐
Elizabeth = Henry VII   Mary    Cecily***= John   EDWARD V   Margaret   Richard = Anne
(1466-1503)(1457-1509)(1467-82)(1469-1507) Viscount (1470-83) (1472)   (1473-83) Mowbray
                                           Welles                                (1472-81)
┌──────────┐
Arthur    HENRY VIII etc
(1486-1502)

┌──────────┬──────────┬──────────────┬──────────┐
Anne =   Thomas    George    Catherine = William   Bridget
(1475-1511) Duke of (1477-9) (1479-1527) Courtenay (1480-1517)
         Norfolk
         (1473-1554)
         │
         Henry Earl
         of Surrey
         (1517?-47)

Margaret = Charles   William   John    George  * Isobel    RICHARD III = Anne     Ursula
(1446-1503) Duke of  (1447-?) (1448-?) Duke of   Neville   (1452-85)   | Neville  (1455-?)
           Burgundy                    Clarence  (1451-76)             | (1456-85)
           (1433-77)                   (1449-78)
           │
           Mary ** = Maximillian    Edward      Margaret         Edward
           (1457-82) of Austria     Earl of     Countess of      Prince of
                     (1459-1519)    Warwick     Salisbury        Wales
                                    (1475-99)   (1473-1541)      (1473?-84)
                                                                 │
                                                                 John & Catherine
                                                                 (illegitimate, no
                                                                 reliable dates)
```

  * illegitimate, possibly to Elizabeth
    Wayte; created Viscount Lisle 1523
 ** son of Elizabeth Woodville and John
    Grey; married 2ndly Cecily Bonvile
*** married 2ndly, c. 1502 William Kyle:
    no issue from either marriage
  + son by 2nd wife
 ++ daughter by Isabella of Bourbon

The Nevilles

THE NEVILLES

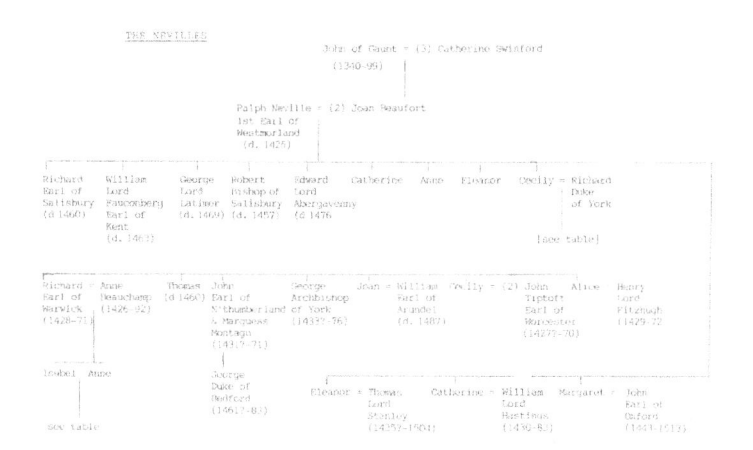

John of Gaunt = (3) Catherine Swinford
(1340-99)

Ralph Neville = (2) Joan Beaufort
1st Earl of
Westmorland
(d. 1425)

- Richard, Earl of Salisbury (d. 1460)
- William, Lord Fauconberg, Earl of Kent (d. 1463)
- George, Lord Latimer (d. 1469)
- Robert, Bishop of Salisbury (d. 1457)
- Edward, Lord Abergavenny (d. 1476)
- Catherine
- Anne
- Eleanor
- Cecily = Richard Duke of York [see table]

Children of Richard, Earl of Salisbury:
- Richard, Earl of Warwick (1428-71) = Anne Beauchamp (1426-92)
- Thomas (d 1460)
- John, Earl of Northumberland & Marquess Montagu (1431?-71)
- George, Archbishop of York (1432?-76)
- Joan = William, Earl of Arundel (d. 1487)
- Cecily = (2) John Tiptoft, Earl of Worcester (1427?-70)
- Alice
- Henry, Lord Fitzhugh (1429-72)

Children of Richard, Earl of Warwick:
- Isobel
- Anne

Child of John:
- George, Duke of Bedford (1461?-83)

Children of Cecily:
- Eleanor = Thomas, Lord Stanley (1435?-1504)
- Catherine = William, Lord Hastings (1430-83)
- Margaret = John, Earl of Oxford (1443-1513)

See table

The Woodvilles

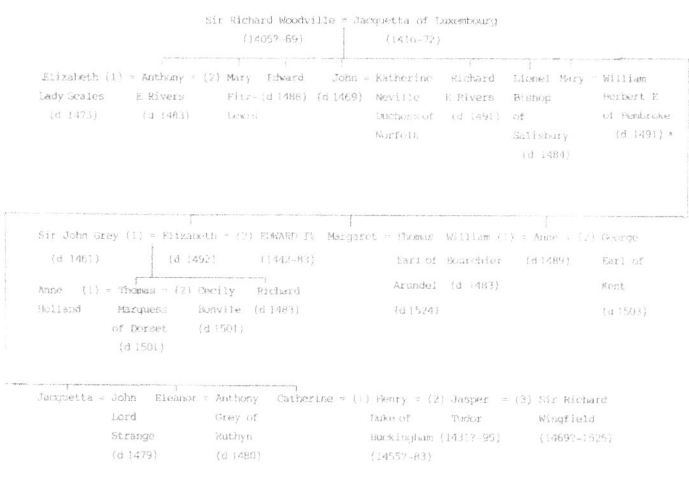

Sir Richard Woodville = Jacquetta of Luxembourg
(1405?-69)   (1416-72)

- Elizabeth (1) = Anthony = (2) Mary Fitz- Lewis (d 1488)
  Lady Scales   E Rivers
  (d 1473)   (d 1483)
- Edward (d 1469)
- John = Katherine Neville, Duchess of Norfolk
- Richard E Rivers (d 1491)
- Lionel, Bishop of Salisbury (d 1484)
- Mary = William Herbert E of Pembroke (d 1491)*

Children of Elizabeth:
- Sir John Grey (1) = Elizabeth = (2) EDWARD IV
  (d 1461)   (d 1492)   (1442-83)
- Margaret = Thomas, Earl of Arundel (d 1483)
- William (†) (d 1489)
- Anne = (2) George, Earl of Kent (d 1503)

Children:
- Anne (1) = Thomas Marquess of Dorset (d 1501) = (2) Cecily Bonville (d 1483)
- Richard (d 1524)

Grandchildren:
- Jacquetta = John, Lord Strange (d 1479)
- Eleanor = Anthony Grey of Ruthyn (d 1480)
- Catherine = (1) Henry, Duke of Buckingham (1453?-95) = (2) Jasper Tudor (1455?-83) = (3) Sir Richard Wingfield (1469?-1525)

* In 1484 Herbert married Catherine, illegitimate daughter of Richard III

Preface

The term "Wars of the Roses" first came into common usage in 1829 with the publication of Sir Walter Scott's *Anne of Geierstein*, which tells of the Swiss involvement in the Burgundian Wars in the wake of the battle of Tewkesbury. Scott had based the name on a scene in Shakespeare's *Henry VI Part 1* where, in the Temple Church Gardens, noblemen choose white or red roses to decide which faction—York or Lancaster—they will support. Otherwise, the civil conflicts were mostly referred to as "The Cousins' Wars", owing to the fact that almost all of the major protagonists were related to each other in some way. While the white rose *was* used as a symbol by the Yorkists, the red rose of Lancaster is not thought to have been introduced until after the battle of Bosworth. Neither did the rival factions have much in the way of connection with the cities of Lancaster and York. The Lancastrian lands and offices were mainly in Cheshire, North Wales and Gloucestershire, while those of the Yorkists were evenly spread throughout England and the Welsh Marches.

Edward III of England and Philippa of Hainault had thirteen children, among them five sons who reached adulthood. All five entered into arranged marriages with powerful English heiresses, as a result of which the first English dukedoms were created: Lancaster, Gloucester, Clarence, Cornwall and York. All of the descendants of these dukes would at some stage of their careers put in claims for the throne.

The eldest son of Edward III—Edward, the Black Prince—died in June 1376, and the king himself died one year later and was succeeded by his ten-year old grandson, the Black Prince's son, who became Richard II. Childless, Richard named Roger Mortimer, 4th Earl of March, as his heir presumptive, but Mortimer died in 1398. The throne was usurped the following year by Henry Bolingbroke, Richard's cousin, who became Henry IV—a move which saw a by-passing of the normal line of succession, and which would eventually result in the Wars of the Roses.

Henry Bolingbroke established the House of Lancaster, and the English throne remained relatively secure until his death in 1413, when he was succeeded by his son Henry V, arguably the greatest of the English warrior kings and one who enjoyed immense popularity on account of his triumphs over the French during the Hundred Years War (1337-1453). Problems—political, social and financial—came about as a result of his unexpected demise in 1422, aged just thirty-five, when the throne was inherited by his nine-month old son, Henry VI.

There had been one notable insurrection mounted against Henry V: the Southampton Plot of 1415, led by Richard, Earl of Cambridge, a son of Edward III's fourth son, Edmund of Langley. Cambridge had been subsequently apprehended and executed at the start of the campaign which led to the battle at Agincourt. His wife was Anne Mortimer, a descendant of Lionel of Antwerp—Edward III's second son. *Their* son was Richard Duke of York, the father of the future Edward IV, whose right to the throne during the early years of Henry VI was, he believed, far stronger than that of any Lancastrian claimant in that *he* was descended from *two* of Edward III's sons—Lionel of Antwerp and Edmund of Langley—while Henry was descended from just one, the king's third son, John of Gaunt. The time was ripe, therefore, to take advantage of Henry's minority and the fierce and bloody squabbles over his Protectorship.

Edward IV has always been overshadowed by his controversial younger brother, Richard III. Such was his reputation that he is often most remembered for his pursuit of pleasure—the archetypal medieval playboy. There was considerably more to him than this. During the first half of his reign, he was an astute military technician, almost on a par with Henry V. He never lost a battle. Edward was a big man, extremely courageous, and a level-headed strategist. He was a personal, approachable monarch, revered and respected by his subjects. The second half of his reign finds him entirely different. With his Treasury solvent after being stretched to the limit financing the quelling of a decade's civil unrest, and with England enjoying a peace marred only by the murky intrigues of his brother, Clarence, Edward found himself at liberty to indulge in his fancies. He lived, loved, and spent more extravagantly more than any king before him. Though devoted to his queen, Elizabeth Woodville, he played the field—there were hundreds of women, and at least one male lover. He threw lavish parties which were the talk of Europe, and sadly ate himself into an early grave, dying while still in his prime, and leaving England to face the most chaotic phase in its history thus far, and with its greatest mystery: the Princes in the Tower.

Henry VI

Margaret of Anjou

1

The Rise of Anjou & The Fall of Suffolk
1443-1454

When the future Edward IV was born in Rouen on 28 April 1442, his father the Duke of York held the appointment of the King's Lieutenant-General, in France. The child's mother was Cecily Neville, the youngest of the Earl of Westmoreland's twenty-three children. [1]

Edward was Cecily's third child, but only surviving son this far. York was the biggest landowner in all England, possessing vast estates in Ireland and Wales. He was ham-fisted, stubborn and generally disliked by the royal court, though his military achievements were second to none. He had campaigned successfully in France, and commanded much respect from the lower classes. York seems initially to have preferred living in France. He was constantly in debt—his chief rival during his French expedition of 1441 had been John Beaufort, the present Duke of Somerset's brother who died in 1444, and a grandson of John of Gaunt by his mistress, Catherine Roet, whom he had subsequently married. Somerset had prevented York from getting vital supplies in 1441 by leading an expedition of his own. This was an abject failure, and York returned to England very much against his will, pawning his jewels and plate in order to see himself through.

Besides being contrary, York was essentially a man who liked to keep up appearances: short of funds or not, he lived his whole life in opulent surroundings. His principal seat was Fotheringay Castle, some eighty miles north of London: it was a gloomy place which achieved infamy in 1587 when Mary Queen of Scots was beheaded there. York's secondary seat was Ludlow, the Marcher fortress near the Welsh border, which he had inherited from the Mortimers. Close by was another favoured residence, Wigmore Castle. A major seat in the north of England was Sandal Castle, near Wakefield. Each of these strongholds would play a major role in the Wars of the Roses.

Immediately after the Parliament of 1447, King Henry VI's uncle, Humphrey of Gloucester, died suddenly:

> He was arrested by Viscount Beaumont, Constable of England, who accompanied the Duke of Buckingham and many other lords. Thirty-two of his servants were also arrested and sent into diverse prisons. Five days after his arrest the Duke was dead...but how he died in unknown, but to God. Some said he died of sorrow; some said that he was murdered between two feather-beds; some said he was thrust into the bowel with a hot burning spit...but no wound can be perceived upon him. His corpse was conveyed to Saint Albans...and five persons of his household staff were hanged, drawn and quartered. [2]

As Gloucester had died without issue, York's claim to the

throne was suitably strengthened, so long as Henry VI did not beget any heirs. The king's closest male heir was the Duke of Exeter. [4] Edmund Beaufort should have been heir-presumptive, but a supplement to a royal act of Parliament declared that the Beaufort family should be excluded from any claim to the throne. York himself was a direct descendant of Edmund of Langley, the younger brother of John of Gaunt and the fourth surviving son of Edward III, so his claim was as good as any. He had adopted the surname Plantagenet in about 1450. [4]

If one is to consider the *female* line of descent, it may be said that York had a stronger claim to the throne than the king himself. His mother was Anne Mortimer, which means that besides being descended from Edmund of Langley, he was descended from Lionel, Duke of Clarence, Edward III's *second* son. Inheriting his mother's lands gave York much of his political clout—this and the fact that he had entered the arranged marriage with Cecily Neville in 1424 when he had been thirteen, and she four years younger. Theirs appears to have been a happy marriage, and the duchess bore him twelve children. Two sons became kings by way of usurpation: one of these and another son died in battle. A fourth perished in the Tower of London. Four more sons and a daughter did not survive infancy. The other daughters married men of importance. Anne (1439-82) firstly married Henry Holland, Duke of Exeter, and secondly Sir Thomas St Leger—Anne's daughter from this first marriage married Edward IV's stepson, Sir Thomas Grey. Elizabeth (1444-1504) married John de la Pole, Duke of Suffolk—their son, John Earl of Lincoln, was nominated by Richard III as his heir. Cecily's third daughter, Margaret, married Charles the Bold, Duke of Burgundy. She would remain Edward IV's favourite sister, though later in life he saw precious little of her.

Suffolk secured for his king the unlikeliest of brides in Margaret of Anjou. Early in 1444 he had led an embassy to France, concluded a two-year truce, and arranged the betrothal in Tours. Margaret came to England without a dowry, landing at Portsmouth in April 1445. Henry is said to have met her dressed as a squire, with Suffolk, offering her a letter which he claimed had been penned by the King of England—a sly move which may or may not have had some bearing on her later attitude towards him. [5] She was escorted to the Tower of London, where she spent the night preparing for her coronation. The next day, 30 May, she was taken to St Paul's in a carriage drawn by two horses trapped in white damask powdered with gold, and crowned. Somerset and Gloucester were in attendance, the latter virulently opposed to the match. There seems little doubt that their attitude towards the new queen contributed towards their imminent downfall.

Margaret had been born on 23 March 1429: the youngest surviving daughter of René Comte d'Anjou and Isabelle de Lorraine, and as such a niece of the French king. Her father had inherited Anjou, Provence, and the Duchy of Bar, and Lorraine was his through marriage. He had also inherited claims to be King of Naples, Hungary and Sicily.

For a time, René had been held prisoner by the Duke of Burgundy, and often he and Isabelle had gone off on some campaign, leaving their daughter to be looked after by her grandmother, Yolande of Aragon. Yolande was Regent of Anjou, from whom Margaret probably inherited many of her less-endearing characteristics. If Suffolk was hoping that her marriage would bring an end to the Anglo-French troubles which were crippling the country's finances, he would be grossly mistaken. Even at sixteen, Margaret was starting to show some of the traits which would become her trademark: in turn she could be spirited, bad-tempered, prejudiced, foul-mouthed, level-headed, courageous, wanton, and psychotically ambitious. The chroniclers almost unanimously describe her as a great beauty.

To such a creature, Henry VI must have appeared as a decidedly bad joke played upon her by a vengeful Suffolk intent on getting his own back on the French. If Margaret was expecting a lusty, muscular monarch with whom to share her marital bed, she must have been sorely and cruelly disappointed. Henry was weak, spineless, absurdly over-pious, disinterested in matters of state, and did not even look like a king.

England had sunk into a bottomless pit of bankruptcy and corruption, headed by Suffolk's government—yet Henry was stupidly benevolent, giving away vast amounts of money and actually *blessing* wrongdoers rather than punish them. From a personal point, sex horrified him, even within marriage. If intercourse did take place, which is doubtful when one considers the king's almost saintly mien, it must have been with great reluctance on Henry's part. He was even advised against the act of 'having his sport' by his confessor, the Bishop of Salisbury. [6] For a full-blooded young woman of Margaret's calibre and breeding, this must have been painfully frustrating. Her husband's celibacy drove her further into the depths of despair, and there seems little wonder why she soon developed a taste for the obvious machismo of some of the more handsome lords which surrounded her at court. In time she would use these, and her feminine wiles, to great advantage in an attempt to rid England of its anarchic state. Unfortunately, in doing so, she would only make matters worse.

In the autumn of 1445, the Duke of York returned to England, and his son Edward was sent to live at Ludlow. York's lieutenancy of France had expired: the office was given to Edmund Beaufort, who in 1448 would be created Duke of Somerset. To soften the blow, in 1447 York was appointed Lieutenant of Ireland, an office he may have been reluctant to accept, for he did not arrive in Ireland until 6 July 1449. On 21 October of that year, Duchess Cecily gave birth to her ninth child in Dublin Castle: he was baptised George, and later became Duke of Clarence. York enjoyed great popularity in Ireland, but still believed that he had been cheated of his heritage by the court faction, and he was naturally homesick.

Meanwhile, back in England the pot was coming to the boil. Richard Neville had married Anne, the daughter of Richard Beauchamp, Earl of Warwick, in 1434. Beauchamp had died in 1439, and the earldom had been inherited by Anne's brother, Henry. Henry died unexpectedly in 1447, leaving his vast estates and enormous wealth to his four-year old daughter. The child had died, and Richard Neville was created Earl of Warwick in his wife's name in July 1449. Thus he became first earl of the realm with immense holdings in Sussex, Hampshire, Essex, Cambridgeshire, Warwickshire, Nottinghamshire, Devon, Yorkshire, Northamptonshire, Kent, Herefordshire, Oxfordshire, Rutland, Staffordshire, Norfolk, Cornwall, Berkshire, Hertfordshire, Wiltshire and South Wales. He also owned Barnard Castle and Middleham, in the 'extreme north'. [7]

For the time being, Warwick and York played little part in the massive upheaval taking place in England. The new queen had to find her footing. An Aragon mercenary, Francois de Surienne, was paid by Suffolk and Somerset to attack the Breton town of Fougeres, contravening the Anglo-French truce. Somerset was not disciplined, probably because Margaret of Anjou was already his mistress, and Suffolk made an impromptu speech when Parliament convened on 22 January 1450, which did little to appease their loathing of him. Within three days, the government was demanding his head. Margaret intervened, and sentence of death was commuted to one of five years' banishment. Soon afterwards, the ship transporting Suffolk across the Dover Straits, the *Nicholas of the Tower*, was attacked by unnamed assailants and he was made to step into a small boat, where his head was cut off with six strokes of a rusty sword. Two of Suffolk's supporters did not go unpunished.

The Bishop of Chichester was murdered by a mob at Portsmouth. The king's confessor, the Bishop of Salisbury, was lynched while conducting mass at a village church in Wiltshire.

In June 1450, King Henry was in Leicester when he was informed of an insurrection in London, involving forty-six protesters gathered outside Blackheath:

> And when these lords [the King's] came to their Captain named Jack Cade, otherwise Mortimer, cousin to the Duke of York as the said Captain names himself, he said he and his people were common to redress many points whereby the King's subjects and commons were grievously wronged; but his final purpose was to rob, as after it shall appear. Wherefore it was agreed that Sir Humphrey and William Stafford should follow the case. At Sevenoaks in Kent they met and fought with the said Captain…and with many others were slain. [8]

The city was held for four days, with much bloodshed, and there was a fierce battle at London Bridge, where Cade set fire to the drawbridge and let the rabble out of the prisons. Typically, Henry granted him a pardon which did Cade little good. Tracked down, he was put to death in Sussex: the corpse was brought back to London, beheaded and quartered, and the head set upon London Bridge alongside those of twenty-one others.

York returned to England in the September, hoping to take his rightful place amongst the King's Council. He was suspicious that Margaret might persuade Henry into naming Somerset as his heir-presumptive, therefore he joined forces with his brother-in-law the Duke of Norfolk and the Earl of Salisbury in an attempt to impeach Somerset of treason, and assert his own power behind the throne. This failed, and despite his enormous rise in popularity York was forced to return to Ireland.

Early in 1452, York supplemented his demands for Somerset's removal by taking up arms. Warwick and Salisbury met with Parliament: it was agreed that if York called a truce, Somerset would be relinquished of his offices. Margaret virulently opposed this—clearly, she was in love with the man. York was captured and held to ransom until he agreed to stand at St Paul's Cross and publicly swear allegiance to her. Warwick and Salisbury, similarly humiliated, returned to their estates where they calmly awaited York's call-to-arms.

King Henry was at Clarendon, his hunting-lodge in Wiltshire, when in August 1453 he suffered what appears to have been complete mental breakdown. His November Parliament was deferred until the New Year, by which time everyone hoped he might have recovered. He did not emerge from his stupor until the end of 1454, by which time matters were truly out of hand and his condition had become public knowledge. Henceforth he would be branded a lunatic.

On 15 October at Westminster, Queen Margaret gave birth to her only child, a son who was baptised Edward. For reasons already explained, the child is unlikely to have been sired by Henry, with two lustier men heading the suspected paternity list: Somerset, and the equally handsome royal favourite, the Earl of Wiltshire. [9] For obvious reasons, the father's name never became public knowledge. If Henry had *not* been sleeping with his wife, his saintly principles would not have precipitated him to confront Margaret with adultery—though it was perfectly acceptable for kings to sleep around indiscriminately and sire bastards which were acknowledged with all the privileges befitting their parenthood, Henry would never have permitted his son to suffer the indignity of being recognised as a royal bastard, brought about by his mother's adultery.

Somerset's influence and power was on the wane. He was arrested and imprisoned in the autumn of 1453. In the December, Warwick was appointed a member of the Royal Council, and the horizon darkened with the gathering war-clouds. The deferred Parliament met again in February 1454, and the Duke of York triumphantly entered London with his twelve-year old son, Edward. Warwick sent a thousand armed men to escort them: the city was said to have ben overjoyed.

The 1454 Parliament was faced with the dilemma of admitting that their sovereign was insane. Attendances were low: for the first time, peers who abstained were fined. Margaret demanded that she be appointed Regent, and Parliament sent out a deputation to ask the king's advice on this. Warwick was included among the examining committee, and reported back that Henry was in a trance, and immobile. Margaret was snubbed. In April, Warwick appointed his father, Salisbury, Lord Chancellor. The Duke of York was appointed Protector of the Realm.

Then, one of Henry's 'miracles' happened. Shortly before Christmas he regained his sanity. Somerset was released from prison, and York was relieved of his Protectorship. Even so, with Somerset's position weakened, York was riding the crest of a wave. His extensive estates up and down the country enabled him to draw more supporters than even the queen thought possible...many of the peerage were squabbling amongst themselves, and saw that much would be gained, monetarily, by supporting the rebel duke. The bitterest fight of all was taking place between the Earls of Salisbury and Northumberland: Henry Percy was Hotspur's son and had married Salisbury's sister, and practically every landowner in England was drawn into the affray. And Salisbury's son, of course, was Warwick!

It is a great pity that no contemporary portrait of Warwick exists. None of the chronicles describe what he looked like, and his character is not always easy to assess. His military ability was unequalled: he was an able commander on land and sea, and was especially popular amongst the men of Kent. He was extremely extroverted, extravagant and kind to those willing to follow his orders and idiosyncrasies to the letter—ruthless to anyone who dared oppose him. Virtually nothing is known of his early years. He favoured the cold, desolate North of England to the stench and iniquity of the London streets, and adored Middleham, in Yorkshire, where he had received much of his harsh military training. Difficulties only stimulated him.

Warwick was determined to save England, and save her he would, though his greed and aggression would eventually destroy

NOTES

1. Westmoreland married twice. Cecily (1415-95) was from his second marriage to Joan Beaufort. Salisbury was her brother. Three other brothers married heiresses to become Lords Abervagenny, Fauconberg and Latimer. Her sisters included the Duchesses of Buckingham and Norfolk.
2. *Chronicles of England*: Vitellius A XVI, *f.*106ro.
3. Henry Holland, Duke of Exeter (1430-75). His grandmother was Henry IV's sister. He married York's daughter Anne in 1447, and they were divorced in 1472.
4. Lander: *Conflict & Stability In 15th Century England.*
5. John Blacman's Memoirs.
6. Storey: *The End of The House of Lancaster*.
7. Richard Neville, Earl of Warwick (1428-71), known as 'Kingmaker'. Henry VI knighted him in 1446 and appointed him joint Warden of the Marches for putting to rights the border scuffles which had resulted since England's truce with the Scots.
8. Vitellius A XVI, *f.*106ro.
9. James Butler, 5th Earl of Ormonde (1420-61), created Earl of Wiltshire in 1449, while his father was still alive. His second wife was Edmund Somerset's daughter, but he left no issue and the earldom lapsed with him.

2

St Albans & Its Aftermath
1455-1456

During the Spring of 1455, Warwick's spies informed him that his enemy, Somerset, was arranging a highly-secretive Council meeting, to be held in Leicester at the end of May. In all honesty, the king was probably hoping for a truce between York and Somerset, but as he was king in name only, his word carried no weight at all and none of the Yorkist lords were invited to attend. Warwick was incensed. He sent word to his father, Salisbury, at Middleham—and to the Duke of York, who had quietly retreated to Sandal. Other messages were dispatched to Warwick's estates: he set up his headquarters at Warwick Castle, and bided his time while watching his army take shape.

By mid-May, Warwick was marching eastwards across the Midlands with over a thousand men. He met up with York and Salisbury on Ermine Street, and was not surprised to find York's son, Edward, marching at his father's side, more than keen to join in with whatever action might take place. Edward, at thirteen, was already a man. He was about six-feet tall, broad-shouldered, very strong, and utterly fearless. Queen Margaret's party, meanwhile, had left London en route for Leicester. With her with Somerset and Wiltshire, Northumberland and Dorset, Lords Clifford and

Dudley, and many other peers of the realm. [1]

The Lancastrian army was said to be a massive one, and with King Henry reported to be in its midst...Margaret had not trusted to leaving him behind because his head, apparently, was still in the clouds.

The Duke of York sent out a message of appeal to the king: he did not wish to seize the throne, but merely wished that the loathsome Somerset might be ousted and tried for his crimes of misgovernment and treachery. This was promptly ignored, and the Yorkists assumed that it was Somerset's intention to march around them and head for Leicester: his army was advancing up Watling Street, but when it came a halt at Watford, on the evening of 21 May, York became suspicious and sent a second message to the king. This too was ignored.

It now became apparent that Somerset was making for St Albans, some twenty miles hence of London. The Yorkist forces, now swelled to around three-thousand, made a frantic dash for the town. Somerset arrived first, at around seven in the morning, and immediately barricaded his army within the market-place—a long, wide street with many openings. He was ill-prepared to do battle, and may have been alarmed at such a prospect, particularly while the simple-minded king was in his charge. The Yorkists drew up in the lush meadows on the eastern outskirts of the town at roughly the same time, and yet another appeal was sent to Henry, now ensconced in St Peter's Street:

> Please it to your Majesty Royal, to deliver up such as we will accuse. This done, you to be worshipped

> as a most rightful King. We will not rest until we have them, or else we therefore to die!

The response, written by Somerset, bore King Henry's seal, though doubtless not for one moment was York fooled:

> I shall destroy them, every mother's son! Rather than they shall have any lord that here is with me, I shall this day myself live and die! [2]

The Yorkists took umbrage: there was little to do but fight, or die branded as cowards. Between the numerous appeals, their number had risen to 5.000, and though medieval reports on the sizes of armies are renowned for their gross inaccuracy, allowing for discrepancies the Yorkist army probably outnumbered Somerset's by at least two-to-one, while additional troops had been brought in by Sir Robert Ogle and Lord Clinton. [3] [4]

The paltry Lancastrian barricades could not keep the Yorkists out: they entered the town via the poorly-defended, thousand yards long Town Ditch. Many of its strategic points had been left unguarded during the lengthy swapping of messages, and in any case Somerset's soldiers had not expected to fight. Thus the royal army was taken by surprise, and began fleeing in every direction, only to be blocked off and cut down by the Yorkist soldiers manning the escape-points. Most of the fighting was concentrated in the area surrounding the market-place, and the battle lasted only thirty minutes with men pressed together like sardines, hacking and stabbing at each other from the neck up, while

Warwick's archers let off lethal showers of arrows from close range. And at St Albans, his soon-to-be-famous battle-cry was first heard:

"Spare the common men! Kill the leaders!"

Considering the limited fighting-space, losses were low on both sides. The Yorkists lost Sir Robert Ogle, the Lancastrian lost Northumberland, Clifford, and Sir Richard Harrington. The royal favourite, Somerset, was axed to death towards the end of the battle, while attempting to hide at an inn. Dorset, Dudley and Buckingham were badly wounded but managed to escape, and according to the chronicle the unspeakably vain Earl of Wiltshire fled the field disguised as a monk, 'For he was afraid of losing beauty.' King Henry had almost done everyone a favour by absent-mindedly wandering into the path of a stray arrow—wounded in the neck, he had been safely escorted to a nearby tanner's cottage. After the battle, a somewhat humble Duke of York was taken to see him: he went down on his knees and craved forgiveness. Naturally, pardon was granted. Then the three victorious Yorkist lords escorted Henry to the abbey, where prayers were said for the dead.

The next day, the Yorkists marched into London, Warwick carrying the victor's banner emblazoned with his famous Bear and Ragged Staff. Behind him, sandwiched between Salisbury and York, rode the king. The battle had achieved little, other than that Somerset was no more and Queen Margaret had been albeit temporarily stripped of authority.

York and Warwick were now supreme in power after the king, and there followed an act of great pretence: the Yorkists were apparently so rueful over what had just happened in the streets of St Albans that not only had they sworn undying allegiance to Henry, they had agreed to pay for masses for the souls of the slain Lancastrian lords. They could afford to be generous: Somerset's offices had been divided between them. Warwick was also now Captain of Calais, one of the most illustrious offices in England, and York was Constable.

The queen, however, had no intention of resting on her laurels, and her party very quickly made up for the lords it had lost. Somerset had three sons, the eldest of which stepped into his father's shoes. Henry Beaufort was just nineteen, and appears to have suffered from some sort of bipolar disorder. He would soon prove as hostile and violent as his father. **[5]** There was a new Lord Clifford and a new Earl of Northumberland. **[6]** Sir John Wenlock, who had survived St Albans and who had formerly been Margaret's Chamberlain, did not join her just yet—for the time being he gave every impression that his loyalties lay with the other side, though when Parliament convened in July 1455, the Commons elected him as their Speaker. **[7]**

After St Albans, the queen's hatred of the Duke of York reached manic proportion, while the sons and brothers of her slain lords thirsted for Yorkist blood. King Henry became mad again in October 1455: though this period of insanity would only last until February 1456, Parliament was not to know this, and on 19 November York once more became Protector.

Warwick, meanwhile, was having problems with the captaincy of Calais. The garrison was being held by the dead Somerset's deputies, who steadfastly refused to acknowledge Warwick's authority: on assuming command, the earl had inherited a massive bill for unpaid wages, and the men were on the verge of revolt. Warwick submitted a plea to Parliament and arrangements were made to offer security to the Staplers of Calais—the wages bill, a staggering £50,000, was settled. In April, the town government surrendered to Warwick's representative, though the earl himself elected to stay in England, aware that his military services would soon be required again.

Towards the end of 1455, in Devon, there occurred an event of indirect significance so far as York's son, Edward of March, was concerned. The Courtenays had been terrorising the West Country for over a year, when a dispute occurred between Thomas Courtenay, Earl of Devon, and Lord Bonvile of Shute. [8] It has been suggested that the problem began as a family squabble over a dog, but as the Courtenays were Lancastrian and Bonvile staunchly Yorkist, it must have gone deeper than this. On 23 October, Devon's son, Thomas, rode to Upcott with a band of thugs to interrogate a man named Nicholas Radford—who was in the invidious position of being Sir Thomas Courtenay's godfather, but also a friend of Bonvile. The interrogation took place, after which Radford was murdered, and his house fired. During the subsequent enquiry, it was revealed that Radford's assailants had used false names. A few days after the murder, Devon and his sons assembled an army in

Tiverton, and marched on Exeter, holding the city until the week before Christmas. Lord Bonvile had taken refuge here: the citizens offered him protection—not because they were on the Yorkists' side, but because they were afraid of the Courtenays. Some of them attempted, but failed, to besiege the Courtenays' seat, at Powderham Castle. Bonvile eventually managed to get out of Exeter. He fled to Greenwich, where he flung himself on King Henry's mercy.

One of Lord Bonvile's friends at the time of his plight was John Dynham, who must have surveyed the attempted siege of Powderham with some interest from his garden at Nutwell, his house on the opposite side of the Exe. Indeed, he may have even organised the siege. **[9]** Dynham's father, Sir John Dynham, had always been an ardent Lancastrian: father and son had clashed frequently over their opposing loyalties. **[10]** His son may not yet have been known to the Yorkists, but within a short time would figure among Edward of March's closest friends and prove a trusted, life-long adherent. Indeed, John Dynham may be said to have almost single-handedly saved the Yorkist cause.

NOTES

1. Henry Percy, 2nd Earl of Northumberland (1394-1455). Thomas, 8th Lord Clifford (1414-55), hereditary Sheriff of Westmoreland.
2. *Paston Letters I*, pp 325-6. *Parl. V*, pp 280-2.
3. The account of the battle, in the Archives de la Cote d'Or, Dijon, was written 27 May 1455.
4. John, 5th Lord Clinton (1410-64).
5. Henry, 3rd Duke of Somerset (1436-64). He fought at St Albans, was appointed Captain of Calais, and was executed after the Battle of Hexham. He never married, was almost certainly homosexual, but left an illegitimate son, Charles, born 1460 and created Earl of Worcester in 1514.
6. John, 9th Lord Clifford (1435-61), killed at Ferrybridge.
7. Sir John Wenlock (c1400-71). Chamberlain, 1450. Lord Wenlock, 1461. He was killed at Tewkesbury and left no issue.
8. Thomas Courtenay, Earl of Devon (1432-61), executed after Towton. Sir William Bonvile (1393-1461), executed after St Albans II. His illegitimate daughter, Anne, married Roger Dynham.
9. For notes on John Dynham V, see Chapter Three.
10. Sir John Dynham IV (1406-58), active in York's efforts to oust Somerset in 1452 before changing sides.

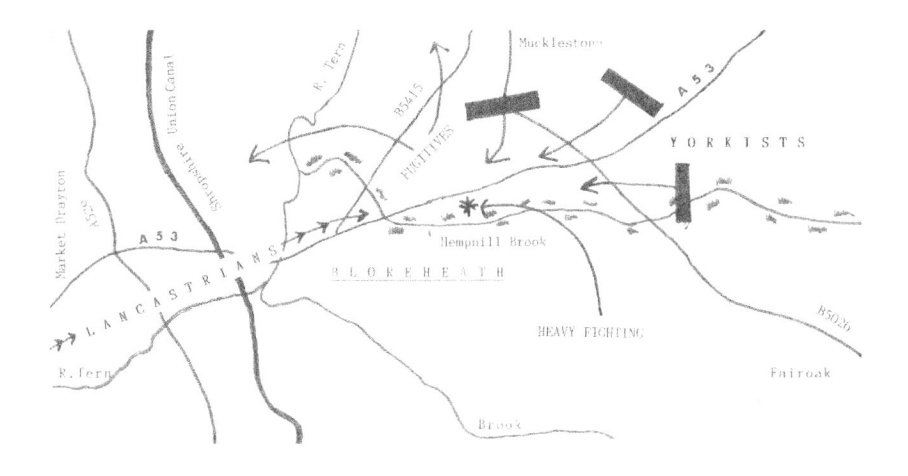

The Battle of Blore Heath
23 September 1459

3

Blore Heath, John Dynham & The Rout of Ludlow
1456-1459

In the Spring of 1956, Queen Margaret took the infant Prince Edward to her manor at Tutbury, and a few weeks later King Henry was dispatched to Coventry. With him was Jasper Tudor, Earl of Pembroke. [1] Salisbury had been discharged of the Chancellorship, and Wiltshire had been appointed Treasurer prior to St Albans. His cowardice during the battle may have riled Margaret for a while, but such was his apparent charisma—not to mention his obvious qualities as a stud—that he was retained as royal favourite. Also on Margaret's side was the king's half-brother, Edmund Tudor. [2]

In September 1456, Margaret summoned a Council meeting at Coventry, in the king's name. Warwick and York arrived, only to be treated with great hostility and humiliation, and there followed several violent scuffles between retainers of the rival factions in the city streets. This resulted in the king's intervention, and the Yorkist lords were instructed to hear the Duke of Buckingham's speech. Buckingham was York's brother-in-law, and he and a number of Lancastrian lords put on an act, going down on their knees and begging Henry to show York no more mercy. Henry, perhaps in another trance, inclined his head, and York and Warwick were compelled to swear an oath of submission before being permitted to leave the Council chamber.

What the Yorkists did not know was that Margaret had contrived to set up an ambush on the outskirts of the city. Buckingham, though a staunch Lancastrian, was repelled by the idea, and forewarned York of the impending peril. He and Warwick managed to get away unharmed. The former retreated to Wigmore, seemingly stripped of political power, while Warwick, accompanied by his wife and two small daughters, went to Calais for the first time. What he observed here saddened him. The garrison was still locked in a bitter dispute over wages, its defences were weak, and the Channel was rife with pirates. Warwick soon saw to things: he treated the garrison with the respect it deserved, and his soldiers reciprocated by swearing fealty to him. Trade increased dramatically, once the seas were made safer for merchant ships.

At this stage of his career, Warwick's military abilities did not reach as far as fighting on the waves, though he was more than eager to learn, and employed shipmasters to teach him the basic navigational skills of the day. He was barely prepared when, in the Spring of 1457, he learned of an imminent attack on the garrison by the French. He crossed to England, where in Canterbury the Archbishop, Thomas Bourchier, granted him an impromptu audience. [3] Kent was with him to the man, and munitions and victuals were sent across from Dover, Sandwich, Lydd and Romney.

The French attack came in August, commanded by Piers de Brezé, Seneschal of Normandy, doubly dangerous because he was a close friend if not actual lover of Queen Margaret, besides being an adherent and favourite minister of Charles VII. Doubtless Margaret had organised the invasion in order to vent her spleen against Warwick, whom she now hated as much as she did York. The strength of the Calais garrison took de Brezé by surprise, and at the last moment he changed course and plundered Sandwich instead. In recompense for having made the garrison invincible, Warwick was appointed Keeper of the Seas.

By the Spring of 1458, Warwick had begun fitting out a fleet in preparation for his return to England—several ships were sent out to scout the Channel. On Trinity Sunday, 28 May, Spanish vessels were observed, approaching from the south-west. Warwick, though greatly outnumbered, gave orders for the attack, and the ensuing battle lasted several hours. Two-hundred Spaniards, allies of the French, were killed and around half as many English. Several days later, Warwick intercepted a Hanseatic fleet freighting salt off the Bay of Bourgneuf. Typically arrogant, he demanded that the ships dip their sails in his honour: they refused, only be attacked and scattered!

In November 1458, Queen Margaret met with her lords in another attempt to oust Warwick from his captaincy of Calais, and replace him with young Henry Somerset. This failed: Warwick was on affable terms with Philip the Good of Burgundy, and was said to be negotiating a marriage alliance on behalf of the Philip's niece, Katherine, the Duke of Bourbon's daughter. [4] Warwick's very 'iffy' friend, Lord Wenlock, acquired a commission from the government to discuss this, and further alliances between 'two English princes and two French princesses', in the hope of a renewed peace with France. [5] The exercise amounted to nothing when all the sides in the discussion suspected, as would be later proved, that Wenlock could not be trusted.

On 9 November, Margaret summoned Warwick to a meeting at Westminster. Seething over his 'bullying' of the Hanseatic fleet, she intended giving him a piece of her mind in a private audience. His men, waiting outside the Council chamber and proudly sporting their Bear and Ragged Staff devices, suffered a tirade of abuse from the royal supporters. A scuffle broke out, a dagger was drawn, and the servants came up from the cellars brandishing knives and cleavers. Warwick dashed into the outer hall, only to be set upon. He escaped to his barge by the skin of his teeth, convinced that this had been an assassination attempt, like the one at Coventry. Margaret claimed that Warwick had provoked the attack, and demanded that he now *resign* his captaincy of Calais—while he retaliated by saying that as Parliament had granted him the office, only Parliament could take it away. On 24 June the queen summoned a Council meeting at Coventry, within which *all* the Yorkist lords were publicly denounced.

York at once began collecting his forces at Ludlow. With him now were his wife and his sons Edward, Edmund of Rutland, George and Richard—along with Lords Wenlock and Clinton, William Hastings, and two of York's young Bourchier nephews. [6]

Soon afterwards, Warwick sent word that he had mustered a force of six-hundred Calicians, said to be among the toughest fighting men in Western Europe. He set sail for England in the middle of September, leaving the garrison in the capable hands of his uncle, Sir William Fauconberg. [7] Before he left Calais, however, his captains demanded that he swear allegiance to King Henry. He did so readily, probably with his fingers crossed behind his back.

Warwick's father, Salisbury, was mustering troops at Middleham, and when he received word from the Duke of York in September, he set off for Ludlow at once. With him were his sons Thomas and John Neville, and around 3,000 men. [8] Throughout the summer, the Queen Margaret had been organising troops from her base in Cheshire, and when she learned that Salisbury was on the march she sent out a massive force, commanded by Lord Audley, to intercept him. [9]

In fact, Margaret had erred in assuming that Salisbury would march directly through the Stoke-Stafford line, and had planned to ambush him at Eccleshall, fourteen miles south of Stoke. Outflanked she may have been, but she was confident because a second army was within striking distance: King Henry was in its midst, as he had been at St Albans, like a royal mascot.

Salisbury was mortified when his scouts informed him that the enemy force numbered 15,000—doubtless grossly exaggerated, though still several times his own number, and he suspected fitter and better-equipped. His own position was well-protected by the River Tern, but he was against doing battle there and then because Warwick's troops had not arrived. Swiftly, he moved towards Blore Heath and the locality known as Hempnill Brook—with Lord Audley hot on his heels—and the two sides clashed during the afternoon of 23 September.

Hempnill Brook in those days was something of an optical illusion. Its bed was some twenty feet across, with sharply rising banks and an elongated, gradual slope. From a distance it appeared no wider than a stream when in fact it was a very fast-flowing river. Its northern side was protected by dense cover, and Salisbury concealed a large part of his army here. The remainder was divided into two equal diagonally-stationed wing formations. Salisbury gave orders for a deep trench to be dug out ahead of his front line: into this were embedded rows of sharply-pointed stakes. The baggage-carts were placed behind the exterior lines, which were themselves immediately behind the most fordable section of the brook. Salisbury's archers were concealed in the wings and centre line.

Audley raised his banner, signaling the first attack. This tore down the slope and mounted the bank, while the Yorkists appeared not to retreat. Not realising this was a trick, Audley sent off the second wave from the southern slope, just as the first wave became impaled on the stakes. The confusion and the ensuing scene must have been horrendous. The survivors from the first Lancastrian wave swerved in a desperate attempt to get away from the hollow, only to crash into the others on their way down. All semblance of order had been lost: adding to the chaos, Salisbury's archers moved in and opened fire at close range.

The river-bed quickly became blocked with the bodies of dead men and horses, as there was no retreat for the Lancastrians either way. The queen had employed the services of the infamous Cheshire bowmen, arrogantly decking them out in livery emblazoned with the newly-adopted Silver Swan device of the Prince of Wales. These badges enabled them to be picked off like flies, while the few who survived found themselves sucked into the melée. Some of the Lancastrians attempted to mount the steep opposite slope of Hempnill Brook, using the corpses of their slain comrades as stepping stones—only to be hacked to pieces by the furious Yorkists who, travel-weary or not, were apparently fitter than their opponents had been.

The fighting continued throughout the afternoon, and one by one the Lancastrian leaders were brought down. Amongst the dead were Dutton, Leigh, Venables, Egerton, Molyneux, Troutbeck and Donne. Lord Audley put up a valiant fight to the very last, only to be cut down by a Yorkist soldier, Roger Kynaston. The battle was over.

The waters of Hempnill Brook are said to have run red with blood for three days after the fighting. It had been an unprecedented victory for Salisbury, proof that even a man of almost sixty could suddenly become a hero. Enemy losses were estimated at around 2,000, though the battle itself proved indecisive.

The Yorkists retreated to Ludlow: over the next few days, many of their wounded died through lack of medical attention. Salisbury's sons and Sir Thomas Harrington had been captured and imprisoned at Chester, though they would soon be released. The Yorkists had Lord Dudley.[10]

Even so, at Ludlow they were just as trapped as the Lancastrians had been in Hempnill Hollow. Margaret was just five miles away, King Henry not much further. There was some relief in the fact that Warwick's Calician troops had arrived: commanded by one of his captains, Andrew Trollope, they had pitched in a field outside the town.

The Yorkists' position became vulnerable when the king's army, reported to be a massive one, began its march towards them, passing through Worcester and coming to a halt eleven miles south of the town at Leominster. As with St Albans, messages were bandied back and forth, again to no avail, and Henry's army set off on the last leg towards Ludlow, travelling much slower than it should have done owing to adverse weather conditions. The Yorkists then learned to their horror that Andrew Trollope and the Calician mercenaries had deserted to join forces with the king.

The Yorkists found themselves in a tight corner. Many believed that the victory at Blore Heath had been a fluke, and in any case they were too exhausted after their last battle to consider the possibility of fighting another. To make matters worse, York, his son Edmund and Lord Clinton had fled Ludlow, and were presumed to be heading for Dublin, as York was still Lieutenant of Ireland.

It was at this point that John Dynham came to the Yorkists' aid. [11] Dynham's father had fought for the Lancastrians at St Albans, as result of which he had been publicly denounced by his headstrong Yorkist son, and subsequently been removed from his will. Dynham had brought a hundred Devonshire soldiers to Blore Heath, most of which had survived to accompany him to Ludlow. Standing at 6 feet 3 inches, he was the tallest man at Edward IV's court apart from the king, and must have cut an impressive figure. Extroverted, he openly condemned York as a potentially useless leader, even in front of his son, and after York's departure drew up a list of seven names: himself, Warwick, Edward, the Earl of Salisbury, John Blount, John Courtenay, and Sir John Wenlock. It would appear that the latter two were only included to prevent them from giving the game away, and so that Dynham could keep an eye on them. Blount was one of Warwick's most trusted captains, now that Andrew Trollope had defected. Dynham's was a wholly unselfish act, and he could not possibly have known at the time that he had taken England's destiny, and that of its future king, into his hands.

It was essential for the Yorkists to reach Calais before Andrew Trollope, and to get there in one piece, and for once Warwick had to bow down to a man of considerably lower rank than himself. Dynham must have been convincing, though of course no one was in any position to argue, and the young Devonian's decision would be final throughout the entire operation. The Duchess of York and her three remaining sons were left to fend for themselves, and the Yorkist lords almost certainly did not know where they were heading when Dynham led them over the little-used bridge behind the castle: after the Rout of Ludlow it became known as Dynham's Bridge, and in his home county Dynham himself became something of a legend, for he would help create one king, and despite the governmental squabbles of the next thirty years, remain in office with two more from opposing factions.

The fugitives probably rode into South Wales, where they chartered a sailing vessel for Bristol. Once at sea, Dynham instructed the crew to head for Hartland Point, that rugged section of the North Devonshire coast famed for shipwrecks and hostile weather conditions. Dynham owned two houses here: Blegberry, perched high on the cliffs near Blackpool Rock, and Harton Manor. After resting for a day or so, the party rode across Devon to the Dynham family's principal seat, Nutwell, between Topsham and Exmouth. Here they were assisted by Dynham's indomitable mother, Joan, who rode into Exmouth to secure them a ballinger and a crew of four. [12]

The party spent two days at Nutwell before embarking from Exmouth, taking Dynham with them. Once at sea and out of sight of the Devonshire coast, Warwick was in charge again. They encountered a severe storm and were stranded for a while in Guernsey, and eventually reached the Calais garrison around 2 November. To their relief, Andrew Trollope had not turned up, and William Fauconberg was still in total command.

NOTES

1. Jasper Tudor (c1431-95), Earl of Pembroke. Knighted 1449, he became Duke of Bedford in 1495. His father was Owen Tudor. He married Henry Stafford 2nd Duke of Buckingham's widow, Catherine Woodville.
2. Edmund Tudor (c1430-56), also known as Edmund of Hadham, elder brother of Jasper. Knighted 1449, created Earl of Richmond 1453. He married Lady Margaret Beaufort and his posthumous son, Henry, inherited his title and later became Henry VII.
3. Thomas Bourchier (c1405-86) was the grandson of Thomas of Woodstock, youngest son of Edward III. He became Archbishop of Canterbury in 1454, and Cardinal in 1467. He crowned Edward IV, Richard III and Henry VI.
4. Philip the Good (1396-1467) founded the Order of the Golden Fleece in 1430.
5. Thielmans: *Bourgogne et Angleterre*. The other marriages were to be Henry VI's son, and Somerset, to the heiress of the Comte de Charolais, and Mary de Gueldres. The latter later married James II of Scotland, and died in 1463.
6. Edmund, Earl of Rutland (1443-60), killed at Wakefield. William Hastings (1430-83), became Lord Hastings in 1461. Executed by Richard III.
7. William Neville (d 1463) Baron Fauconberg, Earl of Kent, 1461. His heiress wife Joan (c1407-90) from whom he inherited his title, came from Skelton Castle in Cleveland, and was said to be a lunatic.

8. Thomas Neville was killed at Wakefield. His brother John (c1431-71) became Lord Montagu in 1461. He was killed with Warwick at Barnet.
9. James Tuchet (1398-1459), 5th Lord Audley. His grandson James, 7th Lord Audley (1463-97) married John Dynham's niece and was executed on Dynham's orders after the Cornish Insurrection.
10. John Sutton (1400-87), Lord Dudley.
11. John Dynham of Nutwell (1433-1501). He became Lord Dynham in 1467 when he married the heiress, Baroness Elizabeth Fitzwalter, widow of the Lord Fitzwalter killed at Ferrybridge. His second wife was Lord Brook's daughter, Elizabeth, whom he married in 1488, two years after becoming Henry VII's Treasurer.
12. Joan Dynham (1412-97). Nutwell is on the Exe and faces Powderham Castle, the seat of the Courtenays. She had nine sons and daughters. Of them Roger (1435-90) married the illegitimate daughter of Lord Bonvile; Margaret married Sir Nicholas Carew (1442-70); Joan married Lord Zouche (1459-1526). Elizabeth married Fulk, Lord Fitzwarin (1445-79); Katherine married Sir Thomas Arundel (1450-85). Another son, Oliver (1442-1500) became Edward IV's chaplain in 1480. When Edward became king in 1461 he granted Joan £80, annually for life, and custody of the lands of Sir Thomas Carew, during Nicholas' minority.

4

Exile In Calais
1459-1460

The Calais Earls, as they became known, spent a total of eight months exiled within the town. Warwick of course was already a legend here, and his friends were cordially received: Salisbury because *he* had sired this legend, Edward because he was a representative of the Duke of York. It is possible that the young Earl of March disliked his stubborn, brooding father, and fortunately he had not inherited these characteristics the way his youngest brother Richard would. Away from York, Edward was let off the leash, so to speak, and allowed to stand on his own feet to begin what would be a life of amusement *and* sound political sense—over the next twenty-four years he would successfully merge the two. Extremely good-looking, he was around 6 feet 4 inches tall—hatted, this would make him appear a veritable giant—slim but muscular, with long blond hair, hazel eyes, and an ever-ready smile. The Calicians were enchanted by his sincerity and charm, and immediately welcomed him into their insular hearts. [1]

Warwick was undeterred by his defeat. He was confident in his personal abilities and aware that his position in Calais was supreme. Within hours of arriving at the garrison he was planning his return to England, and was more interested in his own struggle than that of the bold but fickle Duke of York. Back in England, the people were dissatisfied by the actions of the queen and her unruly court:

> The realm of England was out of all good governance, for the King was simple and owed more than he was worth. His debts increased daily, but payment there was none, and such impositions were put to the people, as taxes, and all that came from them was spent in vain, for he held no household nor mentioned no wars. For these misgovernances the hearts of the people were turned away from them that had the governance: their blessing was turned to cursing. The Queen with such as were of her affinity ruled the realm as she liked, gathering innumerable riches. The officers of the realm, especially the Earl of Wiltshire, disinherited many heirs and did many wrongs. The Queen was slandered that he [who] was called Prince was not her son, but a bastard begotten of adultery, that he should not succeed his father in the crown of England… **[2]**

On 20 November 1459, Queen Margaret summoned a carefully selected Council meeting at Coventry, which subsequently became known as the Parliament of Devils. Twenty-seven people, including the Yorkist lords and John Dynham, were not surprisingly attainted of treason: the forfeited estates of the rebels were shared out amongst Queen Margaret's supporters and friends. Dynham's mother, Joan, managed to hang on to hers, as did the elderly

Countess of Salisbury. York was dismissed as Lieutenant of Ireland, and replaced by Wiltshire. When an envoy was sent to Dublin with a writ for his arrest, York acted totally out of character and ordered a perfunctory trial—the man was hanged, drawn and quartered. In later years, this somewhat schizophrenic trait would be inherited by his son, Richard of Gloucester, particularly with Richard's treatment of Lord Hastings. Wiltshire did not retaliate for the time being, but he would.

In the same act of attainder, Warwick was stripped of his captaincy of Calais—the position was given to Henry Somerset, who by mid-November had mustered a force at Sandwich, assisted by the deserter Andrew Trollope and many of the Calician mercenaries who had absconded after Ludlow. They set sail, only to be fired upon by Warwick's canons as soon as they entered Calais harbour. Undaunted, Somerset refused to return to Sandwich defeated—he and Trollope sailed further down the coast, beached at Scales Cliff, and took refuge as Guisnes Castle. This gave the Kentishmen manning their other ships the opportunity they had been waiting for: taking advantage of the storm which was brewing, they allowed their vessels to be blown into the harbour. Then in typical boastful fashion, Warwick and the Calais Earls donned armour, furs and jewels, and strode down to the wharves to give their visitors a welcome they would hardly forget.

Warwick's archers stood, weapons poised, surveying the scene with amusement. Like him, these were a bloodthirsty lot, ready to dispatch their enemies with a nod of the head. Warwick surprised many by greeting all of his captains kindly—addressing some by their first names, while his friends doled out purses of gold and escorted them to the sumptuous banquet which had been prepared in their honour. Many of Somerset's men, however, were not treated so leniently, least of all the ones who had deserted with Andrew Trollope—these were sent to the dungeons. Then Warwick, contemporarily described as 'that lodestar of knighthood', addressed the remaining men, stating that he had no quarrel with them or any other Englishman. They were given a choice: stay with him and join the Yorkists, or return home. Many believed it was a trick, but one by one they stepped forth, and Warwick was good to his word. The next morning they were safely escorted back across the Channel to Sandwich. As for the prisoners, they were doomed: Warwick gave orders for them to be executed.

Soon afterwards, Queen Margaret attempted a swan-song by sending out a relief expedition from Sandwich, commanded by Humphrey Stafford of Southwick and the new Lord Audley. [3] The leaders were captured, but not severely dealt with: they swore fealty to the Yorkists, and later on were lucky enough to be counted amongst Edward's friends.

During the next two months, Warwick kept a watchful eye on England, waiting for the opportunity to return, while messages were delivered daily by men who readily joined his cause. In the meantime, he had successfully concluded a three-months truce with Philip of Burgundy, who—at a price—supplied him with provisions and munitions, while 'ignoring' the forages into France by Yorkist raiders. Philip disliked Queen Margaret—when his commercial treaty with

King Henry had expired, he had not bothered renewing it. Warwick, however, was not a patient man, and comfortable as Calais might have been, he did not wish to linger here longer than necessary. Early in 1460 he was informed that Lord Rivers was at Sandwich, fitting out ships to come to Somerset's aid. **[4]**

Once again, John Dynham played the hero. On 15 January, while it was still dark, he, Lord Wenlock and three-hundred mercenaries put to sea, disguised as timber merchants. They arrived at Sandwich at dawn and executed a brilliant raid. Lord Rivers and his wife Duchess Jacquetta were surprised in their beds and yielded willingly. **[5]** Their son Anthony Woodville was apprehended in the market place, on his way back to his lodgings at the Blackfriars. He was carrying his armour over his arm, put up a fight, and was beaten up. **[6]** In the meantime, Wenlock had captured the principal ships of the King's Navy. Warwick had wanted Henry's own great flagship, the *Grace Dieu*. The vessel was robbed and despoiled, but not taken because, 'the whyche myghte not be had awey because she was broke in the botome.' **[7]**

The prisoners were treated kindly by Dynham, himself always a genial man, but when the party arrived back in Calais, Rivers and Anthony Woodville were not allowed to enter the town until after dusk, for fear of invoking a riot. A contemporary chronicle, which may or may not have been largely invented, described the ensuing scene in detail:

> My lord Rivers was brought to Calais, and before the lords with eight-score torches. And there my lord

of Salisbury rated him, calling him a knave's son, that he should be so rude to call these other lords traitors, for they shall be found the King's true liege, when he should be found a traitor. And my lord of Warwick rated him, and said that his father was but a squire and brought up by King Harry the Fifth, and sethen himself made by marriage, and also made lord, and that it was not his part to have such language of lords, being of the King's blood. And my lord of March rated him like wise. And Sir Anthony was rated for his language by all three lords in like wise. [8]

This account may have been exaggerated to fit in with the Yorkist bias at the time. Warwick and his faction were not as refined as they have sometimes been defined. Theirs was essentially a man's world where vulgarity and foul language were commonplace—the Yorkists' words to Anthony may have been equally insulting, and certainly Warwick's own manners left much to be desired. Warwick's Kentishmen had been forgiven for supporting Henry Somerset: the Woodvilles suffered no worse a fate than a spell in the dungeons alongside Lord Audley, after which they too joined the Yorkist faction.

 Warwick still could not act without the Duke of York's approval, and soon after Dynham's raid on Sandwich he set sail for Ireland with a large convoy. Dynham was one of the captains: they had an easy crossing and reached Waterford on 16 March. Discussions between the two leaders lasted two months, by which time York had fitted out a fleet of his own. He refused to leave Ireland, however, until Warwick had captured the king: he did not wish to break his oath of fealty to Henry, even if Warwick had broken his.

Queen Margaret, meanwhile, had been informed of John Dynham's exploits, and when the Yorkists set sail for Calais in late May-early June, taking with them the aged Countess of Salisbury who had somehow managed to escape from England to Dublin, they rounded the south coast of Devon to find the Duke of Exeter's ships waiting and were surprised to see that the *Grace Dieu* had been repaired. Exeter had combined forces with a Devonshire knight, Sir Baldwin Fulford, and his fleet was considerably larger than that of the Yorkists. [9] Despite this, Warwick opened fire, and fortunately his legend was so potent, even amongst his enemies: Exeter's captains informed him that they would rather mutiny than attack the Lord of the Seas. Thus the enemy ships turned tail and headed back into Dartmouth harbour.

Warwick returned to Calais, confident there had been a breakthrough. He was told of the vengeful acts perpetrated by the Lancastrians during his absence. The Earl of Wiltshire—another thug who today would probably have been diagnosed as suffering from a bi-polar condition, given his behaviour over the years—and Lords Scales and Hungerford had attacked York's home town of Newbury, seemingly for no other reason than spite. Many people had been murdered, women raped, and a number of important citizens hanged, drawn and quartered. Wiltshire, fearing the queen's wrath (she had taken Newbury from York and given it to the Earl of Pembroke), and on the pretext that he had been about to attack Calais, amassed his plunder into five carracks and sailed to Holland, where he remained until Margaret's temper cooled. What he did not know was that he was deserting her in her hour of need, though needless to say this did not prevent her from venting her spleen. The Master of the King's Ordnance was murdered between Dunstable and St Albans, caught transporting armaments to London. A London lawyer and his co-conspirators were apprehended after attempting to smuggle munitions to Calais, and summarily executed.

On 6 June, Henry Somerset was given power to grant pardon to the Calais rebels, with the exception of Dynham, Fauconberg, John Courtenay and several others. This was an attempt to draw Warwick out into the open, though he had already decided to take the plunge. In England, satirists were busily nailing placards to church doors, pleading for the return of the Yorkists. One such was pinned to the gates of Canterbury:

> Richard duk of York, Job thy servant insigne,
> Edward Earl of March, whose fame the earth shall spread,
> Richard earl of Salisbury named prudence,
> With that noble knight and flower of manhood
> Richard, earl of Warwick shield of our defence,
> Also little Fauconberg, a knight of great reverence...
> **[10]**

On 25 June, John Dynham raided Sandwich for the second time, accompanied by William Fauconberg. 500 troops had been dispatched to the town to replace Lord Rivers' troops: these were under the command of Osbert Mountfort, one of the men who had deserted with Andrew Trollope at Ludlow. Before Warwick could land safely in England, it was necessary to get rid of Mountfort's force, and Dynham probably insisted on John Wenlock going with him because he still did not trust him. This time, however, the Lancastrians were prepared. There was a bitter fight and Dynham was badly wounded in the leg by an exploding bombard, inasmuch that, 'He ever after halted and somewhat limped: yet his courage and policy was so much that he vanquished his enemies, and bore himself so worthily in that enterprise that his praise was great amongst all men.' [11]

Dynham remained in Sandwich, given up for dead, but eventually recovered to fight again and achieve greater glories. The victors took Osbert Mountfort back to Calais: there was no trial, and in the shadow of the mighty Rysbank Tower, his head was hacked off by one of Warwick's sailors, who unceremoniously tossed it into the sea.

Warwick now had additional support in the form of the Apostolic Legate, Francesco Coppini, a peculiar little Italian. [12] Coppini had been sent to England in 1459 by Pope Pius II, though in reality he was little more than an opportunist and an agent for his patron, Francesco Sforza, Duke of Milan. Sforza had asked the Legate to arrange a number of alliances, wherein France would be prevented from supporting Angevin claims to the Neapolitan throne—the claimant was John de Calabria, the queen's brother. The Pope was hoping that Coppini, in his official capacity, might not only bring an end to the strife in England, but also support *him* in his crusade against the Turks. Unfortunately for Coppini, Henry VI had been inaccessible or, more likely, incomprehensible during another attack of madness and hidden from sight, and Coppini had taken this as a snub.

Coppini had left England in the Spring of 1460, and had subsequently turned up in Bruges to find himself courted by Warwick's persuasive charm. The two began writing to each other. As an agent of Philip of Burgundy, who had welcomed him with open arms, Coppini hinted in his correspondences to Warwick that he was only too eager to promote an English invasion of France. Warwick invited him to Calais, and the Calais Earls, together with William Fauconberg, bent their knees before him and received what must have been a pretentious blessing. Warwick then told Coppini that he too wanted to invade France, as proof of his lasting love towards his king. The Legate did not hesitate: he dispatched a letter to Henry, begging him to listen to the Yorkists' pleas. Added to it were the signatures of the Calais Earls. On 26 June 1460, they and 2.000 men set foot on English soil—Warwick excluded, for the first time in eight months. With them was Francesco Coppini.

NOTES

1. When Edward's tomb was opened in 1789, his skeleton measured 6 feet 3 and a half inches.
2. *English Chronicles*,79, Camden Society.
3. Humphrey Stafford of Southwick (1439-69), Earl of Devon, 1469. John Tuchet (c1420-90), 6th Lord Audley, Master of the King's Dogs, 1471. Treasurer to Richard III, 1484.
4. Richard Woodville (c1405-69), Earl Rivers. His seat was Grafton, near Stony Stratford. His father had served under Henry V, and Rivers served under the Duke of Bedford in France, where he was an officer in his future wife's household. He was with the Duke of Somerset in France in 1439, at Rouen with the Duke of York in 1441, and was created Lord Rivers, 1448. Because of his lowly birth and elevation by marriage, his family was never liked.
5. Jacquetta of Luxembourg (c1416-72). She married John, Duke of Bedford in 1433, as his second wife, and became Henry V's sister-in-law. When he died in 1435 she inherited his estates, but before another suitor could be found she married Richard Woodville in 1436. She bore him at least thirteen children, but in what order and when is uncertain. Her father was Pierre, Comte de St Pol de Luxembourg.
6. Anthony Woodville (c1440-83), Lord Scales, and 2nd Lord Rivers. He married, firstly, Elizabeth (d 1473), daughter of Thomas, Lord Scales, hence his title; secondly, Mary, the daughter of Sir Henry Fitzlewis and a grand-daughter of Edmund, Duke of Somerset. He was executed by Richard III.

7. Schofield: *English Historical Review XXXVII*: Dynham's company included a gentleman (his lifelong lover, Philip Atkyn, from Blegberry), two yeomen, a mercer, a merchant, an apothecary, a tailor, a chapman, a butcher and a servant.
8. *Paston Letters*, 506.
9. Sir Baldwin Fulford (c1403-61), of Dunsford. Sherriff of Devon, 1459-61. Arrested by John Dynham, who superseded him as Sherriff, he was executed in Bristol for rebelling against Edward IV.
10. *English Chronicle*, pp 91-4.
11. *Hall's Chronicle,* 243.
12. Francesco Coppini, Bishop of Terni, served under Pius II. Francesco Sforza (1401-66), described as a *condottiere* (leader of a group of mercenaries), elected Duke of Milan owing to his popularity. Coppini's exploits are discussed in 'Pope Pius & The Wars of The Roses', *Archivum Historiae Pontificiae, VIII*, pp 139-78 (1970). He hoped for a Cardinal's Hat after his adventure of 1459-60, but Pius was informed of his double-dealing and in 1461 he was publicly disgraced and demoted to the rank of monk.

5

The Yorkists' Return & The Battle of Northampton
1460

The Yorkists quickly made up for lost time, lingering at Sandwich but long enough to recruit the Kentishmen who would have given their very souls to march—or trudge—behind the Warwick banner. They set off towards Canterbury: heralds were sent ahead to proclaim the happy tidings that the Yorkists were back for good. At the cathedral the leaders knelt at Becket's tomb—piety and devotion were always ready antidotes for bloodshed and violence. Outside, their army had doubled in number and would get stronger with each passing day. There had been a slight hitch when the men of Canterbury might have proved hostile, for wars rarely involved normal citizens who looked upon the trade from both sides in order to earn their living. Opinion was swayed when three captains—Robert Horne, John Fogge and John Scott—elected to join the Yorkists. Thenon the force headed for London. [1]

  The city was held by Lords Scales and Hungerford, and again there was a temporary delay: on 1 July the army pitched at Blackheath, while eager discussions took place. The next morning, Scales and Hungerford retreated to the comparative safety of the Tower: the city gates were thrown open, and the Yorkists entered London to scenes of unprecedented merriment, to be greeted by the Mayor and the Archbishop of Canterbury. Initially, the Londoners only allowed them into the city because they were probably afraid of being stormed by force. On 3 July, however, the Yorkist leaders attended a mass meeting at St Paul's, they solemnly declared by swearing on the Sacred Cross of Canterbury that they intended the king no harm. The next day, Francesco Coppini composed a letter to King Henry, which was also read out at St Paul's, and in such a way that, astonishingly, not even the least gullible amongst his audience saw through the charade:

> On coming to Calais I found almost everything in turmoil, and those nobles all ready to cross to England, declaring that they could wait no longer in the existing state of affairs. Nevertheless, after I had conferred with them and exhorted them to peace and obedience, they gave me a written pledge that they were disposed to devotion and obedience to your Majesty, and to do all in their power…for the good of your realm. They desired to come to your Majesty and to be received into their former state and favour, from which they declare they have been ousted by the craft of their opponents, and begged me to cross the sea with them to interpose my efforts and prevent bloodshed…[2]

The problem was—where *was* the king? For two days, Yorkist spies infiltrated the city streets and taverns, hoping to find some clue as to Henry's whereabouts. Meanwhile, Salisbury, Wenlock and Lord Cobham set about besieging the Tower. [3]

Henry was reported to be somewhere in the Midlands and on Friday 3 July Warwick, Edward and a large part of their army set out to look for him. They were accompanied by a heavenly host of holy men with included Coppini, the Archbishop of Canterbury, the Prior of St John's, and no less than six bishops. [4]

Henry was found to be at Northampton, for the third time in the midst of a massive army. Edward and Warwick arrived here on 9-10 July, and as with St Albans and Ludlow, the Yorkists declared that it was their intention only to speak with the king, not fight against him. It may be said, as a point of digression, that had they been able to do so on these occasions, instead of having to encounter the pugnacious arrogance of Queen Margaret's peers, three battles would have been prevented and hundreds if not thousands of lives spared. This time the protagonist was the Duke of Buckingham, who doubtless would have learned much of his craft from the likes of Somerset and Wiltshire. Some of the Lancastrian peers—Lords Grey de Ruthyn, Beaumont, Egremont and Shrewsbury—were clearly opposed to doing battle. [5] They were however over-ruled: the royal army took up its defensive position, outside the city walls next to the River Nene.

Ultimately, he Lancastrians were confident that *they* would win the day: their men were better-trained, better-equipped and more professional, and had had time to rest after their lengthy march. They scoffed at Coppini's threat that all men who took up arms against the mighty Warwick would be excommunicated. Queen Margaret was not with them, though doubtless her presence would not have swayed opinion: she had conveniently retreated to Eccleshall, in Staffordshire, taking the Prince of Wales with her.

Again, the numbers on both sides may have been exaggerated by the chroniclers: it is likely the Lancastrians had 5,000 men, the Yorkists around 7,000. Though the larger force, the Yorkists were not over-keen to attack because of Buckingham's superior position, and other Lancastrian forces were reported to be approaching from the north and west, which must have been somewhat daunting. A number of messages were sent to the king, though it is unlikely that he saw them—he appears to have entered another period of madness.

Warwick could see no way out but to fight. His army had encamped on Hunsbury Hill, and he now led it along Mere Way towards the locality known as Hardingstone Meadow, skirting Delapré Wood and the grounds of the abbey, and thus coming up against the Nene entrenchments. En route, the army had passed Queen Eleanor's Cross, from which vantage point Coppini and his host watched the ensuing battle with bated breath—though they could not have seen much on account of the weather. It was raining heavily. [6]

The battle began at around two in the afternoon, and was very brief. The right Lancastrian division was commanded by de Ruthyn, the left by Buckingham. William Fauconberg was in command of the Yorkist right, Warwick led the centre: Edward, bearing his father's banner because he did not yet have one of his own, took the left.

The rain formed a cold, solid sheet, and when the attack was called the Yorkists waded thigh-deep into the ditch, blinded by flying mud, each man seeing no further than the man in front of him. They attempted the embankment on the opposite side, but there was a great deal of confusion and many of their horses became stuck in the mud, making their riders prime targets for the Lancastrian archers. The Lancastrians had acquired large numbers of canon and handguns, which could not be fired adequately because of the rain. Handguns, relatively new to the war scene, were accurate once mastered, but were had their disadvantages. There was always the danger of the weapon backfiring in the one's face, and they were slow, taking a long time to load before the operator applied a lighted torch. When one considers that a well-trained archer could fire six or seven bolts a minute, in a tightly-packed battle like Northampton, handguns proved virtually ineffective. [7]

For a time, the Lancastrians appeared to be winning. Then, not unexpectedly in these civil wars, the outcome was decided by treachery. De Ruthyn changed sides, and instead of fighting the Yorkists instructed his men to help them over the barricades. For the Lancastrians, there was little to do but flee the field, and they attempted to cross the flooded Nene via the mill-bridge. The current here ran exceptionally strong, and many were drowned simply by the weight of their armour. Buckingham put up a last fight outside King Henry's tent, only to be cut down. Egremont, Shrewsbury, Beaumont and many more Lancastrian peers were also slain—besides those lost in the river, around three-hundred Lancastrians fell. An anonymous Yorkist archer entered the king's tent and would probably have killed him, had it not been for the intervention of the Yorkist leaders, who not surprisingly fell to their knees and begged Henry's forgiveness before swearing their loyalty. How much of this so-called fealty was heartfelt must only be assumed. They escorted him 'with great reverence' to the nearby Convent of St Mary de Pratis: prayers were said, and the procession moved in to Northampton.

NOTES

1. Sir John Fogge, Edward IV's Treasurer, 1461-7. Robert Horne died at Towton. Sir John Scott Treasurer of Edward's Household, 1461-70.
2. *Calendar of State Papers & Manuscripts Existing In The Archives & Collections of Milan*, translated by Hinds, 1912.
3. Sir Edward Brook (c1415-64) MP for Somerset 1439 and 1442, Lord Cobham, 1445.
4. Robert Botyl, Prior of St John. The bishops were those of Lincoln, Ely, Salisbury, Exeter, Rochester and Canterbury.
5. Edmund, Lord Grey de Ruthyn, Treasurer 1463-4. He became Earl of Kent in 1466, several years after William Fauconberg's death. John, Viscount Beaumont, the third husband of Catherine Neville, an elder sister of the Duchess of York. Thomas Percy (1422-60), Lord Egremont, second son of the 2nd Earl of Northumberland. John Talbot, 2nd Earl of Shrewsbury.
6. Eleanor's Cross, one of the many erected by Edward I on his wife's funeral route to Westminster in 1290.
7. The early handgun was effectively a miniaturised canon with a barrel of approximately eight inches, attached to a wooden or iron stock. Some needed two men to work them. They were in use in England from the late-14th century until just after the Wars of the Roses.

6

Disaster At Wakefield
1460

After the Lancastrian's defeat at Northampton, owing to the treachery of Grey de Ruthyn, Queen Margaret's position was precarious: taking her small son with her, she fled to North Wales. According to the somewhat humorous account written by Pseudo-Gregory, 'Most commonly she rode behind a poor gentleman of fourteen year age: his name was John Combe, born at Amesbury in Wiltshire,' [1]

She cannot have been escorted efficiently, for she was robbed en route, by her own servants, of all her possessions and jewelry. Eventually she reached Harlech, the great fortress on the Caernarvon Coast, where she was granted refuge—and immediately contacted her friend, Jasper Tudor. Angry or despondent the queen may have been: she would not stay out of action for long.

On 16 July the Yorkists entered London, and the people were able to observe that King Henry had been treated kindly—though they probably saw through the pretentious respect, as he was escorted to Westminster, outwardly their sovereign but effectively little more than a puppet, his head and thoughts in a world more spiritual than realistic.

The Tower was still held, but with King Henry in the hands of the Yorkists, there seemed little point in extending the siege. During the Yorkists' absence, Scales and Hungerford's men had run amock, turning the Tower guns on the people, so revenge was only to be expected. Seven officers in the employ of the Duke of Exeter were found guilty by jury, put on display, and hanged, drawn and quartered. Lord Scales attempted to escape: apprehended on the steps of his barge, he was in the words of Pseudo-Gregory, 'Stripped and lay there dispoiled; naked as a worm.'

On 25 July, George Neville, Bishop of Exeter, was appointed Chancellor of England, and Viscount Bourchier made Treasurer. [2] Warwick received a whole catalogue of estates and honours: some were temporary, all brought immense riches to a man who was already the wealthiest magnate in the country. He became Chamberlain of England; Captain of Calais, Hammes and Guines; Warden of the Cinque Ports; Warden of the East and West Marches, Constable of Dover, Steward of the Duchy Honours in Cheshire, Lancashire, Pontefract, Tutbury, Knaresborough and Pickering. Additionally he received the forfeited Yorkshire manors of the Percies and the forfeited Westmorland estates of Lord Clifford, the lands of his lunatic uncle, Lord Latimer [3]; and lordships in Wales formerly belonging to the Earl of Shrewsbury and the Duke of Buckingham. A chronicle of the day observed, perniciously, 'His insatiable mind could not be content, and yet before him there were none in England of the half possessions that he had.' [4]

Edward of March and Lord Wenlock were given seats on the King's Council, dominated by the semi-retired Earl of Salisbury. The Privy Seal was given to Robert Stillington, Dean of St Martin-le-Grand. [5] William Fauconberg later became Earl of Kent.

In August, Warwick, Edward and Salisbury paid another visit to Becket's tomb at Canterbury. Francesco Coppini tagged along, self-assured as ever and still cherishing an invasion of France, even though everyone knew by now that he was a charlatan. There were several council meetings within the town before Warwick crossed the Channel to Guisnes Castle where, in an act of considerable folly, he met with Henry Somerset. The two men embraced on Newnham Bridge. Somerset swore never to take up arms against Warwick again, and was promptly told that he would be able to leave the safety of his refuge without fear of recrimination for his past deeds!

Somerset had entered into a brief homosexual relationship with Charles, Count of Charolais. [6] For some months now, the sexually insatiable Burgundian had been wining and dining his latest conquest, and taking him hunting in the forest at Ardres. Extant of the bedchamber, the two men had little in common save that both were Lancastrian sympathisers, bad-tempered and rash. Somerset is said to have been ethereally handsome: had he not been so, he would not have attracted the attentions of the equally alluring Margaret of Anjou. Charles was also good-looking: unlike those of the Plantagenets, his portrait was executed during his lifetime and is thought to be an exact likeness, though his attractive features were his only redeeming quality. He is described in contemporary chronicles as moody and unpredictable, to which may be added cruel and cold, despotic and calculating.

Neither Charles nor Somerset could have been in the least effete, otherwise they would not have withstood the rigours of their day—similarly the Burgundian heir must have been a good deal tougher than many of his contemporaries, otherwise he would not have earned himself the name, Charles *le Hardi*. [7] His father Philip was, of course, a great friend and ally of the Yorkists, and when he learned of Somerset's plans to hand over Guisnes to his son, he threw a tantrum—Charles' response to this was to offer to command an invasion of England. Thankfully this never took place, and soon after his interview with Warwick on Newnham Bridge, Somerset set sail for England.

In September 1460, the Duchess of York arrived in London. With her were her sons George and Richard, and her daughter Margaret. Edward organised a house for them in Southwark, but within days Cecily was on the move again: York had landed at Chester, and she met him at Hereford. Despite his tight schedule, Edward visited the house daily, arguably getting to know his brothers and sister properly for the first time. Margaret is reckoned to have been his favourite, though in later life he saw her rarely. What kind of affinity he shared with George and Richard may be readily assumed: here was a massively popular figure who seemingly had the world at his fingertips, sharing most of his father's joys and triumphs, while the younger Plantagenets had been forced into the background, transferring from one household to the next, seeing virtually no one of great importance, and gradually getting more and more depressed over what the future might hold for them. Psychologists would agree that there was little wonder these two sons of York turned out the way they did. One sibling's envy of another all too often leads to emnity: add to this an almost complete absence of parental affection and control, and the seeds of delinqency are sown.

York was unsure of what his reception might be amongst his own lords, who had done inordinately well without him for almost a year. He took on a haughty tone and did himself few favours by arriving in London heralded by banners and fanfares, and had the additional gall of *demanding* that Parliament recognise him as their rightful king. He even produced a pedigree which he said proved that the three previous Henrys had been usurpers—true in the case of Henry IV, which meant that his heirs had likewise not been rightful claimants. Simple-minded or not, the current king could not be blamed for his ancestors' discrepancies, and Parliament refused to accept York's claim. An anointed king was a king until death—something which should have been remembered by Henry IV, and of which Edward of March would be reminded eleven years hence. Therefore a compromise was reached. Upon Henry's death, York would become king—something which must have perturbed him greatly, for Henry was ten years his junior, mentally unstable but in good *physical* health and, barring accidents, as a non-military monarch likely to outlive a man raised to live or die by the sword.

York was legally named heir to the throne on 9 November, allegedly with Henry's approval. Nothing was mentioned about the Prince of Wales: the question of the boy's paternity must have been discussed at some time. Almost certainly the Yorkists would have been faced with the same problem that Richard of Gloucester may or may not have resolved to fix twenty-three years later—what to do with powerful political pawns who, though not dangerous themselves, put everyone else on the spot by being who they were. As will be seen, this situation would continue for another decade, until after the battle of Tewkesbury.

Edward of March was well aware that England would never have lasting peace under a puppet king, and most especially while Margaret of Anjou was around. While Edward was listening to his father's claims in London, he was informed that the queen was rallying supporters in the north. Henry Somerset was with her: despite his alleged fealty towards Warwick, he thirsted only for his blood. There was also a new Earl of Northumberland, just as powerful and aggressive as the last one. **[8]**

On 31 October, Edward, York and Edmund of Rutland swore allegiance to Parliament's compromise over York's claim. In a colourful parade, King Henry was taken from Westminster and installed within the Bishop of London's palace. The next day the party rode to St Paul's: Henry was wearing the crown, while Edward carried the train and Warwick himself carried the sword of state. On 5 November, Salisbury was appointed Great Chamberlain of England, and Lord Wenlock became Chief Butler. John Dynham, still described as an esquire—he had turned down a knighthood, claiming that his actions after Ludlow had been exclusively out of his love for the Yorkists, and not for personal gain—was appointed Chancellor of Ireland, succeeding the Earl of Shrewsbury, who had been killed at Northampton. [9]

Edward left London and returned to Ludlow, leaving Warwick and the immensely powerful Duke of Norfolk guarding the king. [10] Thenon he travelled to the Welsh Marches, not only to raise men, but so that he might keep an eye on Jasper Tudor.

On 2 December, York retired to Sandal, in Yorkshire, for the festive season. With him were his son Rutland, and Salisbury and his son Sir Thomas Neville. They were not surprised to learn that a massive Lancastrian force had been mustered ten miles away, at Pontefract, by Somerset and Northumberland, together with the Duke of Exeter and Lords Dacre, Clifford and Roos. [11]

There are various accounts of the Battle of Wakefield. Most are gathered from hearsay, and accurate details of exactly what happened do not exist. If they do, they have never come to light. One account says that Andrew Trollope and Somerset dressed their soldiers as women, another that Sandal was seized by a disinherited Neville. Both accounts are improbable. The likeliest explanation it that, it being Christmas and therefore a time of truce, York and his party were tempted out of the castle and on to Sandal Green, on the pretence that the Lancastrians simply wanted to parley. Why York should have been so naïve to fall into such a trap cannot be known: at St Albans, Blore Heath and Northampton the Yorkists had *wanted* to talk, therefore in a dog-eat-dog situation neither side is likely to have trusted the other.

The fact is that on 30 December 1460 there was a fight—or at least a skirmish—during which York was killed. Edmund of Rutland died too. According to the legend, he was caught fleeing the field and stabbed to death while clutching the sanctuary ring at the Chantry Chapel. History is therefore left with the misleading picture of a handsome prince in his first flush of youth, barbarously murdered by a Lancastrian thug while pleading for his life. Edmund may only have been seventeen, but he was trained in warfare and well aware that, in battle, age has no limits either way, that if one fights and kills, one may *be* killed. Thomas Neville was also killed, along with Sir Thomas Harrington and Sir Henry Radford, though there were few other losses of high rank. [12] The wily old Earl of Salisbury did not die during the battle. Captured and taken to Pontefract, he expected no mercy and was shown none. An inglorious end to a glorious career occurred when he was beheaded, personally, by the Bastard of Exeter.

York and Rutland were decapitated after death—a callous thing to do, even in so violent an age—and their heads, along with those of Salisbury and a number of others, were sent to York to be stuck on spikes above the Micklegate. That of the Duke of York was adorned with a paper crown, a slur on his claim to the throne. [13]

The Yorkists are said to have lost some 2,000 men at Wakefield, and the Lancastrians but a few hundred. What was nothing short of a disaster for one side was a supreme triumph for the other: with one fell swoop, Queen Margaret had managed to rid herself of the better part of the Yorkist faction.

NOTES

1. The chronicler is anonymous, but is known thus because he resumed a chronicle partly written by a mayor named Gregory. A witty writer, he seems to have met most of those he mentions in his work, and to have been present at many important events.
2. George Neville (c1433-76), Bishop of Exeter 1455, Chancellor 1460-7, Archbishop of York in 1464.
3. George Neville, Lord Latimer, Salisbury's brother.
4. *Hearne's Fragment, Chronicles of The White Rose of York*, 23.
5. Robert Stillington (d 1491) was a Yorkshireman. Bishop of Bath & Wells in 1466, was Chancellor 1467-70, and again 1471-3.
6. Charles the Bold (1433-77) 4th and last Duke of Burgundy. Until succeeding his father Philip the Good in 1467 he was Count of Charolais. He married Margaret, sister of Edward IV in 1468. She was his third wife: in 1439 he married Catherine (1429-46) daughter of Charles VII of France; in 1454 he married Isabella of Bourbon (d 1465). Even so, he is known to have had a penchant for young men and boys.
7. Until the end of the 19th century, when historians began calling him Charles le Téméraire.
8. Henry Percy (d 1461), 3rd Earl of Northumberland. He lived at Wressell Castle, 18 miles north-east of Pontefract, and was killed at Towton.
9. *Patent Rolls*, 39 Henry VI, mm 11 & 9.
10. John Mowbray (1415-61), 3rd Duke of Norfolk. He was a close friend of John Dynham, very wealthy but always in poor health. When taken ill on the eve of Towton, he asked Dynham to take over his army.

11. Thomas, Lord Roos, executed after Hexham.
12. Harrington and Radford were probably relatives of Lord Bonvile—the latter almost certainly the Nicholas Radford referred to in the 1455 Exeter rebellion.
13. The figures above the present Micklegate are not the originals.

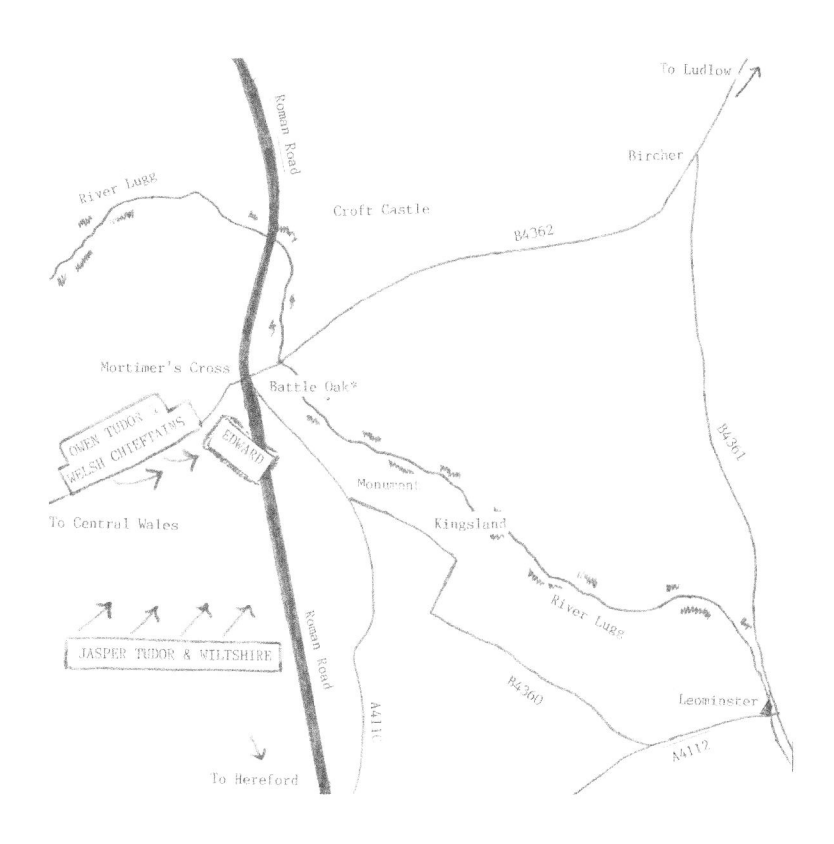

The Battle of Mortimer's Cross,
2 February 1461

7

The Sun In Splendour: Mortimer's Cross & St Albans II
1461

It is hardly likely that Edward of March was shattered by news of his father's death, which would have reached him at Shrewsbury on or around 2 January. Close they may have been, but after Ludlow, when York had clearly left his eldest son to fend for himself, Edward must have had few reservations about his father's character—and in any case he had always leaned strongly towards Warwick, whom he admired and probably regarded as an alter-ego. But he had been inordinately fond of old Salisbury and his brother Edmund, and must have been incensed and hurt to learn that the bodies of his loved ones had been so cruelly despoiled—and equally upset that, for the time being, the heads atop Micklegate would have to stay put because the city of York was a veritable hotbed of Lancastrian activity.

Warwick, on the other hand, would have looked upon York's death as some kind of bonus: as the two Yorkist leaders had differed vastly by way of temperament, so too they had nurtured differing ambitions. York, in his greed, had aimed for the crown. Warwick, the indefatigable warrior 'likened unto another Caesar' had never aimed so high, and his exploits assured him that the people would always be on his side. [1] Now, the earl had exactly what he wanted: King Henry was in his hands, and the pretender to the throne—Edward—was his protegé. On the negative side, he had lost a father he had loved, perhaps the only man whose advice he had taken since John Dynham, the bold squire who had briefly taken over after Ludlow. After inheriting Salisbury's estates, Warwick was now richer and more potent than ever. When on 11 January he wrote a letter to the Pope, amongst others, the battle of Wakefield had already been pushed to the back of his mind. [2]

Contemporaneously, Warwick and Edward set about raising troops. The former was loaned 2,000 marks by the London Council, and commands were sent out to Yorkist captains up and down England. Viscount Bourchier and the Earl of Arundel gathered men in the south, the Duke of Norfolk in East Anglia, and other contingencies were raised by Lord Bonvile and Sir Thomas Kyriell. [3]

Francesco Coppini, whose reign was withering to an end, set about 'reasoning' with Queen Margaret—courting her, then threatening her with 'more than twenty-thousand desperate men.' The Legate advised Warwick against making a definite move before Easter, by which time *he* was hoping to have put England to rights. Warwick invited him into the Yorkist camp, and the cocky little Italian agreed to bless the Yorkists and threatened the Lancastrians with excommunication, should they take up arms against Warwick. When Coppini learned how large the enemy army was likely to be, however, he suffered an attack of the vapours and announced that he wanted to go home. He was escorted as far as Gravesend, in Kent. He boarded a ship at Tilbury, and the pretentions of the past caught up with him:

the ship beached on a sandbank and was attacked by a French privateer before eventually docking at Brill. For Coppini, this represented the ultimate disgrace.

Edward of March, meanwhile, had set off for London with the troops he had gathered in the Welsh Marches. With him were Lords Audley and Grey, Sir Walter Devereux, Sirs William and Richard Herbert, and Humphrey Stafford of Southwick. [4] There had been little time for personal sadness. As the new Duke of York, Edward was now head of his family and, according to his father's claim, heir to the throne. His mother, fearing for the future, had packed her remaining sons George and Richard off to Holland.

Edward had barely begun his journey when news was brought to him from Wales: James Butler, Earl of Wiltshire had returned from Europe with a vengeance—and an army of Bretons, French and Irish. He had joined forces with Jasper Tudor and his Welshmen, and was marching on Hereford. Immediately, Edward turned north.

Queen Margaret had held a secret meeting with the Scots Queen Mother, Mary of Guelders, at Lincluden Abbey on 5 January, and they had formulated a plan. [5] Mary was anti-Burgundian and anti-French: aside from this the two women had little in common. Margaret promised Mary the great fortress at Berwick in return for a Scottish army, with the usual arrangements—in due time, the Prince of Wales would marry Mary's daughter. Nothing was said of Margaret's affair with Henry Somerset—if it was, having heard of his dalliance with Charles of Charolais, it was probably disbelieved.

Margaret arrived in York around 20 January. Somerset was in almost total command of her army, and the force began moving south. With him were Northumberland, Grey of Codnor, Devon, Roos, Shrewsbury, Willoughby, Dacre, Clifford, Wells, Fitzhugh and Greystoke—and, of course, Andrew Trollope. [6]

The queen and the young Prince rode in the midst of this massive, unruly force, attempting to dispel the myth that only women camp-followers of easy virtue tagged along with war-hungry soldiers. The army was decked out in the Prince's new livery of crimson and black with ostrich feathers, and clearly nothing had been learned from Wiltshire's earlier attack on Newbury. The army would eventually pass through Grantham, Stamford, Peterborough, Huntingdon and Royston, leaving nothing untouched in their wake. Towns were plundered, innocent citizens butchered, women raped and houses fired as there seemed to be no end in sight to their mindless violence, encouraged by the psychotic Somerset.

On 2 February 1461, Edward's and Wiltshire's armies clashed at Mortimer's Cross, four miles south of Wigmore. It was Candlemass—a holy day which many of Edward's men deemed unlucky. Fortunately for them, prior to the battle there occurred a phenomenon which Edward with his quick thinking used to his advantage. A parhelion appeared in the sky which he interpreted to be the sign of the Blessed Trinity, and which he immediately adopted as his personal device: the Sun in Splendour. [7]

Incredibly, Edward was still only eighteen and about to reap the glory which he so richly deserved. He is said to have been tactically advised by his friend, Sir Richard Croft, who lived at Wigmore—though it is likely that he was a natural technician, who after Mortimer's Cross left little doubt that no man in England could have made a finer king. Edward knew the area intimately. He had spent many happy hours at Wigmore as a small boy, and it was more than luck that he happened to be in the right place at the right time.

Edward decided that it would be best to allow the Lancastrians to make the first move. For once his own men were well-rested and well-fed, and he was aware that neither Wiltshire nor Jasper Tudor were renowned for military ability. Edward positioned his army west of the River Lugg: at that time it was about twenty feet across, and surrounded by marshland. Also, because of their proximity to Wigmore and the 'sign from above', his men were confident they would win the day quite comfortably.

Details of the battle are scanty. Edward was in full command of the central contingent which opposed Jasper Tudor, while his archers were in a good position on the high ground at his rear. The Lancastrians attempted to cross the river, and were scattered: only Edward knew the most fordable points, and these would have been covered by yet more archers, resulting in much of the fighting taking place extant of the central struggle. Lancastrian casualties were reported to be high—more than 3,000, which accounted for around sixty per-cent of their army. En route to meet up with Queen Margaret's much larger force, they had been surprised by Edward, who they had assumed would have been too involved with mourning his father to raise many men at short notice. The battle lasted all day, but was decisive.

Jasper Tudor and Wiltshire escaped—the latter again donned a meagre habit, and headed for the Welsh hills, where he was taken in. Edward's biggest scoop was the capture of that old Welsh rogue, Owen Tudor. [8] He was taken into Hereford for execution, and his death soon became a legend amongst his people. Even while being led to the block, he steadfastly refused to believe that Edward would kill him. Pseudo-Gregory, who may have been present at the occasion, leaves us with a colourful tale:

> And in that journey was Owen Tudor i-take and brought into Haverfordwest, and he was beheaded at the market place, and his head was set upon the highest grice of the market cross and a mad woman combed his hair and washed away the blood of his face, and she got candles and set about him bremming, moo than a hundred. This Owen Tudor...weening and trusting all away that he should not be headed till he saw the axe and the block, and when that he was in his doublet he trusted on pardon and grace till the collar of his red velvet doublet was ripped off. Then he said, 'That head shall lie on the stock, that was wont to lie on Queen

Katherine's lap,' and put his heart and mind wholly unto God, and fully meekly took his death. [9]

Edward and Warwick do not appear to have been in touch with each other between Wakefield and Mortimer's Cross. Warwick was still in London, though as the men of the south were ready to march with him at the drop of a hat, for the time being there was little for Edward to worry about. Smugly, Warwick had awarded himself his dead father's office of Great Chamberlain of England, and at the end of January his brother John was created Lord Montagu. On 8 February, with great pageantry, Warwick, Wenlock, Lord Bonvile and Sir Thomas Kyriell were elected to the Order of the Garter, and Warwick was informed that the massive Lancastrian army joint-commanded by the queen and Henry Somerset was but a week's march off London.

For some reason, Margaret then decided to change course and enter London by another route. Warwick's spies informed him of the detour: he was on his guard and assumed correctly that the Lancastrians would have to pass through St Albans. King Henry had been at the first battle here, and Warwick wanted to make sure that if there was going to be a second conflict on the same spot that he would be here again—a captive king was a great bargaining counter. The Yorkists set out from London on 12 February: with Warwick were his brother Montagu, Suffolk, Norfolk, Arundel, Lord Bonvile, Sir Thomas Kyriell—and Captain Lovelace, who was in command of the men of Kent. Pseudo-Gregory was here too: he appears to have fought in the infantry, the closest one gets to establishing his identity.

His estimation of numbers is as usual way out: he tells us that the queen had but 5,000 men, and Warwick 100,000. The true estimation may be 20,000 in total, of which just over half were Lancastrians.

As with Northampton, there was treachery afoot when Captain Lovelace smuggled out a detailed plan of Warwick's defences to the queen, which meant that he obviously intended to desert at the critical moment of the battle. Margaret decided against attacking the Yorkists' central line and went for the flank instead—unheard of in those days of chivalry and sportsmanship.

Warwick instructed the Duke of Norfolk to stretch his forces in a line extending for four miles eastwards from the town to the locality known as No Man's Land, a wide patch of heathland near the village of Sandridge: this would block off the two roads leading into the town from Luton, one of which would almost certainly have been taken by the queen. Warwick spent four days preparing his defences, which were unique at the time. The archers were supplied with parvisses—door-sized shields of thick wood, studded with sharp nails and with pivots which enabled them to open, then close again after the arrow had been fired. They were doubly effective because if the archer fell, the nails acted like caltraps and proved disastrous to the roughly shod foot-soldiers. Points of attack and possible escape were strung with nets measuring twenty-four feet by four, with nails fixed at every second knot. Arrows could be fired through these. There were also spiked wooden lattices, fatal to the charging horses. Warwick had learned a little from Northampton in acquiring a large supply of handguns, to be fired by Burgundian mercenaries, and had also employed a number of Burgundian petardiers. [10] The Yorkists' western flank was shielded by archers positioned within the town. Montagu's left wing of Kentishmen was stretched eastwards across farmland and meadow, while Warwick himself commanded the central wing. Never had he been so confident.

During the afternoon of 16 February, Margaret's force reached Luton, swerved to the west, and became engaged in a minor scuffle at Dunstable. The small Yorkist contingent was commanded by the town butcher—it was practically wiped out. Two-hundred Yorkists were slain, and the butcher, whose name is not listed in any of the chronicles, hanged himself in a fit of remorse.

The next day, Shrove Tuesday, the Lancastrians were sighted moving along Watling Street, intent on striking St Albans from the north-west. Their advance guard got no further than the stream of Yorkist arrows. Undaunted, the majority of the army marched across the fields north of the town, breaking into the eastern end of St Peter's Street. The Yorkist archers here were brought down with comparative ease, and by mid-day their left flank was faced with a force much larger than it had anticipated. Similarly, the Lancastrians to the north found themselves flanked on either side by massive Yorkist contingencies, and here the situation appeared decidedly grim. Adding to the confusion, there was a strong wind and it had started to snow. This presented severe problems for the Yorkist hand-gunners, for the powder was blown away, and worse still some of the weapons exploded in their faces. The nets were similarly ineffective, as the queen's troops simply burst into the town, all but collapsing Montagu's wing. By late afternoon the Lancastrians seemed to be everywhere, and there was a compression of confused fighting in the central street of the town, as there had been in 1455.

Vainly, the Yorkists fought on, and might well have been on their way towards winning when Captain Lovelace and his Kentishmen finally decided to desert. The battle was over: the Yorkists fled, leaving King Henry behind—to prevent him from wandering off, as had happened the last time, Warwick had installed him in a house, not that this stopped him from doing so again.

The chroniclers more or less agree that around 2,500 men, mostly Yorkists, were killed in the battle. Edward, Prince of Wales and Andrew Trollope were knighted on the field—the latter had stepped on to a caltrap and announced that he was unworthy of the honour because he had only killed fifteen men. King Henry was discovered sitting under an oak tree, singing, and was promptly reunited with his wife. With him were Sir Thomas Kyriell and several Yorkists who had naively believed the king's promise to protect them if they were taken prisoner. Margaret summoned the Prince of Wales, already developing into a bloodthirsty young lout, and allowed him to choose their fate. He watched gleefully as they were dispatched, sorry only that their deaths were not as gory as he would have liked. Ten years later, this obnoxious creature would get his just deserts, many believed not a moment too soon.

Montagu was captured, but allowed to go free and travel to York. He was Warwick's brother, while the royal favourite Henry Somerset's brother was being held captive by the Nevilles in Calais: Margaret feared reprisals, should anything happen to him. **[11]**

Unlike Northampton and the first battle of St Albans, the Lancastrians lost just one high-ranking adherent: Sir John Grey. His death was not considered too important at the time, but he left behind a pretty young widow who would soon have England rocking on its foundations. **[12]**

NOTES

1. Antonio de la Torre, writing to Sforza from Sandwich, 'The Earl of Warwick, who is like another Caesar in these parts…if they do not quickly send the (Cardinal's) hat, everything will go to ruin.' *Calendar of Milanese Papers.*
2. 11 January 1461, Warwick's letter to the Pope, commenting on the usefulness of Coppini, and adding a reference to 'the destruction of some of my kinsmen.' *Calendar of Venetian Papers.*
3. William Fitzalan, Earl of Arundel. Warden of the Cinque Ports, 1471.
4. Reginald Grey, Lord Grey of Wilton; Sir Walter Devereux (1432-85), Lord Ferrers of Chartley, 1461; Sir William Herbert (c1423-69), Lord Herbert 1461, Earl of Pembroke, 1468.
5. Mary's husband, James II, had died in 1460 while besieging Roxburgh Castle. By 1462 she herself was powerless.
6. Henry, 6th Lord Fitzhugh (c1429-72) was married to Alice Neville, Warwick's sister.
7. Parhelion: a spot on the solar halo which creates one or more mock suns, probably caused at Mortimer's Cross by ice-crystals.
8. Owen Tudor (c1400-61) grandfather of Henry VII. He and Catherine of Valois, the widow of Henry V, lived together (or may have married). Besides Edmund and Jasper there were two daughters (Jacina is alleged to have married Sir Reginald Grey of Wilton), and a third son, Dafydd, is said to have been knighted by Henry VII.

9. William Worcestre in his *Short English Chronicle* (76-7) says Hereford. Gregory errs: Haverfordwest is too far away, and the Yorkists had no control over the far west of Wales. See Ross, 32n.
10. A petard was a kind of medieval firework. It was an earthenware pot on a string, filled with powder and thrown like a Molotov cocktail.
11. Edmund Beaufort (c1439-71), 4th Duke of Somerset, was Henry's next brother. In July 1460 he was captured on the Isle of Wight by Warwick's lieutenant, Geoffrey Gate, and imprisoned at Calais. *Calendar of Milan*, i, 51.
12. Sir John, son of Sir Edward Grey, Lord Ferrers of Groby. His wife was of course Elizabeth Woodville.

Edward IV as a young man

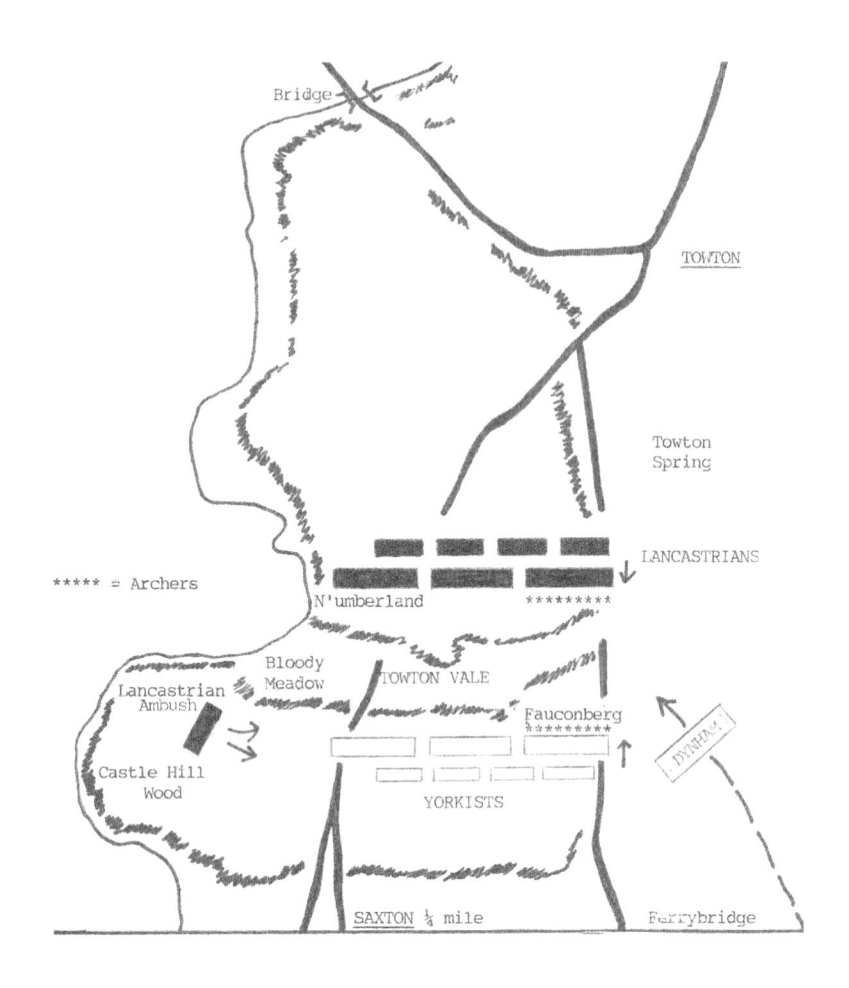

The Battle of Towton
29 March 1461

8

Edward IV: Triumph At Towton
1461

Immediately after the battle of St Albans, the London Council sent envoys to Queen Margaret, informing her that the city gates would be opened to her, but only providing she kept her army under control. The people had learned of the Lancastrians' plunderous march from the north and were terrified of them running amock within the city. Accompanying the envoys were Jacquetta Woodville, and the widows of Lord Scales and the Duke of Buckingham. Margaret sent the larger part of her army back to Dunstable, but demanded food and money for those remaining.

Some of the merchants complied, but the locals took umbrage, attacking the supply-carts and seizing whatever these contained for themselves. There were further problems when the Scottish contingency of Margaret's army, over which she had no control, began running riot on the outskirts of the city. When the people began fighting back, fearing another Jack Cade-style rebellion, Margaret's men began to desert, and she realised that she was beaten. Reluctantly, she took what troops she had left back to York, and these caused as much trouble retreating as they had while travelling south.

Warwick, meanwhile, had no intention of giving in. King Henry was no longer in his hands, so with typical flair he decided to 'make' another. For what man would prove a better king than Edward of York? The Londoners were still hugely supportive of the Yorkists: despite her victory at St Albans, Queen Margaret's recent behaviour and that of her army had rendered her more unpopular than ever.

Warwick and Edward were reunited on 22 February, in the Cotswolds at Chipping Norton or Burford. The former was still licking his wounds after St Albans, while Edward was ecstatic over his expected success at Mortimer's Cross. And when Edward asked where the king was, Warwick announced that *he*, Edward of York, was the king. Historians have given Warwick the nickname, 'Kingmaker', but it must be said that much of Edward's success could only be attributed to his *own* efforts. Unlike many of his contemporaries, he had been blessed with sound common sense and an acute, tactical brain. Unlike his father the Duke of York, Edward was patient and capable of making exactly the right decision, even under extreme stress. This, and his persuasive charm and innate charisma made him the ideal candidate for the throne of England, and he was essentially only interested in fighting for what he believed was right. Edward may or may not have nurtured an ambition to aim so high as the throne: almost certainly he would have got there without any help from Warwick.

News of what was about happen was forwarded to the Londoners, and on Thursday 26 February Edward and Warwick triumphantly entered the city. One propaganda pamphlets read, 'Let us walk in a new wine-yard, and let us make a gay garden in the Month of March with this fair white rose and herb, the Earl of March.' [1]

Edward was elected king by procedure, a custom dating back to the pre-Conquest era, backed by popular demand and local support from whichever magnates were in London at the time. On Sunday 1 March, Bishop Neville addressed 4,000 cheering citizens in St George's Fields: he proclaimed that King Henry had forfeited the people's allegiance by asserting the House of York's claim to the throne—a clever way of twisting words, but true. The crowd roared its appreciation, claiming that they wanted Edward as their rightful king. The possibility of a coronation may have been discussed, though Edward would not have pressed this point, particularly with Margaret of Anjou still at large and undefeated.

On 3 March, a temporary council was hurriedly assembled at Barnard's Castle. Amongst those present were Warwick, the Duke of Norfolk, Lords Fitzwalter, Herbert and Ferrers of Chartley, the Archbishop of Canterbury, and the Bishops of Salisbury and Exeter. [2] It was officially agreed that Edward should be king. On 4 March he listened to the *Te Deum* and attended ceremonies at Westminster Hall and the Abbey. The oath was sworn: he donned the royal robes and cap of estate, and was given the sceptre. Finally, he took his seat in the marble chair known as the King's Bench. The new monarch was a few weeks off his nineteenth birthday.

Immediately after his acceptance, Edward and his adherents set about raising the troops now essential to crush Margaret of Anjou once and for all. On 6 March, proclamations were sent to the sheriffs of thirty-three English counties, advising everyone that he was king: every able-bodied man between the ages of sixteen and sixty was summoned to join the royal army and upon pain of death ordered to commit neither robbery, rape nor sacrilege. Similarly, pardons were promised for any Lancastrian who offered to change sides and join the new regime. As a warning to would-be traitors, a reward of one-hundred pounds was offered to any person who killed one of the following: Sir Andrew Trollope, the deserter at Ludlow and how Henry Somerset's right-hand man; Sir Thomas Tresham, the Lancastrian Speaker at their 1459 Parliament of Devils; Thomas FitzHarry of Herefordshire, who had fought with Wiltshire at Mortimer's Cross; the two Bastards of Exeter, one of whom had beheaded Salisbury after the battle of Wakefield; and 'a certain William Grimsby', who had also been at Wakefield.

Edward, though king, had little money of his own to finance an expedition against Margaret of Anjou: such was their confidence in his abilities, many men paid their own way. Whatever else Edward required, he borrowed. Since July 1460, London had loaned £4,166 13s 4d to the Yorkist cause, and another £4,048 was doled out within three days of Edward becoming king. What else he required, he borrowed from religious houses and churches. [3]

On Saturday 7 March, Warwick marched north via the West Midlands, and began recruiting men. In Coventry, the Bastard of Exeter was caught and executed. William Fauconberg followed on 11 March, with the foot-soldiers. They met up with Edward north of the River Trent—the king had left London on 13 March with the Duke of Norfolk and his army and a large detachment of Burgundian mercenaries riding under the banner of the French Dauphin, the future Louis XI. It was learned that the Lancastrians had taken up battle position north of the River Aire, between the villages of Saxton and Towton.

On 27 March, Warwick's advance guard reached the crossing of the Aire at Ferrybridge. The structure here had been smashed by Lancastrians under a force led by Lord Clifford. Warwick and his second-in-command, Lord Fitzwalter, set off with a contingency to repair it: at dawn the next day they were surprised by Clifford. Warwick was wounded in the leg by an arrow, and Fitzwalter was killed. Warwick sent William Fauconberg, Sir Walter Blount and the Kentish captain Robert Horne upstream immediately, to the crossing at Dingtingvale Valley. Clifford was taken unawares, and the alleged slayer of Edmund of Rutland died with an arrow in his throat when he foolishly removed his gorget. The Lancastrian contingency retreated to join up with that of Queen Margaret. By nightfall the entire Yorkist army, with the exception of the Duke of Norfolk's division, had crossed the Aire and were encamped but a mile distant of the Lancastrians, south of Saxton.

The battle of Towton, fought on Palm Sunday, 29 March 1461, is the bloodiest conflict to have even been fought on British soil. The number of men engaged was exceptionally large: an estimated 40,000 Yorkists and 45,000 Lancastrians.

Henry Somerset's host was positioned on a ridge between the two villages, on York Plain. This rise could only be observed from the west, and Somerset's left was protected by a bog: to his right was a steep slope leading to the Cock Beck, and this was partially wooded. At the time of the battle the terrain was wilder even than it is today: largely uncultivated heathland, open to the elements. The beck itself—again hard to imagine today—was just as dangerous as the one at Blore Heath had been. Because of the inclement weather it was in full spat, six-feet deep in parts; the area surrounding it was boggy and unpredictable. Somerset's frontage, because of his position behind Towton Vale, was narrow and limited: instead of being stretched out in a long line, his divisions stood the one behind the other—not a great military tactic, but unavoidable. His men must have spent an uncomfortable night out in the open: only the leaders and knights would have had any form of cover.

The Yorkists drew up on the opposite ridge, facing their enemies across the shallow dip and able to see them clearly. Edward, Warwick and Fauconberg aside, there were no great peers on the Yorkists' side—the minor ones included Grey de Ruthyn, Scrope of Bolton, Stanley and Clinton. [4] The Lancastrians had many: any onlooker would have observed a greater splash of coloured banners on their side of the ridge. Margaret herself was well out of the way, in York, and if she had ever prayed in her life, she did so now.

Palm Sunday dawned bitterly cold, with a grey sky hung heavy with snow. Norfolk's contingency still had not arrived—the Duke was chronically sick, and would not see the year out. Nothing is known of his exact location at this stage, but Edward ultimately opted to begin without him. The initial challenge was issued by Fauconberg, as the first snow was starting to fall. Little is known of the battle after this. Fauconberg took full advantage of the fierce south wind—his vanguard was facing that of Trollope and Northumberland, across the dip. He ordered his archers to move forwards several paces, fire, then retreat to the main body of the Yorkist army. This was done: the snow suddenly turned to sleet and the Lancastrians found it impossible to distinguish between the sleet and the arrows: hundreds fell in that first volley. The Lancastrians returned fire, but the wind and sleet was in their faces, and their arrows were blown off-course and fell several feet short of the Yorkist front line. Unaware of this, they fired volley after volley until their quivers were empty. Fauconberg anticipated the right moment and sent off another volley—not only of his own arrows, but of the ones sent across by the enemy. Only a few were returned: most became embedded in the ground, forming caltraps for the poorly-shod foot soldiers in the Lancastrians' front ranks.

The Lancastrians advanced in mass confusion down the slope to the spot now known as Bloody Meadow, east of the Cock Beck, and the slaughter here was horrendous on both sides. Some 80,000 cold, desperate men fought hand-to-hand in the treacherous bog which was getting worse by the minute—though here, the snow and sleet was not as bad as it had been up on the ridge. Unlike any other battle in these civil wars, each man had to make his own decision once he ventured into the dip, for the commanders could not get close enough to bawl orders. Edward may have adopted Warwick's battle-cry of sparing the common men and killing the leaders, but it is doubtful anyone would have heard him. In next to no time, men were fighting on a carpet of corpses and snow. Casualties were extremely heavy: men who did not die of their wounds very quickly succumbed to exposure, and the leaders had the invidious task of supplementing the slain with reinforcements. The Yorkists suffered an ambush, south of Bloody Meadow at Castle Hill Wood, but their central and right attack held good until about mid-day, and Edward is said to have been everywhere, urging his men on and proving that he could stand his ground without the famous Warwick. By early afternoon, however, it was becoming increasingly more difficult to find reinforcements, and the scenario in and around the Cock Beck was horrendous. Even minor wounds, no problem in the past, were proving fatal: men who fell were unable to get back up again—crushed by their horses, or trampled to death by their fellows.

Edward realised to his horror that the Yorkists were losing. Then, when crisis point had been reached, a miracle occurred. To the Yorkists' right suddenly appeared the Duke of Norfolk's banner—not held by Norfolk, but by John Dynham. The loyal Devonian, who had beaten the odds to survive his appalling injuries sustained at Sandwich, had relieved his sick friend of his army and marched it through Sherburn-in-Elmet, and along the slushy, freezing lanes towards the battlefield. Immediately, the new recruits took up position.

Dynham's arrival was the turning point of the battle. Without his help, the Yorkists almost certainly would have lost. Now, they quickly made up for lost ground. Dynham's men, in spite of their harsh journey, were fresh and eager to fight. By late afternoon the Lancastrians had begun a slow retreat: this precipitated to mass flight. At this stage in the conflict the enemy losses were particularly heavy, attempting to get up a steep slope, encumbered by armour, with the sleet in their faces and the Yorkists in hot pursuit. Dynham, disappointed that he had arrived late—and unaware that he had saved the day, inasmuch as he had saved Edward's life at Ludlow—refused to give in now, and using his own initiative he and John Wenlock tore after the fleeing Lancastrians with a large contingency, chasing them within a mile of York and dispatching many. There is no accurate account of how many men were killed at Towton, though it was probably around 28,000. This of course would not include the large number who died of their wounds or from frostbite. When one considers the comparatively low population in England at the time, even the lowest estimate is dreadful. [5]

Lancastrian losses amongst the nobility were high: Lords Dacre, de Maulay, Welles, Sir Richard Percy, Sir Henry Stafford, Sir John Heyton, and that scoundrel, Andrew Trollope. [6] The Earl of Northumberland was severely wounded, and died the next day. According to Pseudo-Gregory, forty-two knights were captured and put to death. The Yorkists lost only one man of note besides Lord Fitzwalter—the Kentish captain, Robert Horne.

The next day, the Yorkists entered York and there followed an emotional scene when the heads of York, Rutland and Salisbury were taken down from Micklegate. These were sent to Pontefract, to be interred with their bodies. The Earl of Devon, said by Pseudo-Gregory to have been taken ill in York and thus prevented from fleeing, was executed along with a number of others—their heads replacing the ones that had been taken down. Edward and Warwick were also reunited with relatives who had been captured after St Albans: Montagu, Lord Fitzwarin, and Lord Berners. [7]

Margaret of Anjou, devastated by the news of the Lancastrian defeat, fled with King Henry and the Prince of Wales to Scotland. Soon she would be joined by Henry Somerset, Exeter, Lord Roos, Sir John Fortescue and Sir Humphrey Dacre. [8] The Earl of Wiltshire, who does not appear to have played a major part in the battle, had fled to Newcastle.

NOTES

1. Gregory, 215; *Short English Chronicle*, 77.
2. John Radcliffe (d 1461) married the heiress Elizabeth Fitzwalter, of Woodham Walter, and curiously took her name. She married John Dynham, and died mysteriously during the reign of Richard III.
3. *P.R.O. Warrants For Issues*: E 404/72/1. Number 22.
4. Thomas, Lord Stanley (c.1435-1504), Earl of Derby. He later married Margaret Beaufort.
5. The numbers of dead stated are: *The Paston* Letters, 28,000 of which 20,000 were Lancastrians; *Hall's Chronicle*, 36,776; *Croyland Chronicle*, 36,776.
6. Lionel Welles was the third husband of Margaret, daughter of John, 3rd Lord Beauchamp of Bletsoe. Lord Dacre is said to have been buried in Saxton churchyard, sitting astride his horse. Considering the hardness of the ground and the fact that he was on the losing side, this is extremely unlikely. Henry Stafford was the late Duke of Buckingham's son.
7. William Bourchier (c1416-69). His son Fulk later married John Dynham's sister.
8. Sir John Fortescue (c1394-c1476). Chief Justice on the King's Bench, 1442.

9

The Welsh & Northumbria Campaigns
1461-1463

One wonders about the relationship between the young king and Warwick at this formative stage of the former's career. Edward was nineteen, handsome, brave, loquacious, and his prestige throughout England was unequalled even amongst his enemies. In his own right he had won two battles, whereas Warwick had failed miserably at St Albans.

Regarding the young warrior's other battles, it is certain that Towton would have been lost had it not been for Edward's presence: Grey de Ruthyn had helped his contingency during the first, and Dynham had led Norfolk's army on the king's behalf. Neither of these men had liked Warwick's method of working, and after being forced to preside over the seemingly pointless executions of Somerset's men at Calais, Dynham is known to have loathed him—in later life, Warwick and Edward's brother, Clarence, would make use of this loathing, as will be seen. Now, the boisterous earl found himself overshadowed by his former protégé, who had the power to command and dismiss at will. Warwick had helped Edward attain the dizzy heights of success, but what would there be in it for him now? Warwick could not ascend further and it would have been near-impossible for him to get any wealthier.

The Yorkists spent a leisurely few weeks in York, finding no resistance in a county which was essentially Lancastrian, winning the hearts of the city's most prominent citizens. Edward was able to spread his charm like a soothing balm. He allowed himself to be entertained by Warwick at Middleham, and together they travelled further north to Durham. Here they were warmly welcomed by Bishop Booth, a former adherent of Margaret of Anjou but now firmly on the new king's side. Edward appointed him his confessor. Thenon he travelled up to Newcastle. [1]

James Butler, Earl of Wiltshire had been captured at Cockermouth, along with Doctor Morton and a few others. [2] Morton was held for a while, then released to join his queen. For Wiltshire there was no mercy, and on 1 May he was executed: his head was dispatched south to be set upon London Bridge.

The Scots king, James II, had been killed by one of his own exploding bombards on 3 August 1460, while besieging Roxburgh Castle, leaving behind his eight-year old son, also named James. His widow, Mary of Guelders, had been appointed Regent. For some time her uncle, Philip of Burgundy, had been urging her to support the Yorkist cause, but since Towton the Scots had offered refuge to the exiled Margaret of Anjou and the deposed King Henry. Margaret, of course, would never have been content taking a back-seat, and her promise to secure for Mary of Guelders the mighty border fortress of Berwick still held good.

Early in June, a Scots-Lancastrian force attacked Carlisle, only to be beaten back by Montagu: Warwick's brother was his second-in-command. Towards the end of the month, the Lancastrians retaliated: Lords Dacre, Roos and Rougement-Grey stole across the border to Brancepeth, the Earl of Westmoreland's castle south of Durham. With them was King Henry. Their attack amounted to little: it was scattered by a force led by the Bishop of Durham. What followed was like a medieval game of ping-pong. On 31 July, Warwick was appointed Warden of the East and West Marches towards Scotland. By September the great stronghold of Alnwick submitted. Dunstanborough soon followed suit, though Sir Ralph Percy, its Lancastrian constable, was allowed to stay in command.

It was not considered safe for Edward to travel any further north of Newcastle, and essential that he return to London as soon as possible. Leaving the Nevilles behind, he set off, making overnight stops at Preston, Warrington, Manchester, Chester, Stafford, Eccleshall, Lichfield, Coventry, Warwick, Davenport, and Stony Stratford. He stayed here for two nights, taking time to visit Lord Rivers, who lived nearby at Grafton. His entourage and friends might have thought it strange, or even offensive, to display such obvious friendship towards the Woodvilles: Rivers and his son Anthony had fought for the queen at Towton—the latter was still missing, presumed dead. Later he would turn up safe and well, and with his father be granted a customary pardon. Had Edward' adherents been aware of the goings on at Grafton during those two nights, they might even have proved hostile towards him.

On 12 June, Edward arrived at his palace at Sheen, having ridden more than fifty miles in a single day. He triumphantly entered London on Friday 26 June: the people were overjoyed, but at the back of their minds they must have been thinking that their new king would remain insecure while the former one lived.

Edward's coronation took place at Westminster Abbey on 28 June—a Sunday, which like fighting on holy days was deemed unlucky, not that this deterred him. He was crowned by Archbishop Bourchier of Canterbury, a man who would crown two more monarchs. There was little money to spare—Edward was in debt and the Exchequer coffers empty—but the show had to go on and the people of London were given a day to remember, with pageantry and a bottomless sea of ale and wine. There were further ceremonies when adherents were rewarded for their services: William Fauconberg was created Earl of Kent, Viscount Bourchier became Earl of Essex **[3]**; Wenlock, Hastings and Herbert became lords, and Sir Walter Devereux became Lord Ferrers of Chartley. Other lordships included Ogle, Stafford of Southwick, Lumley, and Sir Humphrey Bourchier. **[4]**

John Dynham, who had previously rejected a knighthood, turned down a lordship, still maintaining that the only honour he wanted was to serve his king, which he would do with all his heart. Edward's brothers, George and Richard, were created Duke of Clarence and Duke of Gloucester.

Edward knew that an uneasy time lay ahead of him. The fact that a crown had been placed upon his head did not mean that his troubles would vanish overnight. London was decidedly pro-Yorkist, and London had acclaimed him as its king, so it would have been easy for his heart to rule his head. Large parts of the country were against him: Lancastrian sympathisers would be active for some time to come. The King's Council, too, was relatively weak: within it, Edward had few supporters, and the only solution to this problem was, he decided, to issue pardons will-nilly and hope that such support would prove permanent. Therefore he opened his borrowed purse and his heart to such undefinable rogues as Montagu and Henry Somerset, when he should not have done.

Problems in Norhumberland were imminent, but Edward ignored these for now. He realised that the only way he would be able to maintain popular support would be by letting as many of his subjects see him as possible, and in August 1461 set off on a tour of the southern counties. With him were Lord Hastings, the Earl of Essex, and a number of judges. The first towns on his itinerary were Canterbury and Sandwich. At a leisurely pace he visited Lewes (23 August), and East Meon in Hampshire, where tenants petitioned him about their rapacious landlord William Waynfleet, Bishop of Winchester. Edward, wise for one so young, recommended that they should bring the matter up at his next Parliament. [5] Proceeding through Salisbury and Devizes, hearing more petitions, Edward arrived in Bristol on 4 September to an unexpected but welcome show of singing and dancing. That he secured the love and the respect of the people here was an enormous bonus, for Bristol then was the second city in England, after

London. Edward stayed at the Mayor's house for almost a week, and personally presided over the trial of the Devonshire traitor, Sir Baldwin Fulford. Found guilty, Fulford was executed on 9 September: his head adorned a spike in the market place until March 1463, when it was removed, 'because it daily falleth down among the feet of the citizens.' [6]

Thenon Edward paid visits to Gloucester and Hereford, and he finally arrived at Ludlow on 18 September. The castle would remain one of his favourite homes—surprising, because it was such a maudlin place, and he was anything but brooding. He stayed here for eight days, granting the town a Charter (dated 7 December 1461), then returned to his royal palace, by way of Stony Stratford and another courtesy call on the Woodvilles.

Wales was hostile towards the new king, and on 8 July Sir Walter Devereux and Lord Herbert had been asked to raise troops in the border counties to suppress problems there and take command of the castles still held in King Henry's name. These included Harlech, Denbigh and Pembroke. The latter was held by the all-powerful Jasper Tudor. In Bristol and Bridgewater, sailors were press-ganged into joining Herbert's fleet, and in August the lords of the Marches were ordered to raise men for Herbert's expedition at their own expense. Herbert set out on 8 September, while Edward was still in Bristol, and met with a great deal of resistance from all the Welsh castles *but* Pembroke. On 30

September this was delivered into his hands—it was later bestowed on him. Within the great fortress, Herbert discovered a four-year old boy, Henry Tudor. No one could have known at the time that within a quarter of a century, this boy would become king.

Henry's mother, Margaret Beaufort, had been born 31 May 1443. As a small child she had married and separated from the son of the Duke of Suffolk. In 1455 she had married Jasper's brother, Edmund Tudor: he had died suddenly in November 1456, and his posthumous child had come into the world on 28 January 1457. Margaret's mother was still living, and Margaret herself was immensely rich—she had retained her Beaufort estates, and much of her two husbands' wealth. [7] Young Henry was left to live with the Herberts for the time being—his father's estates had been confiscated but he was still Margaret's heir, and Herbert had purchased his wardship for £1,000. It was his intention to have the boy marry one of his daughters.

On 16 October, at Twt Hill near Caernarvon, Herbert clashed with a large contingency of Welsh-Lancastrians commanded by Jasper Tudor and the Duke of Exeter. The Lancastrians were defeated, but the leaders managed to escape. Denbigh yielded in January 1462, and Carreg Cennen held out until May. Herbert did not have much luck getting Harlech to surrender, however. Edward would have to wait until August 1468 for this.

Edward's first Parliament opened on 4 November 1461, and

sat with several breaks until 6 May 1462. There were around three-hundred members in the House of Commons, while the House of Lords comprised six earls, thirty-four barons, sixteen bishops, two archbishops, and the Prior of St John. [8] Full houses were not in evidence, and of course none of the peers who were with Margaret of Anjou were invited. The Speaker was Sir James Strangeways, whose address commented on 'the beauty of personage that it has pleased Almighty God to send you.' Compared with the dim-witted, dour King Henry, Edward must have seemed like someone from another world, and he had already proved beyond the shadow of a doubt that he was more than just a pretty face. Strangeways then re-assessed Edward's right to the throne by claiming that the woes of the past were due solely to the murder of King Richard II, in 1400. Many of the peers present had already sworn fealty to Henry: such oaths were now declared null and void to enable Henry VI—now plain Henry of Lancaster—to be attainted of treason. This meant that Henry's lands were forfeit to his successor, who was now solvent again and able to pay off his debts!

In the eschelons of medieval society, the Pastons were not of any particular importance. What makes them vital to this generally poorly-chronicled period of English history is that over a thousand of their minutely-detailed letters have survived. Most appertain to mundane business matters, they are badly written, and their spelling is bad. Their substance, however, is unique, and like Pseudo-Gregory, one or other of the Pastons appear to have been present at most of the major events during the latter half of the fifteenth century.

The elder John Paston (d 1466) was a lawyer of dubious reputation and an acquaintance of Sir John Fastolff, an old campaigner who had amassed a fortune during the French Wars. When Fastolff died in 1469, Paston claimed to have been present at the death-bed and even produced a will within which his 'patron' had bequeathed him some of his estates. The will was contested: nothing came of it and Lawyer Paston moved into Caister Castle with his family. During the next seven years much of his time was spent in London on business, and his wife Margaret was left to fight off the other claimants to the Fastolff lands and bring up an unruly brood of five sons and two daughters. Their letters are not made any easier by the fact that two of these sons were named John. The younger John appears to have been an amiable man, hard-working and honest. The elder John was attached to King Edward's new Treasurer, the Earl of Essex: he was obviously hoping to feather his own nest by acquiring some sort of royal patronage and thus assist his father in his squabbles.

By the time Edward's first Parliament sat in November 1461, Lawyer Paston, recently elected as one of the new members for Norwich, had become involved in a bitter feud with another member, Sir John Howard—a man who had taken office without actually holding any land in Norfolk. [9] Paston alleged that during a scuffle, one of Norfolk's adherents twice struck him with a dagger, that his life had been saved because the thickness of his doublet. This saw a petition being presented to the king, for Howard was a member of the royal household. Paston was twice summoned to London about the matter, but never turned up. On 11 October, his brother Clement wrote to him, warning him of the implications involved in disobeying a royal command, and of the consequences should he dare to do so a third time. Paston travelled to London once more. He was thrown into the Fleet prison for two weeks, and upon his release, Howard imprisoned in his place. Edward then appointed Sir Thomas Montgomery as Sheriff of Norfolk, and peace and order were restored. **[10]**

Constable of England was a relatively new position which invariably meant that the holder could try and condemn without an attending jury. In February 1462 this enviable office was given to John Tiptoft, Earl of Worcester. **[11]** Tiptoft was an intellectual, educated at Oxford 1440-3, but his reputation for cruelty, and for public executions in particular, quickly earned him the nickname 'Butcher'. To curb the still-mounting Lancastrian sympathies throughout England, King Edward appointed a formidable commission or array of twenty-three barons and ten judges, in eight cities and twenty-five counties. Almost at once a plot was uncovered, spearheaded by Sir Thomas Tuddenham, Earl of Oxford, and Oxford's son, Aubrey de Vere. **[12]** These men were arrested and brought before Butcher Tiptoft on 1 February, condemned to death and publicly hanged, drawn and quartered on Tower Hill between 20 and 26 February.

At once, rumours circulated around London that there would be a Scots-French invasion of England from Wales, the north, and the Channel Islands. Charles VII of France had allowed Piers de Brezé to fit out a fleet for an attack on the Channel Islands, and the French already had a hold on Jersey. Then on 22 July 1461 the French king died and was succeeded by his son, Louis XI. The Spider King, as he soon became known, offered a miniscule ray of sunshine by appearing to have a little sympathy with the Yorkist cause—after all, some of his men had crossed the Channel to fight at Towton—and for a time de Brezé was disgraced and the invasion temporarily shelved, at least from the Channel Islands. Unfortunately, de Brezé was still a great friend of Margaret of Anjou, and in April 1462 she and the Prince of Wales set sail from Kircudbright and on 16 April arrived in Brittany, where she was granted an audience with Duke Francis. This did not go well: he refused to have anything to do with her plans, though he did give her money to go and see her father. [13] René of Anjou gave her an even colder reception. Louis XI, however, was excited at the prospect of having a Frenchwoman heading the English government: at a secret meeting in Chinon on 23 June, Margaret agreed to hand Calais over to the French, and two days later a public treaty was signed at Tours. Amongst the signatures were those of Doctor Morton and Jasper Tudor. The invasion would go ahead after all—and who better to lead it than her reputed one-time lover, Piers de Brezé?

Even so, Margaret was to encounter a problem. To reach Calais, she and her army would have to march through Burgundy, which Duke Philip would not allow. William Fauconberg delayed her further by raiding the coast of Britanny in August, preventing her from landing there. By the time she could leave, in October, Louis XI would allow her no more than eight-hundred men, and de Brezé found himself paying for the expedition out of his own purse. He, Margaret and Jasper Tudor and their army set sail for Scotland, where they picked up King Henry and a few extra troops. Sailing down the rugged coast to Northumberland, they landed at Bamborough on 25 October, took the castle, and used it for their base. In next to no time the great fortresses of Alnwick, Dunstanborough, Warkworth and Norham opened their gates to the Lancastrians—their numbers had swollen substantially, en route, and they now presented a serious threat.

Warwick was in Yorkshire, and sent a message to Edward, in London, who responded by appointing him head of a commission of array to suppress the rebels. Edward himself then set off for the north with a impressive force comprising ninety per cent of the English nobility: two dukes, seven earls, thirty-one barons, fifty-nine knights, and 20,000 men. Margaret had expected nothing like this. Terrified, she left the three major castles in the hands of Henry Somerset and Jasper Tudor. King Henry was sent over the border and on 13 October Margaret, de Brezé and Jasper set sail for Scotland, fired with the hope of raising as many men as possibe. Here, their luck ran out. There was a sudden storm, and their ships were wrecked.   Margaret and de Brezé, who cared little for anyone but themselves, left their soldiers to their fate on Lindisfarne and commandeered a fishing vessel which took them to Berwick. At high tide, Lindisfarne was cut off from the mainland and the Lancastrians found themselves stranded. The Bastard of Ogle took it upon himself to launch an attack, which saw some 600 of them being mindlessly butchered.

Edward, essentially a man who loved peace, would have been horrified to learn that one of his own men had taken a leaf out of Queen Margaret's book—had he not been indisposed. He had left York on 19 November, for Durham. Here, he had succumbed to an attack of measles which would put him out of action for several weeks, therefore overall command of the Northumbrian campaign fell on Warwick's shoulders.

Warwick had the good fortune to have virtually all of the Yorkist captains with him, and 8,000 men. William Fauconberg and Anthony Woodville besieged Bamborough, aided by Lords Strange, Say, Grey of Wilton, and the Bastard of Ogle. Dunstanborough was besieged by Sir Ralph Grey, Lords Greystoke, Powys and Scrope, and Butcher Tiptoft. [14] The Duke of Norfolk, from his base in Newcastle, sent supplies, armaments and men to Warwick's base at Warkworth.

The castles did not hold out for long: the Lancastrian soldiers within Bamborough were reported to be starving and reduced to eating their horses. On 26 December it surrendered, Dunstanborough the next day. The soldiers were disarmed and allowed to go free and the captains pardoned.

Henry Somerset and Ralph Percy were captured and taken to Edward, at Durham. Jasper Tudor was offered safe escort to Scotland. Percy promised to turn over a new leaf: Edward allowed him to retain command of the two castles—an act which disgusted Warwick, and which Edward would soon come to regret.

Somerset swore fealty to the king, and he and his cronies set about helping Warwick besiege Alnwick. On 5 January Piers de Brezé re-appeared with a Scots army led by the Earl of Angus. [15] The men of Alnwick joined their allies, leaving the castle undefended, and the next day it fell to the Yorkists.

Edward returned to Fotheringay on 30 January 1463, where he attended the funerals of his father and brother, recently disinterred at Pontefract. Similarly the funerals were held of Warwick's father, brother and recently deceased mother: the corpses of the Nevilles were placed in a chariot and drawn by six black horses to Bisham Abbey on 15 February. Supporting Warwick were his brother Montagu, Lords Hastings and Fitzhugh, the Duke of Clarence, and—representing the king—the Duchess of Suffolk. The ceremony was conducted by George Neville, Bishop of Exeter.

Fresh troubles erupted in Northumberland in March, when Sir Ralph Percy revealed his true colours, allowing a French-Scots force to re-occupy Bamborough and Dunstanborough. Alnwick surrendered to Lord Hungerford, in May—all three strongholds ending up in Lancastrian hands for the third time in less than a year. Montagu, now Warden of the East Marches, went to the rescue. Warwick followed suit on 3 June, assisted by his brother-in-law, Lord Stanley, while word came from London that the king was sending reinforcements. Margaret of Anjou, meanwhile, had joined forces with Mary of Guelders and the young Scots king, in preparation for a full-scale invasion: early in June they besieged Norham Castle, but a few miles from Berwick.

Warwick had gained experience from his winter of 1461-2: the French-Scots army was routed, and retreated across the border. Again, Margeret had been put out of action: she and Piers de Brezé sailed for Sluis, in Holland, leaving King Henry at Bamborough, supposedly in the care of the Bishop of St Andrews.

King Edward, for his part, was collecting money in London for his expedition to the north: he asked the Exchequor for £5,000 for personal expenses, and for another £4,800 to finance Butcher Tiptoft's fleet. The Treasurer, Lord Grey de Ruthyn, pressed the Convocation of Canterbury, then sitting at St Paul's, for additional funds.

On 7 February 1463, while on a visit to Fotheringay, Lord Hastings wrote a letter to Jean de Lannoy, the Burgundian envoy who had recently met the king in London. Hastings was critical of Edward's attitude towards the troubles in the north: 'The King was nonchalantly amusing himself hunting, whilst his servants utterly crush the fools who dare to rebel.' Hastings goes on to write of Warwick's virtues, and of how, 'The Sire de Montagu had pursued the King of Scotland into his own land, ravaged the countryside, killed many Scotsmen so that the Scots would repent and go on repenting till the day of Judgement that they gave assistance to Henry and Margaret.' **[16]**

This letter proves that, despite his wisdom and proved military and governmental abilities, Edward could just as easily lapse into periods of lethargy—a facet of his character which, later in his reign, he would find increasingly more difficult to control.

NOTES

1. Lawrence Booth (d 1480). His half-brother, William, became Archbishop of York in 1476.
2. Master of the Rolls, 1473. Bishop of Ely, 1479.
3. Henry, Viscount Bourchier (c1404-83), Earl of Essex. He married York's sister, Isabel.
4. Humphrey Bourchier, Essex's third son.
5. The petition was heard in the House of Lords on 15 December 1461, when Waynfleet produced several old documents supporting his claim. Judgement was passed in his favour.
6. Schofield, I, pp 197-200.
7. Her mother was Margaret, daughter of John, 3rd Lord Beauchamp of Bletsoe. She married firstly Sir Oliver St John; secondly John Duke of Somerset; thirdly the Lionel Welles killed at Towton.
8. W.J. Dunham: *The Fane Fragment of The 1461 Lords' Journal*, Yale, 1935.
9. *Manners & Household Expenses of th 13th & 15th Centuries*, Roxburghe Club, 1841.
10. Sir Thomas Montgomery (1433-95). His mother was Edward's godmother Lady Say.
11. John Tiptoft (1427-70), Earl of Worcester, 1449, son of the 1st Baron Tiptoft. Married firstly Cecily Neville (d 1450); secondly Elizabeth Baynham (d 1452); thirdly Elizabeth Corbet.
12. Aubrey de Vere, Oxford's eldest son. He married Anne, daughter of the 1st Duke of Buckingham.
13. Francis II (1435-88) last Duke of Brittany.
14. Anthony Woodville was now Lord Scales.
15. George Douglas, 4th Earl of Angus.
16. *Bibliotheque Nationale*, from Schofield, II, 461.

10

Edward & Somerset
1463-1464

There seems little doubt that Edward and Henry Somerset shared a brief relationship. Pseudo-Gregory, writing of the events of 1463-4, observes:

> And the said Sir Harry Beaufort abode still with the King, and rode with him to London. And the King made full much of him: in so much that he lodged with the King in his own bed many nights. The King loved him well, but the duke thought treason under fair cheer, and words, as it appeared. And for a great love the King made jousts at Westminster… [1]

Edward was almost twenty and Somerset twenty-six, so theirs may not be dismissed as an adolescent or experimental fling, while much has to be said Edward's weakness and the handsome Somerset's irascible charm. The former was after all experienced in such matters. He never married, but did supposedly have affairs with Margaret of Anjou and Mary of Guelders, and he also had a bastard son with one Joan Hill. The great love affairs of his life, however, were with men—while obtaining the loyalty of a man like Somerset had enormous advantages for Edward, who might have gone to any length to secure it.

Edward's new love brought its share of problems. The people of England certainly never found out that he and Somerset were sleeping together: had they done so, the consequences might have been unthinkable, and certainly unpardonable when homosexuality was frowned upon by almost everyone, though it was no less prevalent then than it is today. Several kings before Edward had taken male lovers and much more openly, notably William Rufus, Richard II and Edward II—in 1327, the latter had suffered the most excruciating death at the hands of his persecutors (as had his lovers) after making common knowledge of his sexual preferences. The pair's passion was curbed by a riot in Northampton—aimed specifically at Somerset—and Edward reacted by sending him into Wales for his own safety. The King then retired to Fotheringay with his friend, William Hastings, and for several weeks devoted himself the pleasures of hunting and doubtless pursuing females—much to the relief of Hastings, who must have known about Somerset.

How serious Edward was about mounting a full-scale invasion against the Scots may be readily assumed. On 15 August he dispatched a letter to the Salisbury Fathers, demanding that all able-bodied men be ready to join him in Newcastle on 13 September: early in this month he travelled to York, remaining within the county until January 1464.

Somerset's character, at this stage, is not easy to define. Until early 1463 he had been overtly Lancastrian—yet there is no reason to believe that he would not have stayed faithful to Edward, had he been allowed to stay by his side. After his failure to seek refuge in Guisnes: Somerset had become involved with Charles of Charolais, and had seemed genuinely happy with this liaison until being forced out of Guisnes by Warwick. His only hope had been to join his queen, but Margaret had used him the same as she had everyone else. Being with Edward probably reminded Somerset of those balmy days when he had hunted at Ardres with his Burgundian lover, perhaps the only time in his complicated and violent life when he had been truly happy. Edward had offered him friendship, affection and trust. Then, quite suddenly he had found himself ejected from this security.

Somerset may of course have secretly retained his Lancastrian tendencies all the way through his dalliance with Edward: on the other hand his heart may have been dealt a blow that only revenge could heal. In December 1463, he left Wales and travelled to Newcastle, and further rejection: its garrison was manned by former supporters coaxed into supporting the king. Travelling to Durham, he suffered more bad luck: recognised, he fled in the middle of the night, barefoot and wearing only his shirt, and ended up in Bamborough, where he joined King Henry and his clique was augmented by the arrival of Humphrey Neville of Brancepeth and Sir Henry Billingham. [2]

Edward meanwhile made Newcastle more secure by appointing Lord Scrope to captain the town, and reinforce it with men who would hopefully prove more trustworthy than the ones he had expelled.

From his base at Bamborough, Somerset sent out urgent appeals to the Duke of Brittany and Charles of Charolais. He was visited by Guillaume de Cousinot, an agent of Louis XI, thus giving Edward genuine cause for concern that, this time, the French invasion would be for real. [3] The Lancastrians then took Norham Castle and maintained their hold on land south of the Scottish border. Further south, their allies the Cliffords besieged the castle at Skipton-le Craven, and held it in King Henry's name.

In York, on 20 February, Edward hastily summoned a Parliament because of renewed troubles in the Midlands. Warwick was with him. Instead of travelling further north, however, they returned to London for negotiations with the French envoy, Jean de Lannoy. It was a brief sojourn for Edward: upon hearing that Somerset, Hungerford and Roos were laying waste the countryside around Bamborough, he set out for Yorkshire again, leaving Warwick to conclude the business with de Lannoy. A meeting of envoys had been scheduled to take place in Newcastle on 6 March, but safety precautions had to be taken and it was deferred to York for 20 April. Montagu was sent to the Scottish border in the middle of the month to provide a safe escort for the Scots envoys through what was Lancastrian-infested territory. En route to Norham he narrowly avoided an ambush. However, he clashed head-on with the Lancastrians at Hedgeley Moor on 25 April.

Hedgeley Moor was little more than a skirmish, and probably fought on horseback. Somerset, Sir Ralph Percy and Lords Hungerford and Roos commanded the Lancastrians, and it is doubtful that a great many men were involved. Somerset's force was completely overwhelmed, but he, Hungerford and Roos managed to escape. Percy was left for dead on the field. **[4]**

Montagu treated the matter lightly. He met the Scots envoys at Norham, saw them safely to York, then returned to Newcastle.

Somerset, defeated but not disheartened, re-collected his forces and moved south of Alnwick towards the Tyne Valley. From this new base he delivered a fresh challenge which the arrogant Montagu found impossible to ignore. Neither did Montagu go about exacting his revenge in a chivalrous manner, as Edward almost certainly would have. Teaming up with Lords Greystoke and Willoughby, he attacked Somerset's camp in the meadow known locally as The Linnels, three miles south of Hexham, on 14 May 1464, and the young duke found himself trapped. Manoevre within the meadow was extremely limited: many Lancastrians attempted to get away without even trying to fight. The ones who remained stood no chance: by the time they had prepared themselves for battle, Montagu's men had surrounded the encampment, and his archers had opened fire. The escapees were chased into West Dipton Wood, where most of them yielded. Casualties as such were low.

The Lancastrian leaders were captured and brought before Montagu. If Henry Somerset pleaded for mercy, no one listened, and Edward was not around to offer clemency.

Montagu, at the end of his tether, immediately had Somerset and four others executed. That same day his body was taken to Hexham Abbey, where it was interred a few days later. Lords Roos and Hungerford, and a Sir Thomas Findem were later beheaded in Newcastle. Sir Philip Wentworth and several others were executed in Middleham on 18 May. Fourteen more, including Sir Thomas Husey, were dragged before Butcher Tiptoft in York, and as usual he excelled himself by gruesomely dispatching them in two batches on 25 and 28 May. Finally, a Lincolnshire rebel named Sir William Tallboys was found hiding in a coal-pit and executed in Newcastle as late as 20 July.

After Hexham, Montagu focused his attention on the Northumbrian castles. On 23 June, Dunstanborough and Alnwick surrendered. Bamborough, held by Sir Ralph Grey and Sir Humphrey Neville, refused to capitulate, even when all but the ring-leaders were granted customary pardons. Montagu was given little choice but to besiege it with bombards and artillery, and the royal guns were put into action. These had names: Dijon, Newcastle and Richard Bombardel. Grey was badly hurt when one of these brought the ceiling down upon his head, but it was Neville who finally surrendered, and because of this may have been actually pardoned. [5] Grey, who probably would have died in any case, was dragged all the way to Doncaster, to be condemned by Butcher Tiptoft and hanged, doubtless after being beaten up, on 10 July.

King Edward had not been actively involved with the Northumbrian troubles, and it is not known how he reacted to Somerset's death. In any case, he would not have permitted himself to show public remorse, and at least his former friend-lover had not suffered the indignity of having his head put on public display. Also, the fact that Somerset had been given a decent Christian burial so soon after his death proved that Edward must have cared.

For his efforts, Montagu was created Earl of Northumberland, and his personal reward to himself was the signing of an English-Scots truce on 1 June. Edward then moved south. On 14 July he attended a synod in Doncaster, and two days later travelled to Leicester. For the time being, Lancastrian sympathies in England had been curbed, and the north would see nothing of their sovereign for another five years, by which time the tables would have been dramatically turned once more.

NOTES

1. *Gregory's Chronicle*, pp 219-26.
2. Humphrey Neville (ex. 1470). Brancepeth is south of Durham.
3. Guillaume de Rochefort, Chancellor of France.
4. Sir Ralph Percy was the younger son of the 2nd Earl of Northumberland, killed at St Albans in 1455. His elder brother died at Towton. Appointed by Henry VI in 1457, he had served on a number of Lancastrian commissions as late as June 1460.
5. Some reports, notably *Vitellius A XVI f* 125 vo, state that Humphrey was hanged, drawn and quartered in York.

Elizabeth Woodville

11

Edward & Elizabeth Woodville
1464

Between April 1464 and June 1465 there was great mystery concerning the whereabouts of the deposed King Henry. He had disappeared after the battle of Hexham, and the likeliest theory is that he was hidden by sympathisers, or placed with a holy order for safe keeping until an insurrection had been formulated. The recent death of Somerset had of course ensured that no one would consider re-instating a simpleton puppet king in much of a hurry, and most of the Lancastrian leaders were overseas or in hiding.

Margaret of Anjou had arrived at the court of her enemy, Philip of Burgundy. Initially, he had refused to take her in, but he relented, finding the notion of a triple alliance between Burgundy, England and France appealing. At the his court, linked by the common bond of mourning for the man they had both loved, Margaret had befriended Charles of Charolais. He, wishing to avenge Somerset's death and also keen to oppose his father, now offered to invade England. There was one snag—he had no money.

At Philip's court, Margaret was met the chronicler and courtier, Chastelain, and took the elderly charmer into her confidence. As a result he penned a gushing 'biography'. Despite her faults and ruthlessness she remains one of the most fascinating consorts in British history.

Margaret's plight after Hexham, as chronicled by Chastelain, may be exaggerated and at least partially fictitious, but it at least gives us a glimpse of how truly enigmatic and endearing she must have been:

> So a tranquil breeze brought her to Sluys with all the number of her people that she had with her, which was not great. For she arrived there poor and alone, destitute of goods and all desolate; she had neither credence nor money, nor goods, nor jewels to pledge; and her person was without adornment befitting a queen. Her body was clad in one single robe, with no change of clothing. She had no more than seven women for her retinue, and whose apparel was like that of their mistress, formerly one of the most splendid women in the world and now the poorest; she had no other provision except from the purse of her knight, Sir Pierre de Brezé, who himself was in extreme poverty, for he had disbursed and spent every thing in serving her and in carrying on the war against her enemies…he had spent up to 50,000 crowns of his own. It was a piteous thing to see…this high princess dying of hunger and hardship, become forced to throw herself on the mercy of the one in all the world [Philip] whose fame ran as is known, as being most set against her…This noble princess had come there [St Pol] from Bruges in a country cart which covered with canvas like a poor woman going unknown. She had spoken with the Count of Charolais, in Bruges,

who had lent her 500 crowns...she had left her son the Prince of Wales in Bruges, partly from necessity and lack of means to provide for him, partly not wishing to put his person in danger. Not knowing what to do, she dressed herself like a village woman in the garb of a chambermaid to come and seek him out... [1]

Chastelain goes on to describe how, snubbed by Duke Philip, his sister the Duchess of Bourbon had loaned a sympathetic ear while Margaret had recounted her woeful tale: she had her son had had nothing to eat in five days but a single herring; she had borrowed money from a disgruntled Scots archer; she had been attacked by robbers and had begged their leader not to torture her or cut her throat, only to have the robbers fighting amongst themselves over *her*.

As a last resort, Margaret went to see her father: René of Anjou loaned her his Chateau de Coeur, between Nancy and Vichy in the Duchy of Bar, and from this temporary base she gathered about her an impressive group of Lancastrian emigrés including Sir John Fortescue, Doctor Morton, Sir William Faux, Sir Edmund Mountfort, William Grimsby, Sir Henry Roos, Sir Robert Whittingham, the Duke of Exeter and the Bishop of St Asaph. Also with her were Edmund, the new Duke of Somerset (Henry's younger brother), and the same Sir John Courtenay who had sailed to Calais with John Dynham and the Yorkist earls after the rout of Ludlow. [2] Soon, all were plotting again. The new Earl of Wiltshire was at King Alfonso's court in Portugal—

and Fortescue wrote to him, asking for money and 3,000 soldiers. Margaret and the ever blood-thirsty Prince of Wales included letters of their own in the same dispatch—with the exiled queen's customary bad luck, these were intercepted by a French spy and never reached their destination. [3]

With Henry Somerset interred at Hexham Abbey, King Edward's throne was more secure than it had ever been, and the inevitable question arose of finding him a suitable wife, of good stock, who would hopefully provide him with a heir. Edward was twenty-two, and the most eligible catch in Europe. His was a society of cautiously-arranged marriages, where a king was supposed to conform to the dictates of his advisers.

The first would-be match had occurred in 1445 when, aged two, Edward had been considered for the hand of Madeleine, infant daughter of Charles VII of France. A few years later there had been a proposal for him to wed the Duke of Alencon's daughter. The triple-marriage alliance of 1458 has already been discussed, as has John Wenlock's ill-fated mission of 1461, and in 1462 Warwick himself had suggested the king's marriage to Mary of Guelders.

During Warwick's recent meeting with Jean de Lannoy, the subject of a royal union had been brought up again, and in the summer of 1463 the prospective bride had been Louis XI's daughter, Anne. Edward had dismissed the idea as preposterous: Anne was only three years old. Louis next offered the hand of his sister-in-law, fourteen-year old Bona of Savoy. [4] Edward's response was the same: he was not interested in a child, but only in a grown woman he could have sex with at once, without having to wait. Warwick, aware of his former protégé's colossal appetite for sex, had decided not to press. Early in 1464, another would-be queen had been found in Isabella of Castille. [5] Edward rejected this proposal too, instigating a rift between Warwick and himself which would only widen. Also, by this time he was in love with a woman of his *own* choosing.

During one of his visits to Grafton, Edward had been introduced to Lord Rivers' alluring, beautiful widowed daughter, Elizabeth. Her young husband, Sir John Grey, had died fighting for the Lancastrians at the second battle of St Albans, leaving her with two young sons and his title. Edward and Elizabeth had fallen in love, but their relationship had been kept a strict secret—only intimates such as William Hastings and John Dynham may have known, for it was in England's interests that their sovereign should enter into an alliance which would benefit one of the greater Continental powers.

There had been other problems, more pressing: Henry Somerset had still been at large, and Warwick's character was such that Edward had been terrified of displeasing him, in case he suddenly turned against him—or even went over to the other side. It was one thing having one of the dreaded Woodvilles on the Yorkists' side, as Anthony was now—if he turned traitor he could easily dealt with. Wooing and wanting to marry one of their women and make her queen was another matter! As for Edward, his clandestine affair with Somerset had taught him to follow the dictates of his heart, which he now did with an all-consuming passion.

Edward and Elizabeth Woodville are said to have first met under the spreading branches of an oak in the forest at Whittlebury, and the romantic scene is not hard to imagine as akin to a legend by Mallory: the grieving widow, holding her sons by the hand, pleading with the handsome warrior king for the return of her husband's attainted lands. However, it *was* only a legend. Sir John Grey's lands had never been forfeited in the first place. Neither is it likely that Edward was bewitched into Elizabeth's bed by her and her mother, Jacquetta of Luxembourg. Equally absurd is the story circulated at the time that Edward had tried to rape her. Women of all ages—and men—are known to have flung themselves at him.

No contemporary likeness of Elizabeth Woodville has survived: the painting most often seen is a Tudor copy of a lost original. In this she is possessed of the cool, stylised beauty favoured by the artists of the day. In the next century, Edward's grandson, Henry VIII, would receive a very flattering portrait of his bride-to-be, Anne of Cleves, only to recoil in horror when the real thing turned up, literally warts and all. It is quite possible that Elizabeth Woodville was not attractive at all—that where Edward was concerned, true love conquered all and beauty was in the eye of the beholder.

On 23 April, Edward had presided over the Knights of the Garter ceremony at Windsor. After this, he had begun his journey northwards, unaware of the skirmish at Hedgeley Moor, and of Montagu's plans to ambush Somerset. On 30 April he had stopped off at Stony Stratford. The next morning, having told his entourage that he was off on a hunting expedition, he had ridden the short distance to Grafton. With few witnesses present, he and Elizabeth had wed, and several hours later he had returned to Stony Stratford as if nothing had happened. Almost certainly two of these witnesses were Dynham and Hastings: they were with the king most of the time, and a few days after the wedding, Dynham was granted Lord Hungerford's forfeited manors in Devon, Somerset and Oxfordshire, 'for services rendered to his King,'—a singularly generous act on Edward's part which would cause both men a great deal of trouble in the future. [6]

Soon after his wedding, Edward visited Grafton again, as the chronicler, Fabyan, recorded many years after the event:

> And within a day or two after, he sent to Grafton, to the Lord Ryvers, father unto his wife, shewing to him that he would come and lodge with him a certain season, where he was received with all honour, and so tarried there by the space of four days. In which season, she nightly to his bed was brought, in so secret manner, that almost none but her mother was of counsel… [7]

Pseudo-Gregory, reflecting on the king's marriage between 1468-70, gave the impression that his foray into homosexuality had been more widely known than previously thought, but forgave him the indiscretion because Edward had finally done the right thing by choosing his own bride:

> Men marvelled that our sovereign lord was so long without any wife, and were ever feared that he had not been chaste of his living. Now take heed what love may do, for love will not or may not cast no fault nor peril in no thing! [8]

Early in August 1464, Edward attended a preliminary Council meeting in Stamford to discuss proposals for new currency—while his advisers were obviously there hoping that the subject on everyone's mind might be broached: the king's marriage. [9] This did not happen, and with Edward still playing his cards close to his chest, a meeting of the Great Council was arranged to take place in Reading on 14 or 18 September, when it was anticipated that Edward would announce the name of the woman he had chosen, from those previously put to him, to become his queen. [10]

Edward's supporters were confident that he would choose Bona of Savoy—even the Duke of Burgundy had agreed to the match in the end, and Warwick had sent Lord Wenlock across the Channel to be formerly presented to the bride-to-be. Warwick had arranged to personally visit the French court, once the Council meeting at Reading had been dispensed with, which meant he would be meeting the

"Spider King" for the first time. However, once the proceedings opened at Reading, Edward found himself unwilling to keep up the charade. He told the members that for the past five months he had been married to the daughter of Lord Rivers. All were astonished but were probably not horrified or disgusted, as has often been suggested. What caused the most offence was that Edward had failed to consult his friends and advisers, other than Dynham and Hastings, before taking the ultimate plunge. It may well be that he had been apprehensive or afraid of doing so for fear of evoking their outrage. And Warwick, of course, had been made to look silly by sending Wenlock on what may only be described as a fool's errand.

Warwick never forgave Edward: his bitterness and disappointment would escalate to emnity. For now, he contained his anger, though his head was doubtless brimming with dark thoughts when, on 29 September 1464, he and the fourteen-year old Duke of Clarence escorted Elizabeth Woodville to Reading Abbey, where she was publicly accepted as Queen of England.

Because it was late in the year and inclement weather was expected, Elizabeth's actual coronation was postponed until the following summer. The king and queen stayed on in Reading for several weeks, enjoying their honeymoon-proper: then on they rode to Windsor, and finally to Eltham, where they spent their first Christmas together.

NOTES

1. Georges Chastelain (1405-75). *Le Temple de Bocace: Remonstrances Par Maniere de Consolation A Une Desolée Reyne d'Angleterre: Oevres,* Vol 4, 1863.
2. Edmund Beaufort's title was not accepted by the Yorkists, but he is styled Duke of Somerset by Stow (op. cit., 1631, p424). Sir John Courtenay (d 1471), 8th Earl of Devon, 1470, brother of the 6th Earl executed after Towton.
3. John Butler (d 1478), Wiltshire's younger brother. For the letter see *Archaelogical Journal, VII.*
4. Bona eventually married Galeazzo Maria Sforza, Duke of Milan, later assassinated. She was imprisoned by his brother, Ludovico, who was appointed Regent.
5. Isabella of Castile (1451-1504) married Ferdinand of Aragon, 1469. Her father was Henry IV, the Impotent (1425-74).
6. The grant was much opposed and six different commissions were appointed to hear petitions against it. (*Patent Rolls, 4, Edward IV*, p,1, m10; p,ii, mm18, 21,22,23 and 26.
7. Robert Fabyan (d 1513) was a London draper. His chronicle, first published in 1516, is very unreliable but widely read.
8. *Gregory*, 226.
9. The new coins of 1465. Gold: a rose noble or ryal, worth ten shillings; an angel, worth half a mark or six-shillings and eightpence; an angelet or half-angel. Silver: a groat, worth fourpence; a half-groat, a penny, a halfpenny. Copper coins and farthings were no longer minted.

10. The first date is given in Scofield I, 354. Calmette & Perinelle say 28 September. Ross: *Edward IV* (Eyre Methuen, 1975), 91: 'Since Elizabeth's officicial presentation as queen took place on 29 September (*Annales*, 783), and on 3 October Wenlock wrote to Lannoy to inform Louis of the marriage (Waurin, ed Dupont, II, 326-7) it is unlikely that either of these would have been so long delayed if the announcement took place as early as 14 September.'

Charles the Bold
Duke of Burgundy

12

Edward & The Woodvilles/ Warwick & Charolais
1465-1466

Edward had obviously revelled in making his shock announcement to the conclave at Reading, and this was followed by a number of very generous grants, appointments and marriage alliances to members of his newly-acquired family: besides the two sons from her previous marriage, Elizabeth Woodville had five brothers, and seven spinster sisters. [1]

Firstly, Edward attempted to maintain the allegiance of the Nevilles—not an easy task, considering he was not on the best of terms with Warwick, the head of their faction. William Booth, Archbishop of York, had died on 12 September 1464, and Edward now replaced him with Bishop Neville, an extravagant man who celebrated his appointment by throwing what is reputed to have been the largest ever banquet in 15th century England, at Cawood Castle, near Bolton Percy, in Yorkshire. [2] A notable guest, making one of his first public outings, was Edward's twelve-year old brother, Richard of Gloucester, who sat at the table occupied by Warwick's wife and his two daughters, Isabel and Anne. Fifty cooks prepared thousands of sheep and cattle, 400 swans, 104 peacocks, a dozen seals and porpoises, and 13,000 syllabubs.

The promotion of the queen's family, at such rapid pace, outraged much of the nobility, particularly the Nevilles—though even the ebullient Warwick must have been pleased when, in October 1464, the queen's eldest sister, Margaret, was betrothed to his nephew, Lord Maltravers. [3] Of her remaining sisters, Anne married Viscount Bourchier [4]; Eleanor married Anthony, the eldest son of Lord Grey de Ruthyn; Martha married Sir John Bromley; Mary was betrothed to William, the son of Lord Herbert [5]; Katherine married Henry Stafford, the grandson and heir of the Duke of Buckingham. [6]

Sir Thomas Grey, Elizabeth's eldest son from her first marriage, married Anne Holland, the daughter of King Edward's sister, the Duchess of Exeter, in October 1466—Anne had already been betrothed to Warwick's nephew, George Neville (Montagu's son and heir). It subsequently emerged that the queen actually bribed the Duchess with 4,000 marks to allow the marriage to take place. [7]

A '*maritagium diabolicum*' is how one chronicler described the event of January 1465, when the queen's 19-year old brother, John, was forced into a marriage with the 66-year old Dowager Duchess of Norfolk—who had managed to see her way through a trio of husbands, and who would outlive this one by fourteen years. [8] Not only this, it was denounced as an absurd match by Edward's friends and subjects alike: many considered it downright distasteful, and Warwick must have thought that Edward was really rubbing salt into his wounds, for the Duchess was his aunt.

Elizabeth's younger brothers, Edward and Richard Woodville, do not appear to have been given any great favour with the king, though later in life they would be known for keeping him company during his endless amorous pursuits. Neither were found wives, and Richard never married at all, sparking rumours that his designs on Edward were the same as Somerset's had been. [9] The fourth brother, Lionel, became Dean of Exeter at twenty-five, and in 1482 was ordained Bishop of Salisbury. [10]

Elizabeth Woodville's accounts do not suggest an extravagance in keeping with most medieval consorts. Neither did marriage make her inordinately wealthy: nothing had been taken from royal revenues to provide for the Woodvilles, a point which must be stressed in her defence. [11] She and her family *were* grasping—not for monetary gain, but for power. The Nevilles, who never stopped believing that England and its king owed everything to them, were on the other hand arrogant and renowned for instigating any amount of violence to achieve their aims. It is interesting to note that Elizabeth's marriage settlement was considerably less than that of Margaret of Anjou. Edward bestowed upon her the royal palaces of Sheen and Greenwich, and Ormond's Inn, the town-house in Smithfield. [12] Of course, wherever Elizabeth stayed during Edward's absences, her household bustled with members of her clan: Lord Berners (Humphrey Bourchier's father) and Sir John Woodville were her highest-paid officers, and her ladies-in-waiting included her sister Lady Anne Bourchier, and Elizabeth, her brother Anthony's sickly wife.

On 4 March 1466, Elizabeth's father, Lord Rivers, replaced Sit Walter Blount as Treasurer. On 20 May he was created Earl Rivers, and if this was not enough, on 24 August 1467 he would succeed Butcher Tiptoft as Constable of England. His annual income from these officers was £1,300, plus his portion from the King's Council, though Edward gave him no land: Rivers was already one of the wealthiest magnates in England on account of the vast dower estates of his wife, Jacquetta.

Rivers' eldest son, Anthony Woodville, was also suitably rewarded, and apart from one or two recorded outbursts of bad temper and foul language, appears to have been the least rapacious of a grabbing family. Like his father he too was already extremely wealthy by way of his wife, Elizabeth, the heiress of Thomas Lord Scales, and in November 1466 was granted the lordship of the Isle of Wight, and the castle at Carisbrooke. The following year he was appointed keeper of Portchester Castle, in Hampshire. Anthony is generally regarded as having been over-pious, and in later life made pilgrimages throughout Europe. He was an early patron of William Caxton, was said to be moody and melancholy, and professed to wearing a hair-shirt under his splendid peacock's finery. He was the only Woodville to receive praise from the scurrilous pen of Dominic Mancini, who wrote:

> He was a kind, serious and just man, and one tested by every vicissitude in life. Whatever his prosperity he had injured nobody, though befitting man. **[13]**

Elizabeth's coronation took place at Westminster Abbey on Whit Sunday, 26 May 1465, officiated by Archbishop Bourchier. It was a grand occasion for which the king spared no expense: £280 was spent on cloth of gold, cups and basins of gold, and crimson and scarlet robes for the heralds and kings-at-arms. The queen's chairs were provided with bay and white coursers. There were pageantries and tournaments, and forty Knights of the Bath were ordained: these included John and Richard Woodville, Lord Grey de Ruthyn, Buckingham and Maltravers. The closing tournament, which included participants brought over by Elizabeth's uncle, Jacques of Luxembourg, was won by Lord Stanley. If this disappointed Anthony Woodville, hailed as England's finest sportsman, Edward immediately began making arrangements for what he promised would be a tournament of tournaments, for which the main attraction would be a contest between Anthony and the 'rightly-famed' champion, Antoine, Bastard of Burgundy, reputed to be the best in Europe. There would be hitches here, and the bout would not take place for another two years. **[14]**

Edward and Elizabeth would have ten children. The first was born 11 February 1466, which must have come as a big relief because they had been married a year before the queen fell pregnant, a long time when one is waiting for an heir to the throne. Edward was not disappointed that the child was a girl: his wife was only a few years older than him, and had plenty of time ahead of her. The child was baptised Elizabeth, and like her mother would one day become queen of England. The Duchess of York and Jacquetta of Luxembourg were chosen as godmothers: Warwick, still feeling disgruntled, was godfather.

Warwick returned to Westminster for the baptism and the churching of the queen: in the latter he represented the king, who by tradition was not allowed to participate. He sat at the same table as the visiting Bohemian traveller, Gabriel Tetzel, who wrote a colourful account of his experiences in England: having eaten enough his fill of the sumptuous sixty-course banquet, he was invited to stand in an ante-chamber and observe the queen, sitting in a golden chair which had been placed on a dais. Her mother and several of the king's sisters knelt at her feet, and during the repast Elizabeth spoke to no one. Tetzel concludes that he and his travelling companions had hoped to hold a tournament in London, that Edward had not allowed this, and that subsequently they had given away their tilting horses and armour to save them having to be carted back across Europe. [15]

Isabella of Bourbon, the second wife of Charles of Charolais, had died on 26 September 1465. By now, Philip of Burgundy was ailing, and a great many of his responsibilities had been passed on to his son. With no male Burgundian heir, should Charles die, a re-marriage was of paramount importance. [16] To this aim an envoy, Guillaume de Cluny, arrived at the English court early in 1466 armed with the feasible proposition that Edward's 19-year old sister, Margaret of York, might marry Charles. [17] Edward was aware of Charles' sexual leanings—having shared the same lover he would have been hard put not to have been—but expressed his approval, even though Margaret was all but betrothed to Don Pedro of Portugal. [18] Not only this, he suggested a match between his brother, George of Clarence, and Charles' daughter, Mary. [19] Edward knew too that Clarence was very much under Warwick's influence—Warwick wanted him to marry his daughter, Isabel—and probably thought it best to have Clarence out of the country as soon as possible. [20]

On 22 March 1466, Warwick, Hastings and Lord Wenlock were appointed to negotiate with France and Burgundy over these matters: they arrived in Calais on 15 April and went straight to the court of Charles of Charolais, in Boulogne. Why Edward had entrusted Warwick and Wenlock on such a delicate mission gives rise to conjecture: Hastings was never anything but honest and trustworthy, while Wenlock had always been a loose canon, and Warwick had a few ideas of his own.

This was Warwick's first meeting with Charles, and he may have been surprised, having heard all the 'effeminacy' stories, to see for himself how hard-edged this man was.

Charles was anything but effete, and not at all like his father: very powerfully built, he was wholly lacking in patience and morals, and extremely bad-tempered. Contemporary accounts state that when he paced a room, shoulders hunched and eyes focused on the ground, he gave the impression that he was burning from the inside. From boyhood he had thrown himself into all manner of violent games: he jousted fiercely, and regularly "chastened his blood" by enforcing a sexual continence which hardly befitted a prince. No evidence suggests that he experienced any pleasure out of being alive. [21] Charles was stubborn, ambitious, and hard-working both day and night: the portrait which hangs in a Berlin museum, probably executed at the time of his relationship with Henry Somerset, is a far contrast to the mentally unstable figure Warwick encountered now, and even he must have found him foreboding. Charles knew, of course, that Warwick and Louis XI of France were only hoping to propagate the downfall of Burgundy, and he must have been hard put to conceal his contempt.

Having achieved nothing, Warwick returned to Calais three days later, and was met by Louis XI's ambassadors who offered a new proposal: on 24 May a land-and-sea truce was sealed for a period of twenty-two months, and a peace conference scheduled for 23 October. Louis promised not to assist the Lancastrians in any way during this period, so long as Edward refused to aid Charles of Charolais or the Duke of Brittany. Louis offered to pay Edward 40,000 crowns annually, or for the duration of whatever agreement was reached to provide Margaret of York with a European prince of her choosing: the usually parsimonious French king even agreed to pay for the wedding *and* the dowry!

Four would-be suitors were named, and when Warwick returned to London, he and Edward shook hands on the deal.

NOTES

1. The dates and order of birth of Lord Rivers' children are not known. Elizabeth is thought to have been born between 1436 and 1440.
2. William Booth (c1390-1464). Cawood Castle belonged to the Archbishops of York.
3. Thomas, son and heir of the Earl of Arundel.
4. William Bourchier (d 1483).
5. William Herbert (c1455-91) later exchanged his earldom for that of Huntingdon and in 1484 married Catherine Plantagenet, the illegitimate daughter of Richard III.
6. Henry Stafford (c1455-83) 2nd Duke of Buckingham. His father died in 1458. His grandfather the 1st Duke was killed at Northampton. Henry was executed by Richard III and his widow married Jasper Tudor.
7. George Neville (c1461-83), Duke of Bedford, 1470; Sir Thomas Grey (1455-1501) Marquess of Dorset, 1475, the great-grandfather of Lady Jane Grey. Anne died in 1474. The next year he married Cecily Bonvile, Lord Harrington's daughter and William Hastings' step-daughter.
8. Catherine Neville, elder sister of the Duchess of York. Her other husbands were John Mowbray 2nd Duke of Norfolk; Thomas Strangeways; and the Viscount Beaumont killed at Northampton.
9. Edward was killed fighting for the Bretons in 1488; Richard (d 1491) 3rd and last Earl of Rivers bequeathed Grafton to the Marquess of Dorset: the 2nd Marquess swapped it with his cousin, Henry VII, whence it became Grafton Regis.
10. Lionel died in 1484.

11. A R Myers: *The Household of Queen Elizabeth Woodville, 1466-7*, Bull, John Rylands Library (1967-8) I, pp 207-35 and pp 443-81.
12. The house was in Knightsriders Street, now Giltspur Street.
13. Dominic Mancini: *The Usurpation of Richard III*, ed & translated by C.A.J. Armstrong, 1969.
14. Antoine (1421-1504) Bastard of Burgundy.
15. Gabriel Tetzel accompanied Lord Rozmital, the brother-in-law of George of Podebrad who became King of Bohemia in 1458.
16. Isabella had married Charles in 1454.
17. Guillaume de Cluny, protonotary and later Bishop of Thérouanne and Poitiers.
18. Don Pedro had been proclaimed king by the Catalan Independence Movement. He died 29 June 1466.
19. Mary of Burgundy (1457-82).
20. Warwick only had two daughters: Isabel (1451-76) and Anne (1456-85).
21. Paul Murray Kendall: *Louis XI*, pp 111-12.

Margaret of York, c.1468

Antoine, Bastard of Burgundy

13

The Burgundian Alliance
1466-1468

Richard Plantagenet, about to enter the political arena at this time, remains the most controversial royal figure in British history, a fact unlikely to change until essential details concerning his character and alleged deeds are brought to light. Modern historians have done much in recent years in an attempt to 'clear' his name, and some headway has been made, particularly with the discovery in September 2012 of his remains beneath a Leicester car park. At the opposite end of the scale to Shakespeare's villain with the withered arm and fondness for eating live frogs there are the fanciful novelists, mostly wishful-thinking females, who have over-whitewashed his character by turning him into some kind of 15th century Sir Galahad, which he most certainly was not.

Indeed, the modern myth of the medieval knight is as far from the truth as it possibly could be. Men came in all shapes and sizes: the chances of being incredibly handsome or downright ugly were no different amongst the upper classes then than they are today. Only the privileged were afforded an education, and many of the great magnates could neither read nor write. Chroniclers were overtly kind and sympathetic towards the lords they favoured, even if these did not warrant sympathy—or flagrantly scurrilous, as is proved by the prejudiced jottings of the likes of Sir Thomas More. Life-expectancy was different then only because many men died young by way of acts of violence, battle or execution, many women died in childbirth, and medicine was primitive. Personal hygiene was not what it should have been: it was not uncommon for even the wealthiest nobles to have rotten teeth, lice, and body odour because they had no reason to make a great effort before presenting themselves to their lesser-ranking public. Venereal disease was rife, amongst all the classes.

England in the 15th century was with very few exceptions male-dominated. Richard belonged to this world, and had it not been for the Tudor propagandists would not have stood out for any reason, other than he was a fearless and able general, extremely loyal towards his brother the king, and himself possessed of all the makings of a good ruler. It is true that later in life he did at times behave irrationally, but when one considers some of the bloody events he was compelled to live through, there is nothing to condemn him for in this respect. Even the accomplished, handsome Edward IV, when his hand was forced, was capable of perpetrating unpardonable acts of great cruelty. Such was the age these men lived in.

Edward's youngest brother was born on Monday 2 October 1452, at Fotheringay Castle. Virtually nothing is known of his first seven years: he probably lived at Fotheringay, seeing little of his parents or elder brother until shortly before the rout of Ludlow. That he was a weak, sickly child may be certain: part of a rhyming account of the Duke of York's children and their order of birth, written around 1456, stated that 'Richard liveth yet'. **[1]** It is possible that the young Richard caught every childhood malady going which left him frail and spindly, and we now know that he suffered from scoliosis of the spine, possibly on account of a breech birth, and for which in those days there was no cure. His remarkable spirit and courage of conviction, however, enabled him to overcome whatever weaknesses he may have had once he began to develop as a youth and man. He is said to have practised rigorously with the sword and axe, and his youth spent in desolate but healthy north—as opposed to the fetid streets of London, certainly contributed to his astonishing fitness. As a grown-up, Richard was neither lacking in muscle nor short of stature as was believed—above average height, he stood at around 5 feet 9 inches. A facial reconstruction of his skull, in 2013, revealed him to be better than average-looking—handsome, in fact. Also, unlike his elder brothers, he was cautious of his well-being and constitution, and did not share their gluttony for food, drink and sex.

While the Woodvilles appeared to be over-running Edward's court at Westminster, other things were happening at Middleham, in Yorkshire. Warwick believed that if he could woo George of Clarence and Richard of Gloucester on to his side, then Edward would see the Woodvilles for what they were, and return to the Neville side of the fence. Clarence was a push-over for Warwick's persuasive charm: arrogant, shallow, not very bright, and out to oppose Edward in any way that might see him bettering himself and his Neville cousin. All Warwick had to do was to promise his daughter Isabel's hand in marriage, and Clarence was his for the taking: until Elizabeth Woodville gave Edward a son, Clarence was heir to the throne. It is possible that Warwick may have already had aims to marry his youngest daughter, Anne, to Richard—the youth had been an integral part of the Warwick household since the age of twelve, when he had been sent to Middleham as an 'apprentice in knightly pursuits', therefore he had had time to get to know the girl. She, however, was only ten years old, and Richard was not Clarence. He was not easily impressed by Warwick's half-meant promises of power and riches, and saw that they served only as a means of re-achieving his self-greatness by ousting the Woodvilles. As the web of intrigue involving Warwick and Clarence intensified, Richard gradually found himself pulling away. In February 1467 Edward appointed he, Warwick and Montagu on a commission of oyer and terminer to enquire into a dispute in York. Here, Richard learned, if he had not known already, that by enlisting the services of Chancellor Neville, Warwick had deliberately contravened the king's wishes by asking the Pope for the dispensation which, because they were related, would enable Isabel and Clarence to wed.

By February 1467, France and Burgundy were eager for a marriage-alliance with England. Edward was still intent on his sister marrying the Burgundian heir, while Warwick was set on opposing him by allying with France. A Burgundian embassy had been received in England in December 1466:

negotiations had been chaired by Earl Rivers, Hastings and Bishop Stillington, but matters had been hindered because Duke Philip had refused to abrogate his earlier ban on the importation of English cloth. Adding to the confusion, the Bastard of Bourbon arrived in London to discuss an extension of Louis XI's truce and *his* plans for Margaret's future. Edward refused to see him, and unwisely handed him over to Warwick.

Meanwhile, negotiations continued with Charles of Charolais, and in April an English embassy set out for Bruges. Arrangements been finalised for the long-awaited trial of strength between Anthony Woodville and the Bastard of Burgundy, and Edward knew that to have Warwick hanging around when this took place might be tempting fate: he appointed him and Lord Wenlock on a commission to visit the French court to further discuss Louis XI's proposals. The party set sail from Sandwich on 28 May, accompanied by the disgruntled Bastard of Bourbon and a gift of six hunting hounds for the dog-mad Spider King.

Louis received the party warmly, showering them with expensive gifts: silver cups for his friends, and for Warwick a jeweled cup costing 2,000 livres. Warwick saw through the charade: as with Charles of Charolais, behind the kindly exterior lurked a man of malicious intent. Louis said that he was eager to defer the marriage between Margaret of York and Charles of Charolais—a suggested suitor was Philipe de Bress, the Duke of Savoy's son, and concluded that the Burgundian territories might be petitioned off by allowing Richard of Gloucester to marry his second daughter Jeanne, using Holland, Brabant and Zeeland as part of her dowry. [2] Louis added that if Warwick *really* wanted to get at Edward, why not enlist the help of Margaret of Anjou to re-instate Henry VI? Warwick scoffed at this. The Lancastrian cause was dead: Edward had recognised the mighty puissance of Warwick once, and would do so again.

On 29 May, one day after Warwick had left England, the Bastard of Burgundy's small but colourful fleet was met at Gravesend by the Garter King of Arms, and the next day the procession made its way into London. With Antoine was his father's best friend and favourite envoy, Louis de Gruthuyse. [3] The party lodged with the Bishop of Salisbury—an authority on Burgundian affairs—at his palace on Fleet Street. Here, Antoine was greeted by some of the king's friends and over the course of the next few days practiced for the tournament. At forty-six he was in his prime as a jouster, and considered unbeatable. Unlike his father he appears to have been an extremely likeable man: gently unassuming, better-looking than Philip, and bearing none of the more distasteful characteristics of his half-brother, Charles. Only Anthony Woodville would bring out the worst in him.

On 2 June, the king entered London with great pageantry: before him rode Anthony Woodville, the English champion, bearing the sword of state. The preliminary speech upon his entry to the city was delivered by Edward himself: the Speaker, George Neville, Archbishop of York, whose task this should have been, had sent an excuse saying that he was too ill to attend. Edward smelled a rat: he had suspected Neville of double-dealing over the Clarence dispensation, and when this was clarified later in the week—added to which Edward was informed that the Archbishop was hoping that Warwick would contrive to award him a Cardinal's Hat—Edward decided on a showdown. Since Clarence was involved, on 8 June he forced him to ride out with himself and eleven others, including Lords Dynham and Herbert, to Archbishop Neville's house at Charing Cross. [4] Here, George Neville was formerly but politely stripped of his office and made to hand over the Great Seal for safe keeping to Robert Kirkham, Keeper of the Rolls. In the light of the emergency, Kirkham would hold on to the Seal until the next cabinet reshuffle, when Bishop Stillingon would be created Chancellor and the Privy Seal given to Thomas Rotherham. [5]

The Great Smithfield Tournament was described in considerable detail by the Burgundian court official, Olivier de la Marche, in his memoirs. [6] The lists, measuring ninety yards by eighty, were set up near Queen Elizabeth's townhouse: on either side were lodges, or grandstands—a large one for the king and his company, and a smaller one for the Mayor and city officials. Oddly, de la Marche does not record women as being present at the spectacle, which may have been an oversight: though seven months pregnant

Elizabeth and her ladies are unlikely to have been excluded from so prestigious an event. [7]

Arrangements were made by Butcher Tiptoft and Sir John Howard: the latter officiating for his cousin, the young Duke of Norfolk, hereditary Earl Marshall, who was too ill to attend. [8] There was much merrymaking on the streets of London, and this went on for a week while Parliament was prorogued.

The main event between Anthony Woodville and Antoine of Burgundy began on Thursday 11 June. King Edward was dressed in purple and wore the Garter: he carried a thick staff, which may suggest that he was already on the way for the obesity which would ruin his health later in life. Anthony entered the field first, heralded by Clarence and the Earl of Arundel, each carrying a 'frog' helmet. [9] After bending their knee to the king, both men retired to their pavilions to arm themselves. During their first charge, both champions used lances, and missed. During the next they carried swords: whether Anthony swerved deliberately is not recorded, but Antoine's horse rammed his saddle and dropped down dead, pinning him under its weight. Luckily, only his temper was bruised, and Anthony was accused, in no mean terms, of bending the rules by having a saddle which was illegal. This first fray was quickly sorted out by Butcher Tiptoft, who prevented a fist-fight by declaring the mishap to have been an accident. When asked if he wished to resume the match, Antoine sulked off to his lodgings where he told de la Marche, 'He has fought a beast today—tomorrow he will fight a man.'

The next day the two champions fought on foot, with spears and axes: the spears were confiscated and the match resumed with each man battering the other with the blunt end of his axe. There was much strong language in what was no longer a chivalrous contest, but a bitter duel which became so violent that the king himself stepped on to the field to stop the proceedings. Edward probably regretted this, for the crowd was having enormous fun. Edward knew, however, that his brother-in-law would never stand a chance of winning against the Burgundian—a huge man possessed of herculean strength who would not have been satisfied until his arrogant opponent collapsed in a bloody heap in the middle of the arena. Even so, the pair lashed out at each other while leaving the field, and Edward made them shake hands and swear 'to love together as brothers-in-arms' and never fight again.

The revelry and pageantry of Smithfield was but a subterfuge for the negotiations going on between Edward and the Burgundian emissaries, and on Sunday 14 June he and Elizabeth put on a sumptuous banquet at the Grocer's Hall: Edward had specifically chosen the venue to emphasise English-Burgundian trade relations. Antoine was still feeling decidedly bitter, and probably would have welcomed a re-match with Woodville. Soon after the banquet, news was brought to him that his father, Duke Philip, had died—an event which also cut short Warwick's negotiations with Louis XI. Antoine is said to have been devastated, for he had been closer too Philip than his legitimate son, Charles, and when the Burgundian court poets began penning their eulogies, one contained the lines:

> Adieu mon bastard Anthoine
> Et tous mes enfants naaturelz.

Antoine left London on 24 June, though Louis de Gruthuyse and his envoys stayed behind to finalise negotiations with the king. Edward and Louis became firm friends, and though the king did not know it at the time, this friendship would be of vital importance a few years hence.

Ironically again, Warwick landed in England on the very day of Antoine's departure. With him was Louis XI's embassy, headed by the Archbishop of Narbonne and Jehan de Popincourt. **[10]**

Needless to say, Warwick was not given an ecstatic welcome by the king, and he moved into the rooms at the Bishop of Salisbury's palace, recently vacated by the Burgundians. From here, he pressed Edward into granting the French envoys an audience. There then followed a charade which was typically Warwick. The next day, the envoys were ferried to Westminster in barges especially decorated for the occasion: here they were met by a grinning Clarence and a humiliated Lord Hastings, in the company of Anthony and John Woodville. Clarence himself presented the envoys to the king, and Louis XI's proposals were read out by Jehan de Popincourt. Edward was not interested, aware that Warwick had been in contact with his brother, the ousted Chancellor. That same day he and most of his family retreated to Westminster—plague had broken out in London—leaving Warwick well aware that if he was dedicated to any alliance, it was not the French one.

Warwick's wounds were already smarting, and Edward would add insult to injury. The French envoys were permitted to remain at Windsor until 14 July: when they left, all they took with them were a few mastiffs for the French king, and some hunting horns. Warwick, and Montagu and his wife escorted the party as far as Canterbury, then Warwick alone saw them off from Sandwich. He had made himself look a fool in Louis' eyes, and when he returned to Middleham it was to plot his revenge of the king who had turned him over in favour of his queen's relatives.

Edward was now on good terms with Burgundy, or at least as was possible with the new, tetchy Duke, and on 6 July concluded an alliance with King Henry of Castile—not a great admirer of the French. Edward was also negotiating with John II of Aragon, and had already treated with Ferdinand of Naples. [11]

Charles of Burgundy was not as affable as his father had been: Edward annoyed him by nullifying the statutes of 1463 and 1465 which had prohibited Burgundian imports into England. On 27 November a treaty was drawn up for thirty years of 'free intercourse of merchandise': this was discussed at the Diet of Bruges on 15 January 1468. [12]

Next day, the marriage treaty between Margaret of York and Charles of Burgundy was sealed: it was ratified on 14 March, and a dowry set for 200,000 crowns, 50,000 of which Charles insisted should be paid on the actual wedding day. Edward had problems raising such a vast amount and the event, scheduled for 4 May, had to be deferred until 3 July. He knew that his merchant backers were not all in agreement with the Burgundian commercial treaty, and as such it would not have been apt to ask Parliament for money. Luck came to the rescue, when news arrived that Louis XI had encroached on the Duke of Brittany's territory. Francis asked for aid on the form of archers when his six months truce with France, signed on 6 January, expired. In Greenwich, on 2 and 3 April, an Anglo-French conference took place wherein it was agreed to supply 3,000 English archers at two months' notice: it was essential that Brittany should remain intact, and Edward's condition was that if any part of Normandy should be taken during the campaign, it should be handed back to him. This presented a great opportunity for the pugnacious Duke of Burgundy, and an even greater one for the English king: with a Burgundian alliance, Louis might be prevented from causing trouble in the future.

News of a probable war with France formed an integral part of Bishop Stillington's speech to Parliament on 17 May: satisfactory alliances had been concluded with Burgundy, Brittany, Aragon, Naples, Denmark and Castile, and this met with universal approval. Revenues were forthcoming—Edward now had the down-payment for his sister's dowry, and the men of England were honing their weapons. It was agreed that the dowry would be paid by Gerard Caniziani, the London representative of the Medici

Bank: the agent acting for Duke Charles, in Bruges, was Thomas Portinari. **[13]** This business concluded, Edward's third Parliament closed on 7 June.

The invasion, of course, did not take place. Louis XI persuaded the Duke of Burgundy to sign a truce with him which would last until 1 August, and commanded his troops to attack Brittany the moment the Franco-Breton truce expired on 15 July. Edward did not let Duke Francis down: on 3 August he ratified the clause in his agreement which demanded troops for Brittany, and on 10 September Lord Mountjoy led a force of 3,000 archers across the Channel. Anthony Woodville further commanded a 4,000-strong naval force, at Edward's expense, intent on invading France. However, 'On the same day, Duke Francis—unable to resist the French invasion any longer without immediate aid, came to terms with France, and by the treaty of Ancenis agreed to abandon his allies.' **[14]**

The story circulated that Margaret of Anjou, armed with a small force at Harfleur, was herself preparing to invade England in the October, therefore an English fleet was commissioned to skirt the Channel, only to be battered by storms and forced on to the Isle of Wight in the November. Edward had wasted his money, though he did manage to retake Jersey from the French. **[15]** And the Duke of Burgundy, dealing with Louis XI behind Edward's back at the Treaty of Péronne on 14 October, swore not to aid the English if they mounted an invasion of France. Edward could do nothing for the moment but put his plans on ice.

Many must have felt truly sorry for Margaret of York when she set out for Burgundy on 18 June 1468. Here was an attractive young woman of twenty-two, doomed to spend the rest of her life in a foreign land, with an aggressive, mentally unstable homosexual husband she would almost certainly dislike. The task of escorting the bride-to-be on the first stage of her journey was assigned to Warwick, which indicating that Edward still trusted him and hoped for renewed allegiance. Edward had spent Christmas at Coventry, with an armed guard of two-hundred archers, and had insisted upon having Clarence with him to keep an eye on him. Early in January he had summoned Warwick to a Council meeting with every intention of letting bygones be bygones: Warwick had refused to attend while Lord Herbert and the Woodvilles were there, and Edward had offered a compromise by getting Warwick to make up with Herbert and by keeping the Woodvilles out of sight. Warwick had been wholly against the Burgundian marriage alliance, and felt genuinely aggrieved for the king's sister. The first stopping-off point was Stratford Longthorne, in Essex. Margaret spend several days at the monastery here: with her were her three brothers, Warwick, and the queen. Thenon she was escorted to Margate, where she took ship on 23 June. Amongst those waving her off at the harbour were Anthony and John Woodville, Sir John Howard, Lord Wenlock, and the Duchess of Norfolk. Also here were the Paston brothers, and Pseudo-Gregory. The marriage alliance was effectively a kick in the teeth for Louis XI, who had tried his utmost to prevent the papal dispensation from coming through (Charles and Margaret were distant cousins) by spreading the rumour that Margaret had an illegitimate son. It was reprehensible that the bride should have had her character and reputation defiled in such a way, when that of the bridegroom was black as sin.

The couple were married at Damme, just outside Bruges, on 2 July: the ceremony was conducted by the Bishop of Salisbury, doubtless with a tear in his eye. For Margaret it would be a lonely, unhappy life from now on. Charles' loathing of the female body equaled that of Henry VI, and subsequently he and Margaret would spend little time under the same roof. Her one consolation was that she grew to love her step-daughter, Mary, and she became a close friend of Charles' mother, Isabella of Portugal, an indomitable woman unafraid of stating that she was the rightful Queen of England. [16] Edward was always within easy reach, but Margaret of Burgundy was too proud a woman to wish to burden her brother with personal problems—she had, after all, entered the marriage of her own volition. [17]

Ten days of festivities followed the wedding, in non-stop pouring rain. Jousting was led by Antoine of Burgundy, who entered the lists dressed as 'The Knight of The Golden Tree' who had received a letter from 'The Princess of Unknown Isle', concerning a chained giant who is being guarded by a dwarf. John Paston the younger wrote home to his mother:

> As for tidings here, but it be for the feast, I can none send you; saving my Lady Margaret was married on Sunday....at five of the clock in the morning. Many

> pageants were played in her way in Bruges to her welcoming, the best that ever I saw. And the same day my Lord the Bastard took upon him to answer twenty-four and gentlemen, within eight days at jousts of peace…and they that have jousted with him into this day, have been richly be seen, and himself also, as cloth of gold, and silk and silver…I heard never of none like it, save King Arthur's court. [18]

Antoine would, of course, have loved to have fought with Anthony Woodville, but this was not possible because of their oath sworn at Smithfield, and it was ironically sad that the great Burgundian's jousting days were brought to an end by a kick from a horse while he was escorting a friend on to the field. But if the younger Paston was enjoying himself in Bruges, Pseudo-Gregory was not. Sarcastically, he recorded that the Burgundians 'showed no more favour unto Englishmen than they would do unto a Jew,' and added that the English horses were better treated than the English visitors.

NOTES

1. Gairdner, quoting Vincent on Brooke, 622-3.
2. Calmette & Perinelle, pp 81-7.
3. Louis de Bruges, Seigneur de a Gruthuyse (d 1492), created Earl of Winchester, 1772. The peerage was cancelled by Henry VII in 1500.
4. John Dynham had married Baroness Elizabeth Fitzwalter in March, and still against his will been created Lord Dynham, though he did not begin using the title until 9 July. Regarding the Chancellor's illness, *Annales* 786 states that he *was* ill at the time of his dismissal.
5. Thomas Rotherham (1423-1500), later Bishop of Rochester, Bishop of Lincoln, Archbishop of York. Chancellor 1474-83.
6. Olivier de la Marche: *Memoirs*, 4 vols edited by Beaune & d'Arbaumont, Société de l'Histoire de France, 1883-8.
7. Princess Mary, born 11 August 1467, died at Greenwich 23 May 1482, and buried in St George's Chapel, Windsor.
8. John Mowbray (1444-76) 4th and last Mowbray Duke of Norfolk. John Howard (c 1430-85), 1st Duke of Norfolk of the Howard family, created Duke in June 1483 by Richard III.
9. The helmet had a slit like a frog's mouth which allowed the knight to see while his head was down during a charge. When he threw his head back at the moment of impact, he was not able to see at all.
10. Antoine du bec-Crespin, brother-in-law of Piers de Brezé, Archbishop of Narbonne.
11. Ferdinand I (1423-94), infamous for his cruelty and treachery.

12. Rymer: *Foedera XI*, pp 591-600.
13. Gerard Caniziani (d 1484). In 1473 he became a naturalised Englishman.
14. Scofield, I, 473.
15. Margaret's plan, mentioned in *Annales* 792 but dismissed by Scofield, I, 477. Calmette & Perinelle however, 104 n3, state that Louis XI had provided her with seven ships at Rouen.
16. It has been suggested that Isabella's mother, a daughter of John of Gaunt and Blanche of Lancaster, had left her the crown in her will.
17. On 30 September 1467, Margaret had thus addressed a Great Council at Kingston.
18. *Paston Letters II*, 317-9.

14

The Northern Rebellions & Edgecott
1468-1469

After saying goodbye to his sister, Edward returned to London to face whatever perils fate had in store for him. Basically, there were three threats: Margaret of Anjou; the fermenting Lancastrian cause in England now further aggravated by Louis of France; and Warwick. On 1 June 1468, the parsimonious French king authorised his treasury to finance Jasper Tudor with 293 livres, a flotilla of three ships and a paltry fifty men with whom he hoped the ever-troublesome rebel would mount an invasion of Wales.

 Jasper landed in the Dyfi estuary, near Harlech, on 24 June, only to find the mighty garrison still held by William Herbert. Unpeturbed, Jasper marched towards the north coast of Wales, and was by now said to have 2,000 men. He reached Denbigh, which he sacked and burned along with parts of Flintshire before being defeated by Herbert and his brother Richard on 3 July. Herbert had around 8,000 men, and two wings of his army descended on Harlech on 14 August. By this time Jasper had escaped—he eventually turned up in Brittany—and of the defenders of Harlech, two were taken to London to be executed, while the others were pardoned. On 8 September, Edward rewarded Herbert for his services by granting him Jasper Tudor's title, Earl of Pembroke.

Harlech was but one of many problems facing Edward: insurrections and petty landowner squabbles were commonplace all over England. Early in 1468 an courier named Cornelius was arrested for carrying seditious letters: he turned out to be one of Margaret of Anjou's agents, and when tortured by having his feet roasted on a griddle revealed the name of a fellow conspirator—Hawkins, one of Warwick's servants. Hawkins was designated guinea-pig for the so-called 'Duke of Exeter's Daughter'—the first rack to have been imported into England—and confessed several names. One was Lord Wenlock, who Edward arrested but quickly released—he was Warwick's friend, but Edward refused to believe him a traitor, despite all the warnings he had received since Ludlow. Another was Sir Thomas Cook, a wealthy draper. Cook had been Lord Mayor of London 1462-3, and had loaned money to the king. He was suspected of financing a disreputable cause—this could only mean Margaret of Anjou—and thrown into prison. While Cook was conveniently indisposed, Earl Rivers' and Sir John Fogge's servants ransacked his town house in Broad Street, stealing jewelry and plate worth £700, and a tapestry depicting The Siege of Jerusalem worth £800. Rivers' wife, Jacquetta, had been after this for some time, and had tried to buy it from Cook—who had refused to sell, inciting her and her husband's anger sufficiently for Rivers to wish to set him up. Cook was tried for treason on a trumped-up charge: the judges could not get this charge to stick, and instead were told to find him guilty of misprision—the concealment of knowledge by a public figure of a felony or treason, without being actively involved in the crime. Hearing the case was Sir John Markham, Lord Chief Justice of the King's Bench. Cook was given a huge fine and re-committed to prison until this was paid. There then followed an independent enquiry to investigate the cost of the damage to the house on Broad Street—Cook's claim was for £14,000 and this was offset against his fine, leaving a shortfall of £8,000. The queen, who had hoped that Cook might be executed for treason, resulting in his lands and wealth being forfeit to the Crown, revived the old demand known as the 'Queen's Gold', which allowed her to claim ten per cent of whatever the king claimed. She and the Woodvilles then petitioned Edward to dismiss Sir John Markham—he would be stripped of his office the next year. Why Cook was persecuted is unclear. It has been suggested that Edward was out to ruin him, but this seems unlikely. The most plausible explanation is that Jacquetta of Luxembourg had been so eager to get her hands on the tapestry, she would have gone to any length to do so—even if this meant having an innocent man put to death. [1]

More calumny followed, which would lead to later repercussions. Early in November, rebels Henry Courtenay and Thomas Hungerford were arrested in Wiltshire, and imprisoned in Salisbury. On 16 January they were hanged, drawn and quartered at Bemerton, outside the town, and soon afterwards Courtenay's lands given to Humphrey Stafford of Southwick, who became Earl of Devon. The Earl of Oxford was arrested and imprisoned, but released after turning king's evidence: this resulted in a number of men being executed on Tower Hill on 28 November.

In the Spring of 1469, the first signs of open warfare surfaced. The northern rebellions of this year are very confusing. Contemporary accounts differ: they are scanty, muddled, and may be based on hearsay or second-hand gossip. Ross devotes an entire appendix to the uprisings. [2] Vergil's account is unreliable and discusses only one rebellion where the leader is referred to as Robert Hulderne. Montagu is recorded as having defeated Lord Herbert, while the Earl of Devon is not mentioned at all. Warkworth describes Robin of Redesdale's insurrection, but says nothing of the one led by Robin of Holderness. Vitellius says little other than the rebels executed the Woodvilles. The very name Robin may even be fictitious: legends were rife in medieval England, and the name may have been invented by the rebels themselves, after the adventures of Robin Hood, who had served the good of the common people by fighting against the barons' injustices, as they believed they were fighting now.

The first uprising occurred towards the end of April, when a large band of disgruntled men flocked to the standard of a rebel-leader known as Robin of Redesdale. It has been suggested that he was Sir John Conyers of Hornby, Warwick's cousin by marriage—or his brother, Sir William Conyers of Marske. [3] Montagu, still in the north and still on King Edward's side, routed the rebels in this part of the country, but their leader escaped. A second Robin turned up in the then East Riding district of Holderness to begin what began as a local grievance against a tax on corn, imposed by St Leonard's Hospital, in York. This then developed into a major rebellion when the so-called Robin of Holderness pressed for the restoration of Henry Percy to the earldom of Northumberland—this young man had been held captive in the Tower of London since his father's death at Towton. Montagu had no intention of allowing the Percys to lord it over the Nevilles in the north: Robin of Holderness was captured in York, and beheaded without his identity being properly established. Later he was dubiously unmasked as one Robert Hillyard, though the truth may never be known.

During the first week of June 1469, Edward set off on a pilgrimage to East Anglia, to visit the shrines at Bury St Edmunds and Walsingham. With him were Richard of Gloucester, Earl Rivers, Anthony and John Woodville, Sir John Howard, Louis de Bretaylle, and Edward Brampton. [4] Learning of the troubles in the north, the king decided to investigate for himself: he asked the royal wardrobe to supply him with banners and standards, forty jackets of damask and velvet with roses, and a thousand jackets in his colours or murrey and blue. [5] Around 18 June, he and his retinue entered Norwich, arriving in the middle of a dispute between the Pastons and the Dukes of Norfolk and Suffolk. [6] The gist of this was petty: the young Duke of Norfolk wanted to get his hands on Caister Castle, which the elder Paston was intent on keeping. Similarly, Sufflolk had laid claim on the manor of Hellesden, a part Sir John Fastolff's estate 'bequeathed' to Judge Paston some years before. Edward had intervened already on 18 January, the day that Hungerford and Courtenay had been executed, so he was not in the best of moods. He had written John Paston a stern letter, summoning him to the Council of Westminster. By 12 March the dispute still had not been settled: some of Norfolk's men had felled trees, drained the ponds, and stolen Paston's fish. Subsequently, several other landowners had joined in with the fray: Anthony Woodville, a cousin of Anne Haute—one of Paston's neighbours—now supported Suffolk, as did Sir Edward Brampton, who was accused of currying favour with the king. Edward had to pass through Hellesden to get to Walsingham, so he saw for himself the damage inflicted by Suffolk. Even so he decided that the best policy would be to remain neutral and leave the matter to the relevant authorities.

Accompanied by Norfolk and Suffolk, the royal party left Norwich on 21 June: they reached Castle Rising on 24 June, and Lynn two days later, spending the night at Croyland Abbey. The next morning, they sailed up the river to Fotheringay, where the queen was waiting. Here they rested for several days: as usual, when pressed, Edward was in particular hurry to get on with things. This time, his lethargy would almost cost him his crown.

Warwick, meanwhile, was back in Kent, having arrived in Sandwich early in May to witness the rebuilding of his flagship, *Trinity*. He was still Warden of the Cinque Ports and Captain of Calais. With him were Clarence and Archbishop George Neville. The dispensation for Clarence's marriage to Isabel had come through: on 28 June Warwick wrote to his adherents in Coventry, announcing the arrangements for the wedding. On 4 July he was joined by his brother-in-law the Earl of Oxford, eager to get even with the king for executing his father and brother. [7]

In London and the south of England, Warwick's supporters had broadcast the rumour that Edward was a bastard, and therefore Clarence, as the Duke of York's eldest legitimate son, was the rightful King of England. This followed an alleged statement issued by the Duchess of York, five years earlier, when Edward had married a Woodville—such was Cecily's loathing of these people, it was said, that she was willing to fabricate the story that he had been conceived in adultery, even if it meant him losing the crown. Such a statement would have been hard to disprove, had it been true, for Edward resembled neither of his brothers. The English masses, Warwick believed, had always enjoyed a juicy scandal, and it mattered little to him that he lacked support from much of the nobility, for the common people had always been England's backbone. With them on his side, how could he even think of failure?

Warwick already had thirty ships patrolling the Channel: he knew intimately of Edward's movements in the Midlands and was pretty certain that Edward knew nothing about his. A few days after Oxford's arrival, the party crossed to Calais. Isabel was already there. The wedding, conducted by George Neville took place on 11 July.

The next day, Warwick issued a proclamation to which was attached a copy of the rebels' petition: the men of Kent were asked for their aid towards ridding England of the king's favourites—the Woodvilles, Sir John Fogge, Lord Audley, and the new Earls of Devon and Pembroke. Attention was also drawn towards the wrongs committed against three English kings: Edward II, Richard II and Henry VI. Warwick begged the men of Kent to join up with him in Canterbury, and set a date: 16 July. They had never let him down before, and did not disappoint him now. On 18 July he left the town with a considerable force, and they marched on London. The city did not resist, loaned him £1,000, and he set off for Coventry at once to meet up with Robin of Redesdale.

On 7 July, meanwhile, Edward's party had ridden through Stamford, to Grantham. Thenon they had ridden by way of Nottingham to Newark, to be greeted with the chilling news that Robin of Redesdale had an army three times the size of theirs. Edward realised that Warwick was at the root of the trouble, and as the Woodvilles were prime targets for Warwick and his faction, Edward acted wisely by sending them away: Earl Rivers and John went to Wales, Anthony returned to Norfolk. Edward himself retreated to Nottingham, where he set about raising troops. He had already asked Coventry for a hundred archers on 5 July. Lord Herbert was on the march from Wales, and Humphrey Stafford was en route from Devonshire: Edward was hoping that they would reach him ahead of Redesdale's force from the north and Warwick's from the south. As a last resort, Edward wrote a letter to Warwick and Clarence in which he urged them to prove that they were not 'of any such disposition towards us, as the rumour here runneth.' **[8]**

He was wasting his time.

The battle of Edgecott, fought on 26 July 1469, or at least the manoeuvres leading up to it, are confusing. Herbert and Stafford were on their way to the king, and Edward was expecting their forces to combine. On 25 July, while approaching Banbury, they quarrelled over the town's restricted billeting arrangements. Stafford appears to have had the superior force, at least where archers were concerned: he moved to Doddington Castle, on the Oxford Road, and struck camp within the bailey. Herbert's army, of little use on its own, halted between the villages of Thorpe Mandeville and Wardington, thus blocking off the roads from Daventry and Northampton. Neither faction knew the exact location of Redesdale: Herbert had anticipated that the fight would take place in a flattened valley called Danesmoor, four miles north-east of Banbury. In fact, Redesdale was closer than he thought, and Herbert suddenly found his position very vulnerable: he was desperately short of archers, and there was the added fear that his men, aware of the precarious situation, might desert. He realised therefore that he had but the one option—to attack and hope for the best. He took the first hill north of Danesmoor with comparative ease and few losses, though there appears to have been little or no cover. The second hill afforded him access to the Thorpe Mandeville road, though in taking this,

his archers were severely depleted. At this stage in the battle, Herbert could have held back and waited for Stafford's reinforcements, but he foolishly opted to press on. At Cudworth Hill he came unstuck: Redesdale clung to the crest, and his army rapidly fanned out into two divisions and surrounded him. Even so, Herbert might have fought his way out of an exceedingly tricky situation, had it not been for the sudden interjection of an army of amateur mercenaries led by the Lancastrian Sir John Clapham, who blocked his rear. Herbert assumed this was Warwick's vanguard, and pressed on. Meanwhile, Stafford had arrived and was watching the fierce fighting from a safe distance. Realising Warwick's main army would turn up at any time, he executed a swift about-turn. This was not cowardice on his part, but sound common sense.

Losses were heavy: some 2,000 Welsh, and 1,500 or more English. William Herbert and his brother Sir Richard were captured and brought before Warwick, in Northampton. He gave orders for them to be executed as traitors the next day. This was flagrantly unlawful: traitors could only be executed for taking up arms against their king, and their king happened to be Warwick's enemy.

Edward left Nottingham on 29 July, and headed south towards Northampton to meet Herbert and Stafford, unaware of their fate until he reached the gates of the city. Here, most of his men deserted, and he dismissed the few who remained, though the lords stood by him. At Olney, in Buckinghamshire, on his way back to London, he was captured by an army led by George Neville. Much of what happened was Edward's own fault. In times of lethargy he was unquestionably his own worst enemy, never seeming to accept the fact that treachery could, and did, exist within his own circle of family and friends.

Warwick meanwhile refused to curb his thirst for blood, and resumed exacting his revenge on Edward's favourites. Lord Rivers and John Woodville—the queen's father and brother—were tracked down in Monmouthshire, and brought into Coventry where they were beheaded on 12 August. Sir Thomas Herbert was executed in Bristol. Humphrey Stafford was caught by a Bridgewater mob and dispatched five days later.

William Herbert had been allowed to write to his wife: he gave her instructions for his burial, and for various bequests, and told her to take up 'the order of widowhood', which meant that she would be saved from a second marriage, and thus retain his lands and look after the interests of their children, and his illegitimate daughter, Maud. [9] Lady Herbert's charge, Henry Tudor, was in considerable danger: she took him to her family's home, at Weobley in Herefordshire, and Margaret Beaufort immediately set about fighting for custody of her son. Eventually, the boy was put under the protection of Sir Richard Corbert, who had married Lady Herbert's niece. Henry was taken to Hereford and handed over to his uncle, Jasper Tudor, for safe keeping.

NOTES

1. *Great Chronicle of London*, 207-8, 213. Cook later supported the Re-adeption of Henry VI, whence he claimed damages of £14,666.
2. Ross: *Edward IV, Appendix IV*, pp 439-40.
3. Sir William Conyers (d 1495). Sir John's son was killed at Edgecott.
4. Edward Brandon, later Sir Edward Brampton (d 1508) was known as 'The Portuguese Jew'. He had settled and been baptised in England, and later supported Richard III before returning to Portugal.
5. Scofield, I, 491-2.
6. John de la Pole (1442-91), 2nd Duke of Suffolk. He had married Edward IV's sister in around 1460. They lived at Wingfield.
7. John de Vere (1443-1513), 13th Earl of Oxford.
8. *Paston Letters, V*, 35-6.
9. Nicolas: *Testamenta Vetusta*, 1826.

15

Edward's Apprehension/ The Lincolnshire & Exeter Rebellions 1469-1470

On 2 August 1469, Edward was brought before his 'liege lords'—Warwick and Clarence—in Coventry. If the rebels had expected their royal captive to prove troublesome and demanding, and thus offer them the opportunity to dispose of him, they were disappointed. Nothing is recorded of any subsequent conversations between the two parties, but Edward is understood to have conducted himself in a gentlemanly manner. He knew (or at least hoped) that Warwick would never have dared put him to death, and he was patient to bide his time and let the awkward situation work itself out. The rebels escorted him to Warwick Castle, and in late August, under cover of darkness, set off with him to Middleham. None of his lords appear to have been with him, so it may be assumed that during the early days of Edward's apprehension, Warwick had allowed these to disperse.

On 12 August, Warwick attempted to buy the loyalty of one of Edward's closest friends, William Hastings, by appointing him Chamberlain of North Wales. The Prior of St John became Treasurer on 16 August, and the next day Warwick rewarded himself with Lord Herbert's offices of Chief Justice and Chamberlain of South Wales. Prior to this he issued writs for Parliament to assemble in York on 22 August. The reason for this Parliament is uncertain, though some believed it was to discuss whether or not Clarence should have been offered the throne. **[1]** The choice of venue was blatantly obvious: Warwick's kidnapping of the king had turned out to be an open ticket towards violence, particularly in London where Edward's popularity was at its most potent. Charles of Burgundy threatened the city with yet more bloodshed should its people turn their backs on their king. In East Anglia, there was a renewed effort to oust the Pastons from Caister Castle. Clarence intervened, but to no avail: Norfolk was adamant that he would listen only to the king. He besieged the castle for several weeks, and even though severely short of victuals, John Paston held out until 26 September when one of his men and two of Norfolk's were killed in a scuffle. **[2]** There were squabbles in Lancashire between the Haringtons and Stanleys, and in Gloucestershire between the Talbots and Berkeleys. There were fears of an uprising in South Wales, and an urgent commission of array was appointed, headed by Lord Ferrers. Adding to the confusion, Humphrey Neville of Brancepeth and his brother Charles mounted an insurrection along the Scottish border in support of Henry VI. Warwick set about suppressing this, but found he could not raise troops while Edward was being held captive. He was given little choice but to set him free. By 10 September Edward was in York, and with his assent, Warwick amassed his troops and culled the rising. The Nevilles, Warwick's distant cousins, were brought into York on 29 September, where Edward presided over their executions.

Edward now re-assumed full control and asserted his authority by summoning many of his chief magnates and closes friends to join him at Pontefract: these included his brother Richard, Lords Hastings and Dynham, Suffolk, Montagu, Howard, Mountjoy, Arundel, Buckingham, and Essex. Only then did he feel confident to return to London, leading more than a thousand men. Warwick's brief reign was over. George Neville trailed after the royal party, stopping off at The Moor, in Hertfordshire, to collect the Earl of Oxford. [3] He petitioned Edward for an audience, obviously to worm his way back into his affections, and received a curt message: Edward would see him when *he* wanted to, and not before. The king then rode into London, accompanied by the Mayor, two-hundred craftsmen in blue, and twenty-two aldermen in scarlet. By mid-October he was back at Westminster. John Paston, writing home, was not sure what to make of the situation:

> I wot not to suppose therein. The King himself hath good language of the Lords of Clarence, of Warwick, and of my lords of York and Oxford, saying they be his best friends. But his household men have other language; so what shall hastilly fall I cannot say. [4]

Montagu had opposed Warwick and scored triumphs for the Yorkists at Hedgeley Moor and Hexham, therefore Edward saw no reason not to take him into his confidence now. Had he been able to see into the future, he would have had second thoughts. Edward still did not have a son, though he loved his three daughters dearly. Given Warwick's ruthless character, he realised that he was lucky to be alive, that the next time he might not be so fortunate. The heir to the throne was his three-year old daughter, Elizabeth, and Edward decided that for safety's sake she should be married to Montagu's son, George Neville. [5] This meant that if he died before Elizabeth Woodville bore a son, Clarence would be prevented from becoming king. Edward also took measures to curb the Nevilles' power in the north by releasing Henry Percy from the Tower and reinstating him to the earldom of Northumberland—a title currently held by Montagu who, in compensation for his losses became Marquess Montagu. Additionally, he received the greater part of the Courtenay estates formerly belonging to Humphrey Stafford of Southwick, and in January 1470, his son became Duke of Bedford.

Edward then set about rewarding the most loyal of his supporters. Sir John Howard became Lord Howard and on 17 October, Richard of Gloucester became Constable of England, and was further granted Lord Herbert's Welsh offices—the ones which Warwick had bestowed on himself. On 25 October, the Prior of St John was stripped of his post of Treasurer, and replaced by William Grey, Bishop of Ely.

On 29 October, twenty-six commissions or array were issued: three to Edward's friend, Lord Dynham. Warwick and Clarence were excluded for obvious reasons, though they were commanded to attend the Great Council meetings of November 1469-February 1470. Dynham's whereabouts during Edward's apprehension are confusing, though he must have been nearby—for on 9 November he was granted stewardship of Humphrey Stafford's castles, manors and boroughs in Devon and Cornwall, thus becoming the most powerful lord in the West Country.

Despite his recent ordeal, Edward was prepared to let bygones be bygones: Warwick and his rebels were granted pardons for all offences committed before 11 October 1469, and the betrothal between Edward's daughter and George Neville went ahead. The king further emphasised his alliance with Charles of Burgundy by swearing the Oath of the Golden Fleece, and Charles in return was invested with the Garter. Warwick and Clarence, however, still had not learned their lesson and promptly set about exploring new horizons. Warwick was confident in that, if he had 'made' one king, he could just as easily make another—Clarence.

Warwick's opportunity came early in January 1470 in the wake of a disturbance in Lincolnshire: his second cousin, Lord Welles—along with his son, Sir Robert, and his brothers-in-law Sir Thomas Dymoke and Sir Thomas de la Lande—attacked the Gainsborough manor of Sir Thomas Burgh. [6] Goods were stolen, the house razed to the ground, and Burgh forced to flee to London, where he craved an audience with the king. Such acts of petty violence were not uncommon, but Edward took an especial interest in this one: Burgh was his Master of the Horse. Furthermore, Welles had always been fiercely Lancastrian. He and Dymoke were summoned to Westminster—but not before Warwick had dispatched secret messages into Lincolnshire, sparking off another insurrection in support of Clarence and himself. Clarence had also sent his chaplain and another priest into the county, to advise Welles to raise troops and bide his time until Warwick left the capital to send out the call to arms.

News of the conspiracy was leaked: placards were nailed to the doors of churches, denouncing Warwick and Clarence as traitors. On 4 March, Edward dispatched a letter to Coventry: he was leaving for the north, and ordered that troops be waiting for him when he reached Grantham eight days hence. Sir Robert Welles immediately broadcast the rumour that the king would 'come thither and utterly destroy those that late made commotion there,' and the people of Lincolnshire were warned that 'the King's judges should sit, and hang and draw a great number of the commons.' [7] Warwick had promised to join Edward on his march, and seems to have been believed—which shows how truly gullible the king could sometimes be. Clarence had ordered Welles to begin the uprising on 4 March, and he now purposely delayed his brother by putting on a pretend show of family loyalty—inviting him to their mother's house at Baynard's Castle. Edward even believed Clarence when he informed him that he and Warwick had every intention of *suppressing* the rebellion, and he rewarded them by giving them a commission or array for Warwickshire and Worcestershire.

Edward, accompanied by Hastings, Arundel, and Henry Percy reached Waltham Abbey, Essex, on 7 March, to learn that Welles had mustered an army. Two days later, Lord Welles, the rebel's father, was summoned to Edward, by now in Huntingdon, and ordered upon pain of death to write to his son and call off the rebellion. On 11 March, Edward journeyed to Fotheringay, with Lord Welles as his prisoner, and Sir Robert Welles plans were thwarted: he had intended meeting up with Clarence and Warwick and their reputedly massive army in Leicester, but now changed course and headed for Fotheringay in the hope of rescuing his father and smashing the king. His army, of which little is known, pitched at Empingham, near Stafford. Edward gave orders for Lord Welles and Dymoke to be executed, and travelled overnight the fifteen miles to Empingham with such speed that the rebels were taken by surprise—they fled with such panic, throwing off their thickly-padded jackets, that the rout became scurrilously known as Lose-Coat Field. Calm as ever, Edward then retreated to Stafford, now well aware that Warwick and Clarence were behind the rebellion.

Why it took Edward so long to discover the obvious is a matter for conjecture, yet he was in a forgiving mood and sent an equerry, John Donne, after the rebels with the command for them to appear before him. [8] They refused, thinking that if he had been capable of executing Welles and Dymoke, he would show them no mercy. Edward pursued them: his army reached Grantham on 14 March. Sir Robert Welles was captured, and confessed that the rebellion had been organised by Warwick and Clarence, with the intention of putting Clarence on the throne. On 19 March, he was executed in Doncaster. Meanwhile the rebel leaders headed for Manchester, anticipating help from Sir Thomas Stanley, married to Warwick's sister. Richard of Gloucester, in Wales, assembled a small force: on the Hereford-Shrewsbury road, Stanley's men were scattered, and Stanley sent word to the rebels informing them that more help would not be forthcoming.

Clarence and Warwick turned tail and rode south. The king was unable to travel beyond Rotherham because the fleeing rebels had stripped the countryside of provisions: he turned towards York, arriving here on 22 March, to be told of other uprisings up and down the country. Robin of Redesdale had resurfaced to team up with Lord Scrope of Bolton: again the rebellion was backed by Warwick. It soon fizzled out when Montagu was appointed to head a commission or array.

On 25 March, the day that Henry Percy was finally restored to his title, Warwick and Clarence were formerly declared traitors.

Sir Hugh Courtenay of Boconnoc was a nephew of Edward, 3rd Earl of Devon, and a cousin of Henry Courtenay, allegedly executed in 1469 on the orders of Humphrey Stafford of Southwick [9] Prior to Edward assuming the crown, his sympathies were Lancastrian: since then, despite being appointed on a number of royal commissions he seems to have been loyal towards his rebellious family. By the Spring of 1470 he was openly supporting Warwick and Clarence. On 16 March, Edward appointed a commission of array to Lord Dynham and his brothers-in-law Baron Carew and Lord Fitzwarin—Baron Carew to arrest Boconnoc, William Courtenay of Powderham, and several members of his family. [10] On the same day, Dynham was appointed Keeper of the King's Forests for Exmoor and Neroche, for life. Dynham and his commissioners travelled the few miles from Nutwell to Exeter with a thousand men, but instead of capturing the Courtenays, they themselves were taken by a force much larger than their own, and imprisoned within the Bishop's palace. Here they were solicited for help by Isabel Neville, who had arrived in the city on 18 March. Dynham refused, though Clarence's wife was eight months pregnant, and his party's treatment at the hands of Boconnoc cannot have been pleasant, for the consumptive Nicholas Carew, died within a few months of his ordeal. Boconnoc then besieged the city, and for twelve days no provisions were brought in: still Dynham refused to capitulate, even when the Countess of Warwick arrived with her youngest daughter Anne and joined in with the plea—so much can be said for his loyalty.

Warwick and Clarence reached Exeter on 3 April, and the former must have been reminded of their escapade after the rout of Ludlow, when Dynham had organised their escape to freedom. Dynham, however, was never less than a king's man, and even when threatened with execution refused to budge. It was only when the evil Clarence had Dynham's baby son (ironically named George) kidnapped and threatened to kill him that he yielded—loaning the rebels money to head for Calais, but sending word at once to Lord Wenlock, Warwick's deputy in Calais, urging him not let them in. Wenlock proved reliable for once. Warwick and his rebels set sail from Dartmouth, and reached Calais on 16 April. Polite messages were exchanged between him and Wenlock, but the rebels were refused admittance. Wenlock provided two casks of wine for Isabel, who had gone into labour. Her baby was born dead and dropped into the sea. Undeterred, Warwick sailed along the Normandy coast. He had attempted to rescue his flagship, *Trinity*, from Anthony Woodville at Southampton, and there now followed a fierce sea-battle with Anthony and Lord Howard, wherein several hundred men were killed. Even so, Warwick scored a victory by getting the Bastard of Fauconberg to defect: together, on 20 August, they attacked and plundered a Flemish convoy outside Calais harbour, and insulted Charles of Burgundy by stealing the ships as well. Lord Howard gave chase and recaptured some, but by now Warwick's ships had reached the mouth of the Seine, at Honfleur. Here, he was greeted by his friend, the Archbishop of Narbonne, and word was sent to Louis XI that this time Warwick meant business: he would topple Edward IV and restore Henry VI to the throne. **[11]**

Many of Warwick's men were captured at sea, and brought before Butcher Tiptoft in Southampton. Their treatment was horrific. One or two were executed 'normally'. Twenty sailors were hanged, drawn and quartered, and their bodies 'reassembled' and 'spiked' by having sharpened stakes inserted into their rectums and pushed through their bodies until these came out at the neck, onto which their heads were impaled.

Clarence never forgave Dynham and always held him responsible for the death of Isabel's child: he set him up on a number of occasions, and for several years menaced and blackmailed the Dynham family. After Clarence's death in 1478, Dynham was granted money from the issues of the manors of Sampford Courtenay and others in Devon 'in recompense for having been compelled by George Duke of

Clarence to pay the latter divers great sums of money.' **[12]**

Edward arrived in Exeter on 14 April, having ridden almost three-hundred miles in eighteen days. He was met by the Mayor at the East Gate, and lodged within the city. The next day, Palm Sunday, he attended a ceremony at the cathedral: before leaving, he gave the city his huge two-handed sword, and granted further commissions of array to Dynham and his brothers-in-law. **[13]**

NOTES

1. *Calendar of Close Rolls, 1468-76,* pp 85-7; Calmette & Perinelle, op. cit., 108.
2. John Paston, elder (b 1442); John Paston, younger (1444-1503).
3. Archbishop Neville's mansion later belonged to Cardinal Wolsey. It was rebuilt in the 18th century and renamed Moor Park.
4. *Paston Letters, V*, 63.
5. George Neville (c 1461-83). He never married and died at Sheriff Hutton.
6. Richard Lord Welles, elder son of the lord killed at Towton. Sir Thomas Dymoke was the hereditary King's Champion and had officiated as such at Edward's coronation in 1461. Sir Thomas Burgh, MP for Lincoln 1467 and 1478, had acquired his property through his wife, Margaret, the daughter of Thomas Lord Roos, killed after Hexham.
7. The first statement from *Calendar of Close Rolls 1468-76*, pp 137-8; the second from *English Historical Documents, 1327-1485*, Vol IV, ed Myers, pp 302-3.
8. Sir John Donne of Carmarthen was married to Elizabeth, sister of Lord Hastings. The Memling triptych of him, his wife and daughter may be seen in the National Gallery.
9. J.A.F. Thomson: 'The Courtenay Family In The Yorkist Period,' BIHR, 1972, pp 233-5.
10. Fulk Bourchier (1445-79), the first husband of Dynham's sister, Elizabeth. As previously stated, Nicholas Carew married another sister, Margaret. They died within days of each other and are buried in St Nicholas' Chapel, Westminster Abbey.

11. Thomas Neville, Bastard of Fauconberg (1429-71). William Fauconberg's illegitimate son.
12. *Calendar of patent Rolls, 18, Edward IV*, p, ij, m. 10
13. *Calendar of Patent Rolls, 10, Edward IV*, m. 9d. Commissions issued on 2 June to Dynham, Carew and Fitzwarin, for Devon and Cornwall.

16

Edward's Flight & The Re-Adeption of Henry VI
1470-1471

In order to restore Henry VI, Warwick was faced with the daunting task of meeting and winning over the woman he had helped send into exile, the one person in the world who hated him as much as was possible for one person to hate another: Margaret of Anjou. He knew only too well how homesick her similarly exiled supporters were feeling. But how would they react, returning to England under the banner of the Bull and Ragged Staff?

Louis XI, the wily Spider King, was more than eager to help: with Edward out of the way this cold, thoroughly heartless man would have a better chance of overthrowing Charles of Burgundy. On the negative side, of course, there was the very real threat of an Anglo-Burgundian attack on France, but this was a risk Louis was willing to take: already he had pleaded innocence over the Bastard of Fauconberg's ambush of the Burgundian fleet. Louis made a rare dip into his purse and sent for Margaret of Anjou: she and her son were escorted from their house in Bar to meet him at Amboise. Louis put the proposition to her with sickly sincerity: a marriage proposition between Edward of Lancaster and Warwick's daughter, Anne.

On 22 June, in Louis' presence, Warwick and the fiery queen met at Angers: Margaret kept him on his knees for a quarter of an hour while he begged her to forgive him for his past deeds. Clarence was not here to witness the charade: he was in Calais with his wife, and Warwick had temporarily replaced him with another protégé, the young Earl of Oxford, who had managed to escape from England. Margaret was horrified at the thought of her beloved son marrying a Neville, and refused to have anything to do with the alliance. Her father, René of Anjou, was summoned to persuade her and she relented: even so, she refused to hand over the prince to Warwick, who she believed perfectly capable of duping her and having the boy put to death, something she herself would have done, had their roles been reversed. Her quest for power equaled his and she reluctantly signed a thirty years truce and instructed her Chancellor, Sir John Fortescue, to draw up an agreement stating that Warwick would become Governor of England once Henry VI had been restored. Louis then agreed to pay for Margaret's upkeep, and that of her son and his bride, until such time as Warwick had England under his control—as a safeguard he insisted upon Jasper Tudor and the Earl of Oxford accompanying them on their expedition.

The betrothal between fourteen-year old Anne Neville and the eighteen-year old delinquent prince took place at Angers Cathedral on 25 July 1470. Oaths were sworn on a piece of the True Cross—to break such on oath, it was said, meant death within the year. Louis swore allegiance to Warwick, who swore to support Henry, while Margaret swore never to get back at Warwick for past deeds. [1]

Exactly what Anne Neville thought of her enforced match may only be imagined. Raised by Margaret of Anjou and influenced by Somerset and Wiltshire—either of whom could have been his father—Edward of Lancaster can hardly have been the noble, chivalrous man Anne had hoped to have as a husband. Much of her life had been spent within the closed confines of Middleham, far from court intrigues and the corruption of her father's circle, and she is said to have been a quiet, shy girl. When discussing Edward's character, it is sufficient to say that, during his 'honeymoon', he insisted upon taking his bride on a visit to the infamous Montfaucon gallows, in Paris, where a hundred men could be dispatched at once, and where their bodies were often left hanging for years. Such was his infatuation with grisly manners of death. [2] Warwick cannot have cared much for his daughter's wellbeing to lumber her with such a psychotic spouse, and for Anne Neville it was to be but the beginning of another chapter in her sad, short life. For the time being, though, there would be a little respite: the marriage could not be consummated until the necessary dispensation arrived, so for now Anne did not have to share a bed with this brute. She and her mother went to live with Margaret of Anjou at Amboise.

Warwick began preparing his invasion of England. On 31 July he travelled to Valognes, unaware of Clarence's latest intrigues. From here, he maintained contact with his supporters in England. Messages were smuggled across the

Channel by the Earl of Shrewsbury and Lord Stanley: Montagu may already have been thinking about changing sides. Warwick was pressing for an insurrection in the north to lure King Edward away from the south. Support from one invaluable ally would not be forthcoming: Chancellor Neville was under armed guard at The Moor. The time was ripe. Warwick's men were half-crazed with the urge to fight—against who did not matter so long as he was paying them well—and he had additional support from the Admiral of France, Louis Bastard of Bourbon. There was a last-minute hitch when one Anglo-Burgundian fleet blocked the exit from Honfleur, while others prevented his ships from leaving Hogue and Barfleur. His men grew restless over unpaid wages—they had been paid once, but after the delay only rightfully demanded more. On 21 August they were ordered to march from Valognes to Barfleur and board ship: they refused, and ran riot in the town. Finally, on 9 September the Anglo-Burgundian blockades were scattered by violent storms. Warwick seized the opportunity and set sail with some sixty French ships: with him were Clarence, Oxford, and Jasper Tudor.

Four days later the rebels landed at Plymouth and Dartmouth. Jasper set off for Wales, Warwick and his party for Exeter. Lord Dynham received word that Clarence was in the vicinity with a large force, and fled to Hartland with his entire family, leaving the way open for the Lancastrians to march across Devon and collect supporters rallied by the Courtenays. Messages were sent ahead, proclaiming that all Lancastrians attainted by Edward would be pardoned so long as they swore allegiance to King Henry...and Warwick hammered home his 'peaceful intentions' by warning his men that the death penalty would be enforced for robbery and rape. His army was augmented by the forces of Stanley and Shrewsbury, and by the time he approached Coventry he was reported to have 30,000 men. In Kent, news of his landing had caused his ever-faithful Kentishmen to run amock. They swooped on London, plundering Southwark and the southern suburbs, where Flemings became their prime targets. Warwick's plan for a pretended insurrection in the north had worked: his brother-in-law, Lord Fitzhugh of Ravensworth, instigated the trouble and Henry Percy informed the king that he had no way of putting it down. There was no word of Montagu, and a very suspicious Edward had set off from Yorkshire early in August, with by Richard of Gloucester, Lords Say, Howard and Hastings, Butcher Tiptoft and Anthony Woodville. The queen, six months pregnant, had been lodged within the Tower: extra artillery had been brought in, including a number of large guns from Bristol.

Edward meanwhile had reached York, expecting Warwick's force to land on the east coast, and feeling relatively unperturbed because he was confident of Montagu's backing. Even when he realised that he had been duped, he chose to linger. Richard was appointed head of a commission of oyer and terminer, and on 26 Warden of the West Marches towards Scotland. Edward then turned south, sending word to Montagu to follow with the army he had raised at Pontefract. He was at Doncaster when news came in the middle of the night that Montagu had changed sides during the night and was hot on his heels with 3,000 men.

Trapped, Edward realised he would never muster support at such short notice, that this was Ludlow all over again. At once he, Richard, Hastings, Anthony, Lord Say and a handful of others jumped on to their horses and rode swiftly for Anthony's house at Middleton, in Norfolk. From here they piled into small boats, were almost drowned in a gale, and on 30 September reached King's Lynn, where they commandeered a ship. On 2 October they set sail and several days later beached near Alkmaar, in Holland. As with the flight to Calais in 1459 this was no easy trip: they were chased most of the way by Hanseatic ships, managed to get away, and because he was desperately short of money Edward paid the captain for his services by giving him his rich gown lined with marten-furs.

For the second time in his life, Edward had been forced into exile. This time, however, it was due to his own mismanagement.

News of Edward's flight reached London on Monday 1 October, and violence erupted. Further riots were instigated by a Lancastrian zealot, Sir Geoffrey Gate, who gave orders for the prisons to be opened. The rabble was let loose on the city: added to the looting and pillaging which was still going on, this caused mass chaos and such was the violence that the queen fled the Tower during the night and took sanctuary with other members of her family at Westminster. The next day, the Yorkist Chancellor and his council took similar measures and escaped to St Martin-le-Grand, near St

Paul's. On the Wednesday, the Tower surrendered to Sir Geoffrey Gate and the Mayor: King Henry was brought out of captivity—a dithering, dirty mess—and transferred to the opulent apartments which had been prepared for the queen's lying-in. He may have been unaware of what was happening to him: even so he was treated with kingly reverence. Archbishop Neville, who had somehow managed to evade his guards, arrived in London on 5 October, and also ensconced himself within the Tower. The picture was completed the next afternoon when Warwick, Clarence and their motley crew cruised into the capital.

King Henry was dressed in a long, blue velvet gown and conveyed to St Paul's, and installed within the Bishop of London's palace. Clarence moved into The Erber, the former London home of the Earl of Salisbury, while Warwick himself lodged with the puppet-king. On 13 October, Henry was put on public display and taken to St Paul's to be re-crowned. In an act of mock-sincerity, the Earl of Oxford carried the sword of state, and Warwick held the train—well aware that he, and not Henry, was King of England. The coronation speech was modified to exclude the words 'and also King of France'—Warwick did not wish to offend Louis XI, who had after all paid for the exercise. Upon this day the so-called Re-Adeption of Henry VI began.

Edward and his fellow fugitives arrived in The Hague on 11 October 1470: he contacted Louis de Gruthuyse, and soon afterwards went to stay with him at his mansion in Bruges. Edward does not appear to have been unduly worried over the changing tide of fortune, or that a great deal of controversy surrounded his flight. Philip de Commines blamed this on Edward's lethargy, and commented that 'he was more handsome than any man then alive, but he thought of nothing else but women far more than is reasonable, and looking after himself,'—aspects of his character which have never been doubted. Commines goes on to suggest that Edward could have put up a fight against Montagu because he himself had 3,000 men. Ross discusses the king's 'crumbling authority' and lack of popular support, which is a more likely theory: the fact that Edward was in the north of England when Warwick landed, an area known for its hostility, could not have helped even if he had attempted to rally for support—the northern lords who were not his enemies would have chosen to sit on the fence, as they had often done in the past, waiting to join whichever faction had the greatest advantage. [3]

Warwick meanwhile seemed to be undergoing a temporary change of personality. He was ruler of England in all but name: King Henry was too mad to remain coherent for any length of time, and Warwick's was the invidious task of achieving and maintaining the support of those Yorkist lords who had risen high by serving Edward. He therefore decided that peace, not recrimination, must be the order of the day. Several of the more prominent Yorkists—Norfolk, Wiltshire, Mounjoy, Cromwell and Archbishop Bourchier—were arrested, ticked off, and released again. On 15 October writs were issued for lords to attend the Parliament scheduled for 26 November, but there were notable exceptions: top of the list was Lord Dynham, still 'exiled' in Hartland.

Of Warwick's supporters, Archbishop Neville was re-appointed Chancellor, and was returned the Great Seal: Stillington, the Yorkist Chancellor, was still in sanctuary. Jasper Tudor regained Pembroke Castle from Lord Herbert's widow, and thirteen-year old Henry Tudor was brought into London on what may have been his first excursion into England. This proved humiliating for Clarence, signing himself Earl of Richmond—Henry's title—and after two weeks, the boy and his uncle were sent back to Wales. The Bishop of Coventry and Lichfield was appointed Keeper of the Privy Seal; Sir John Plummer, a rich London grocer, became Keeper of the Wardrobe; Sir Richard Tunstall became Chamberlain and Master of the Mint; Sir Henry Lowys became Comptroller of the Household, and Sir Thomas Cook was appointed an alderman. [4]

Warwick himself became King's Lieutenant of the Realm, Great Chamberlain *and* Lord High Admiral, and the Prior of St John re-assumed the treasurership. The situation within Westminster was described as 'Neville regime in Lancastrian costume', but there were few honours for Montagu and Clarence: the former was restored to his wardenship of the East Marches, while Clarence was offered nothing in return for his 'loyalty' other than the return of his forfeited lands.

The Earl of Oxford temporarily appointed Constable of England, primarily to try and condemn the most feared man in England, certainly as far as the nobility was concerned: Butcher Tiptoft. He was sentenced to die on 17 October, but when his time came the crowds were hysterical, and blocked his walk to the scaffold, wishing only to tear him to pieces. Order was restored, and the next day he went to the block, asking the executioner to sever his head with three strokes, representing the Blessed Trinity. It was a fitting end for a barbarous thug. On a lesser note, the now immensely powerful Oxford had become a patron of the Pastons, and John Paston had suddenly found himself better-equipped to recover Caister Castle from his Norfolk enemies.

On 2 November 1470, in Westminster Sanctuary, Elizabeth Woodville gave birth to Edward's long-awaited first son. Warwick afforded her every luxury, considering the adverse circumstances: her mother and Lady Scrope were in attendance, and her butcher supplied her weekly with two sheep and half a beef—she later rewarded him for his overwhelming loyalty by allowing him to load a ship, *Trinity of London*, with ox-skins, tallow and lead at any English port. The sub-Prior of Westminster baptised the child Edward, after his father: Lady Scrope and the Prior and Abbot of Westminster were god-parents.

Whichever way Warwick looked at it, England now had two kings, two queens, and two Princes of Wales who were both heir to the throne. Thus, in the November Parliament, Edward and his brother Richard were attainted: no records of the Re-Adeption Parliament have survived, so there is no way of knowing who else was attainted, though Lord Dynham and the six others barred from the Parliament must have been, and there was further humiliation for the Duchess of York: the tale was revived that she had conceived Edward during an extra-marital affair with an archer named Blayburn—which meant that her eldest legitimate son, Clarence, was heir to the throne should anything befall Margaret of Anjou's son, Edward of Lancaster. Clarence had thus publicly branded his own mother as an adulteress and a whore. Even so, Duchess Cecily attempted to make her son see the error of his ways by trying to persuade him to turn his back on Warwick and support Edward, behind the scenes, before Margaret arrived in England.

The French king, meanwhile, was expecting action for the money he had 'lavished' on Warwick's plot to overthrow Edward. The Prince of Wales had promised to send an army of English mercenaries to help him against Burgundy: by December 1470, nothing had happened, and Louis sent his ambassadors to England in the hope of spurring things along, while Warwick promised than an army would be forthcoming. Louis was by no means a patient man, and by the end of the month had taken decisive action by denouncing the Treaty of Péronne and amassing troups along the Burgundian border at Picardy. Duke Charles' hackles were at once raised. On 2 January 1471 he met Edward at Aire, near St Omer—the first time in three months that he had had the decency to acknowledge him.

With Edward was Louis de Gruthuyse: neither man had any feeling for Louis and this probably showed. Nevertheless this and a further meeting at St Pol, on 7 January, was conducted with great courtesy, and Charles agreed that though he would publicly refuse to assist his brother-in-law, he *would* provide him with men and money on the sly. Subsequently several Dutch ships were fitted out at Veere, on the island of Walcheren, and Edward was given 50,000 florins, amounting to around £20,000.

Edward next secured loans or gifts from other sources, notably from the Calais merchants whom he had befriended during his first exile. He then got in touch with Clarence and Henry Percy: the former was a push-over, and young Percy was terrified that Montagu would attempt to snatch back his lands and title. Edward also negotiated with Duke Francis of Brittany, and the Hansards: they eventually promised to supply him with fourteen ships, and men to serve him for two weeks and one day after his return to England. In Bruges, Anthony Woodville negotiated for more ships, and Edward's developing fleet in Flushing was further augmented in February by the arrival of two English sea-captains, Steven Driver and John Lister. On 19 February, Edward set off for Flushing, and on 2 March he embarked on the great Burgundian flagship, the *Antony*. His fleet comprised thirty-six ships and some 1,200 men. For several days, proceedings were held up by bad weather, but on 11 March 1471, Edward finally set sail for home. [5]

NOTES:

1. The couple were not allowed to be formerly married because they had a common great-grandfather, John of Gaunt. According to Calmette & Perinelle, pp 139-40, they were later married at Ambroise, probably on 13 December. Whether the marriage was consummated or not is a matter for conjecture.
2. The structure, measuring 40 feet square by 20 feet tall, stood outside the city walls, near the present Place de Colonel Fabien. Built in the late-13th century it was destroyed in 1760.
3. Philip de Commines, 185, Penguin Classics, 1972.
4. Richard Tunstall (d 1492) secured an annuity of £40 in 1453 for informing Henry VI of Margaret of Anjou's pregnancy. Cancelled by the Duke of York the following year, it was restored, reduced to 56 marks in 1456. Tunstall served both Edward IV and Henry VII.
5. According to Warkworth and Waurin, 900 English and 300 Flemings with handguns. *The Arrivall of Edward IV* states 2,000.

Edward IV, in later life

17

Edward's Return & The Battle of Barnet
1471

The Bastard of Fauconberg's fleet had plundering Spanish, Breton and Portuguese vessels in the Channel for some time, financed by Warwick's pirates. Warwick's spies scouted the south coast, the likeliest place for Edward or Margaret to land. Inland, Edward's friends and known adherents were watched. On 27 February 1471, Warwick travelled to Dover: the Prior of St John had been dispatched across the Channel to collect Margaret and her son, only to return empty-handed. Warwick sent word to the French king: he was eager to invade Burgundy but could not do so until the queen arrived, for to leave England 'unattended' might have weakened his position as its governor. He was informed that Margaret and Edward of Lancaster were at Honfleur, fearful of making their journey because King Edward was about to begin his. Louis meanwhile had already set the ball rolling. Amiens had been taken, and he and his army awaited Warwick at Beauvais. The English Calicians were laying waste the countryside around Boulogne. His hands tied, Warwick could do little more than return to London, where the city was agog with excitement pending Edward's return. The Mayor, feigning illness, had taken to his bed. Sir Thomas Cook, himself preparing to take flight, stepped into his shoes.

Warwick continued collecting men for his invasion of Burgundy, though the idea was starting to lose its appeal, while waiting for news from Kent of the queen's arrival. No one knew exactly Edward would land, but every area was catered for. Kent was able to take care of itself. Montagu was in Pontefract with a large force: the eastern counties were guarded by Oxford and Scrope of Bolton. Clarence was in the West Country with Somerset and the Earl of Devon: Baron Carew had died and been replaced as Sheriff by one of the Courtenays. Jasper Tudor was in Wales. Therefore it seemed obvious that, wherever they landed, Edward and his meagre force would easily be put down.

By 12 March, Edward's fleet had reached the Norfolk coast: this was Anthony Woodville territory, and the Yorkists hoped for support from the Dukes of Norfolk and Suffolk. Two of Edward's officers, Sir Gilbert Debenham and Sir Robert Chamberlain, went ashore only to be told by the Archbishop of Canterbury and the Bishop of Rochester that it was not safe to land. Norfolk was in custody and the area was rife with the Earl of Oxford's supporters. Edward set sail at once for Yorkshire. There were violent storms and his fleet was scattered, though with his customary good fortune only a ship-load of horses was lost, and on 14 March, at Ravenspur on the mouth of Humber, he finally stepped on to his beloved English soil. The other ships landed safely along the coast, and the force was reunited early the next day. [1]

Yorkshire was as dangerous a place to land as any. The nearest town to Ravenspur was Kingston-on-Hull: the mostly-Lancastrian populace refused to allow Edward in until he had convinced them that he had *not* returned to England to reclaim the crown, but to recover his ducal inheritance. He even produced papers signed by Henry Percy to this effect. On 18 March, he marched to York, and leaving his army encamped outside the city walls he was greeted by the recorder, Thomas Conyers, and two of the city's most prominent citizens, Robert Clifford and Richard Burgh. According to the sometimes unreliable chronicler, Warkworth, he then entered the city with just seventeen men and, bearing the white ostrich feather of the Prince of Wales, swore allegiance to Henry VI. Thenon he travelled to Sandal, near Wakefield, well aware that Montagu's army was but ten miles away, at Pontefract.

Warwick's brother neither resisted nor assisted, primarily because he was in an area which fell under the cast-iron jurisdiction of Henry Percy, but possibly because he was testing the water before deciding which side to support. Edward headed south. In Doncaster, William Dudley joined him with 160 men: 600 more were waiting in Nottingham under the command of Sir James Harington and Sir William Parr. Sir William Stanley and Sir William Norris brought 3,000 into Leicester. There was also bad news: Oxford, Exeter and the new Viscount Beaumont were in Newark with a massive enemy force. [2] Edward had come this far, and would not submit. He marched to confront them, but they fled during the night and joined Warwick's main army in Warwickshire. Then, to his horror,

Edward learned that Montagu was on the move: he was at his rear, chasing him south.

Edward's army, probably in excess of 5,000, reached the outskirts of Coventry on 29 March, ten years to the day since Towton. Warwick was within the city with a force of 6,000, waiting for Oxford and Montagu to arrive with enforcements—and, he hoped, the Duke of Clarence. Knowing that the odds were stacked against him, Edward challenged Warwick to come out into the open and do battle. He refused, and this went on for three days. Realising that he was wasting his time, on 2 April Edward moved the eleven miles to the city of Warwick on what would be the first leg of his journey to London. The castle was taken, and a message sent to Earl of Warwick offering him the customary pardon, should he surrender. This of course fell on deaf ears.

Edward received news of his brother, en route from Somerset. On 15 March, Clarence had sent a letter from Bristol to Henry Vernon, of Haddon Hall in Derbyshire—asking for assistance and news of the activities of Percy, Stanley and Shrewsbury. Further letters were dispatched during his march from the West Country: even when Clarence reached Banbury he was unsure which side he would be fighting for. By 3 April, he too had decided to join Edward, probably for no other reason than his side was the better-advantaged. He, Edward and Richard of Gloucester were 'reunited' on the road between Banbury and Warwick, in a public show of sham emotion: Clarence went down on his knees to the king, kissed Richard, and delivered a perfunctory speech to their two armies. Edward almost certainly saw through him: in any case, Clarence had brought 4,000 men with him, a good enough reason for Edward to welcome him back into the fold. Similarly, by this time Warwick's army had been well augmented by the combined forces of Montagu, Exeter and Oxford, and the position could have been ratified had he accepted Edward's renewed challenge to do battle, which he did not. Edward began marching again, and reached Daventry on Palm Sunday, 7 April, and at this point of his account the author of *The Arrival*, who so far has stuck to the hard facts, offers light entertainment. [3]

Edward, never superstitious of making war on 'unlucky' holy days, had always had great faith in spiritual phenomena. He attended Mass at the parish church in Daventry: an alabaster shrine of St Anne was attached to a pillar near the altar, but because it was Lent, its linen-fold doors had been closed. Suddenly, they opened a fraction and closed again—then flew wide open and remained so. There would have been a logical explanation for this, but Edward conveniently remembered that he had prayed to St Anne for guidance while at sea. Needless to say, his army reacted with expected enthusiasm.

Hearing that their 'second' king was almost upon them, Londoners were thrown into a state of abject confusion—there was still no news of Margaret of Anjou. Henry was paraded through the streets—the chronicler erroneously tells us with Archbishop Bourchier holding his hand and Lord Zouche carrying the royal sword, while a horseman dangled two fox-tails from the end of a pole. [4] The people treated this farce with the contempt it deserved.

Henry was a decidedly bad joke: soon, a *real* king would be arriving, one possessed of brains and brawn...

On 10 April, Edward had reached St Albans. The next afternoon, Maundy Thursday, he made an exultant entrance into London, and went to St Paul's, where the customary offering was made. He then marched to the Bishop of London's palace and took charge of Henry. The two kings are said to have shaken hands and Henry is reported to have said, 'My cousin of York, you are very welcome. I know that in your hands my life will not be in danger!' Edward must have been touched: Henry, Archbishop Neville and several clerics were placed under guard in the Tower. Edward then went to Westminster, where the crown graced his head but for a moment before he dashed off to be reunited with his queen, and to see his son for the first time. This done, he packed his family off to his mother's house for the night: later they would be transferred to the safety of the Tower. Philip de Commines, writing of Edward's entry into the city, knew more than most about court intrigues. Though following hearsay, he was pretty close to the truth:

> From what I have been told three factors helped to make the city change its mind: first the men, who were in the sanctuaries, and his wife, the Queen, who had given birth to a son; secondly the great debts he owed in the city, which made his merchant creditors support him; thirdly, several noblewomen and wives of rich citizens with whom he had been closely and secretly acquainted won over their husbands and relatives to his cause. [5]

On Saturday 13 April, Edward led his army along Watling Street—in the midst of it was King Henry. Edward's army had been further augmented by forces brought in by the Bourchiers and Lord Howard, though it was still smaller than Warwick's. What neither side could have known was that Margaret of Anjou and her son had landed in Weymouth that very day, or that Somerset and the Earl of Devon had swerved from their march on London to go and meet her. Edward was severely criticised for wanting to do battle in the Easter period: he probably thought he had little choice, for no one would have put it past Warwick to attack him while he was at his devotions.

After a twelve-mile march, Edward and his army of roughly 8,000 reached Barnet. Night had fallen. Warwick's advance guard had been there since the afternoon. There was a scuffle and Edward's advance vanguard beat them back from the streets of the town towards their main army, which had approached from St Albans on the road which ran through Kitt's End, between Wrotham Park and the present golf course—they were encamped right across the road on the high ridge stretching south from Hadley Green to Barnet. Warwick's right was commanded by Oxford, though the chroniclers do not agree upon who was in command of the centre: some say Somerset—who almost certainly was en route to meet his queen—while others agree that it was Montagu, a much more likely theory. His left was commanded by the Duke of Exeter and Warwick himself, who would also have supervised the reserve, if there was one. Again, nothing is certain, for even eye-witness accounts of this battle are muddled.

Edward had already cleared the streets of the little town, and now thought it prudent to camp closer to the enemy—this was extremely difficult, moving such a large number of men under cover of darkness, and he almost erred by moving too close before settling down for the night in St John's Fields. Edward himself was in command of the central flank which also included Clarence: like Warwick and Montagu, he still did not trust his brother and knew from first-hand experience at Northampton how easy it was for commanders to change sides at the crucial moment. Hastings and Lord Say were in command of his left, while eighteen-year old Richard of Gloucester took the right. King Henry was stuck amongst the reserves, and goes down in history as the only English king to be present at several major battles and not play an active role—or any role at all, for that matter.

Edward's mistake of coming too close to his enemy paid off handsomely during the preliminary stages of the battle. Warwick was eager to get on with things: he had the better artillery, probably more ammunition, and throughout the night maintained a cannonade. Edward had given orders that no fires should be lit, though it was bitterly cold, and the enemy missiles passed harmlessly over the heads of the men in his front ranks.

Easter Sunday dawned misty: this developed into fog, with visibility down to almost nil. Edward's soldiers had spent an uncomfortable night bedded down on the cold, boggy ground, so their spirits low when his commanders awakened them. At 5 am, the order was given to advance the banners: silently, they trudged towards the enemy front line, bumping into one another.

Horses played little or no part in this battle. As with Towton, most of the fighting was done on foot—though Edward is said to have been mounted on a white steed—and again like Towton, the adverse weather conditions turned out to be in the Yorkists' favour. Warwick's archers, clumped together within his central flank, sent off a few volleys of arrows, but the thick blanket of fog made it impossible to perfect an accurate aim, and in next to no time the opposing front lines clashed head on. Oxford, on Warwick's right, smashed into Hastings' flank: it was scattered and pursued all the way into Barnet, where the rumour spread like wildfire that the Yorkists had lost the day. Richard, on Edward's right, had no direct opposition so he attempted to get at the Duke of Exeter's division on Warwick's left by ascending the tricky incline near Monken Hadley. This proved no easy task, for neither he nor Edward were over-familiar with the area. Richard was on the verge of defeat when Oxford suddenly re-entered the fray. His men, having made a bad job of chasing Hastings' men into Barnet, had set about looting and pillaging the town. Some 800 of them were brought back into the battle, but by this time the two sides had changed position and they immediately came up against Montagu's men. The fog was still patchy in places, but in the confusion the Radiant Star device of de Vere was mistaken for Edward's Sun in Splendour and they were assailed with arrows. Treason was suspected—Oxford left the field, followed not only by many of his own men, but a great many of Montagu's as well.

It was still only 9 am, and Edward's reserve had been used up. It appeared to be the most critical stage of the battle, and he risked his ace by surging forward with his central line. Warwick's men had witnessed Oxford's flight: Montagu had been brought down, it was reported, while coming to his brother's aid, and Exeter was also dead. Demoralised, the enemy crumpled. Victory was Edward's.

Edward wasted no time. He gave orders for Warwick to be brought before him, promising that his life would be spared. He was too late: Richard Neville, attempting to flee the field, had managed to get as far as the horse-park at Wrotham Wood. No longer in his prime, the weight of his armour proved too much for him, and he was brought down by a group of Edward's soldiers who wrenched open his visor and plunged a knife into his throat.

It is estimated that 1,500 men died in the battle, and many more were killed during the mopping-up operation in the locality known today as Dead Man's Bottom. According to John Paston, 1,000 of these were Lancastrians. The Paston brothers had fought on Warwick's side: both were taken prisoner, and granted pardons. On 18 April the elder Paston wrote to his mother saying that his brother had been wounded in the arm by an arrow, but that they were both well, and that their patron had escaped to Scotland along with Viscount Beaumont.

Other than Warwick and Montagu, the Lancastrians lost no one of note. The Duke of Exeter, mistaken for dead, had been stripped of his armour: after the battle he was smuggled away by his servants and took refuge in St Martin's Sanctuary. Eventually he would spend four years in the Tower (where he had been born during his father's governorship) in great luxury with a coterie of servants. Edward lost Lord Say, Sir Thomas Parr, Sir John Lisle, Humphrey and Viscount Bourchier, and Lord Cromwell. Sir William Blount died of his wounds, while Richard of Gloucester and Anthony Woodville were slightly hurt.

The next day, the bodies of Warwick and Montagu were brought into London on the back of a cart. Clad only in loin-cloths, they were put into rough wooden coffins and displayed on the pavement outside St Paul's—to let the people know that they were well and truly dead, and to offer a stern warning to would-be traitors. After a few days, Edward allowed them to be moved and they were interred in the family vault at Bisham Abbey. During the reformation, the abbey was destroyed. Warwick's remains were discovered, but what became of them is not known. All that is left of the Warwick legend is a pair of mutilated alabaster effigies within the parish church of Burghfield, in Berkshire, thought to represent his parents, the Earl and Countess of Salisbury.

NOTES

1. Ravenspur is thought to lie beneath the sea some two miles east of Spurn Head. Henry of Derby landed here in 1399 when he came to usurp the throne from Richard II.
2. William (1438-1507), 2nd Viscount Beaumont. In 1487 he is described as mad, and cared for by Oxford, who later married his widow. William Dudley (d 1483), Bishop of Durham 1476. Younger son of the 6th Lord Dudley.
3. *Historie of The Arrivall of Edward IV In England*: Camden Society, 1838. It is the best and most accurate chronicle written during Edward's reign, and was probably written by a chaplain. He almost certainly was an eye-witness at most of the events he writes about.
4. John, Lord Zouche (1460-1526) was a brother-in-law of Lord Dynham. Though a friend of Clarence, he was not in London at the time and in any case would have been too young. The sword-bearer was Ralph Butler, 7th Lord Sudley, who died aged over eighty in 1473.
5. Philip de Commines, 194.

18

The Battle of Tewkesbury & The Death of Henry VI
1471

Margaret of Anjou had opted to set sail from Honfleur on 24 March 1471: bad weather held her up, and she did not reach Weymouth until 13 April. Gone was the reckless, passionate girl who had arrived in England three decades earlier to become its queen. Margaret was forty-two, and hardened by eight years of exile and hatred. Gone were the amorous conquests and the handsome young gigolos: only one young man mattered now—her son who, if he had been fathered by Somerset or Wiltshire, had certainly inherited their psychotic streak. Her army consisted mainly of French mercenaries, and an odd assortment of would-be commanders. Edward of Lancaster was seventeen. At the opposite end of the scale were Lord Wenlock and Sir John Fortescue, well into their seventies, the Prior of St John, and Doctor Morton. The Countess of Warwick had travelled independently to Portsmouth: at Southampton she had learned of her husband's death, and realising that she was now the wealthiest heiress in England and still marriageable even at forty-four, she had entered the inviolable sanctuary at the nearby Beaulieu Abbey.

On 15 April, Margaret was joined at Cerne Abbey by Somerset and Devon. For a while she was despondent, and considered returning to France. Her son and her lords persuaded her to stay: she resumed her quest and her party left for Exeter. Devonshire was almost entirely Lancastrian in its sympathies, for the Yorkists lords were still in hiding and as yet knew little of the events of the last few weeks. Thenon she made her way via Taunton and Wells (where Robert Stillington's soldiers plundered the Bishop's Palace and broke open the prison) towards Bath, by which time the size of her army had increased dramatically. Margaret was utterly convinced that her strength now lay in Edward's weakness: after Barnet his men would be tired, and if *she* did battle now he would have insufficient time to replace the men he had lost and reassemble his army. News came to her that her friend Jasper Tudor was raising troops in Wales, and she already knew that the Bastard of Fauconberg, still patrolling and pirating the Channel, was about to besiege London.

After Barnet, Edward had dismissed his men, but between 18 and 26 April, fresh commissions of array were issued to fifteen counties, and from his base at Windsor, Edward set about re-assembling his artillery train. He was expecting Somerset to join Jasper Tudor and march through Reading towards London, and was cautious of leaving the capital open to attack: though the Lancastrians were rumoured to be short of money and ammunition. Alternatively, Somerset and Jasper could have been heading for Cheshire and Lancashire, and when on 24 April Edward learned that this was indeed the case, he set off and via Abingdon reached Cirencester on 29 April. Thenon he moved to Malmesbury in Wiltshire, where he learned that Margaret had obtained men, munitions and money from the citizens of Bristol, and that Somerset's vanguard was encamped at Sodbury, on the Bristol-Malmesbury road. Edward pitched camp at Sodbury Hill, ten miles north-east of Bristol, and prepared to do battle. This turned out to be a ruse. Somerset had set off to catch up with Margaret's army: en route for the Severn, this had already reached Berkeley, and after a brief rest had completed the fourteen miles to Gloucester, under cover of night, marching across some very rough territory indeed. Edward received this rather disconcerting news on the morning of 3 May, and at once gave chase, leading his troops along the old road which crossed the western scarp of the Cotswold ridge. It was a very hot day, and the Yorkists' march was not that much easier than that of their enemy: men complained of hunger and thirst, but the victory which had just taken place at Barnet, coupled with the fact that Edward had never lost a battle, spurred them on. Edward then sent a message ahead to the Governor of Gloucester, Sir Richard Beauchamp, ordering him not to open the gates of the town to the Lancastrians. [1] Beauchamp complied, and also barred the way to the bridge over the Severn, forcing Margaret to head for the next crossing at the ford near Tewkesbury. By this time it was getting dark, and her men were extremely foot-sore and fatigued. They encamped within the castle ruins, half a mile south of the town. A few hours later, Edward's army reached Tewkesbury, by way of Cheltenham, still relatively fresh after an astonishing thirty-six mile march. They settled down for the night at Tredington, three miles from the enemy front lines.

Somerset had selected an excellent defensive position on a ridge a mile south of the town, near the present hospital. The Severn was to his right, Swilgate Brook was to his left, the River Avon and Tewkesbury Abbey behind him. In front of him were 'foul lanes and deep dykes and many hedges with hills and valleys, a right evil place to approach.' The centre was commanded by Edward of Lancaster, under the supervision of Lord Wenlock. The left was commanded by the Earl of Devon. Margaret had retreated to the town to await the outcome of the battle. The Lancastrians had 6,000 men, Edward a thousand less, but his troops were better conditioned and because *their* leader had never lost a battle, in better spirits. Richard of Gloucester was in command of Edward's left, and immediately facing Somerset: to his left was an area of marshland. Edward commanded his own centre, assisted by Clarence whose every move was watched, while Hastings took the right. Edward also had 200 detached "spearmen" placed in a concealed position on his army's left, close to the edge of Tewkesbury Park. These were probably mounted lancers, and were there for a specific purpose: Edward had earlier observed the wooded hillock, the perfect spot to execute an ambush, and the men were given orders to act not on command, but on initiative.

The battle, brief but the most decisive of Edward's reign, took place on the morning of 4 May. It began with the customary exchange of arrows and missiles, though the

Lancastrians were sorely lacking of the latter, and when Edward's division lurched forwards to tackle the enemy front line, it was impeded by prickly hedges and scrubland. This offered Somerset the opportunity to swing around the by-lines and attempt to attack Richard's flank. The spearmen, finding no ambush on the hillock, suddenly swooped down the slope and Somerset was caught between them and Richard's wing. His men immediately resorted to flight, and there was mass panic amongst their ranks. Had Wenlock attacked Edward at this point while the king was still at a disadvantage, the outcome might have been in the Lancastrians' favour. He did not: the entire army turned and ran towards the field next to the Avon, still known as Bloody Meadow. Here, the massacre was not unlike those at Towton and Blore Heath: the few Lancastrians who survived the carnage were drowned in the river.

Somerset, meanwhile, had re-entered the battle and ridden back to the central line, furious over Wenlock's incompetence. But instead of giving the old man a piece of his mind, he smashed in his skull with a battle-axe! Exactly why Wenlock remained inactive at such a crucial stage of the battle is unknown. He could not have been considering desertion or surrender, for Edward's patience had been tested to the limit and there would have been no pardon this time. It is a well-known fact that because of his double-dealing over the years, neither side like or trusted him, and it may well be that Wenlock had had enough and *wanted* to die. Surprisingly, after killing Wenlock, Somerset made no attempt to resume command of his army—had he done so, Edward of Lancaster might have been sent off the field to join his mother, and his life would have been spared. He was slain, along with the Earl of Devon, Somerset's brother John Beaufort, Sir John and Sir Thomas Seymour, and 2,000 others, of which 500 were Yorkists.

Exactly how Edward of Lancaster died is not known. Hall states that he was brought into Edward's tent and cut down in cold blood by Richard of Gloucester—if this is true, no one deserved to die more brutally than he who, even at the age of seven, had taken great delight in watching men being quartered. Warkworth adds that 'he called to Clarence for succour.' *The Arrivall*, the most reliable chronicle of the time, says, 'Edward, called Prince, was taken, fleeing to the town wards, and slain, in the field.' The *Tewkesbury Chronicle* and *Three Fifteenth Century Chronicles* more or less agree, so this must be deemed the likeliest theory, and on this charge at least Richard may be exonerated.

Somerset and a number of other Lancastrians had taken sanctuary in Tewkesbury Abbey, perhaps unaware that the establishment had not been granted a charter of papal bull, and as such was not an official sanctuary. Edward hammered on the doors, and promised the Abbot that everyone inside would be pardoned—only to violate the holy law and have them dragged outside. The common soldiers and several lords—Sir John Fortescue, Sir Henry Roos and Thomas Ormond—*were* pardoned. The title of Constable of England had been bestowed upon Richard, while Lord Howard was the Earl Marshall.   Seventeen men were tried, including Somerset, the Prior of St John, Sir Thomas Tresham and Sir Gervaise Clifton. Not surprisingly all were sentenced to death, and on Monday 6 May were beheaded in Tewkesbury market place. They were however spared from quartering, and all were given decent burials in the town, or in the Prior's case interred within his priory at Clerkenwell. A callous act on Edward's usually clement part this may well have been, as his critics have pointed out—however, experience had taught him that pardoning rebellious die-hards never worked out in the long run. Thus these men deserved nothing less. Indeed, when one considers Edward's attitude and frame of mind after the battle of Tewkesbury, one wonders if he would have kept his promise, after Barnet, and *pardoned* Warwick. It is very doubtful.

After Tewkesbury, Edward's troubles were far from over, and reports came in of insurrections in the north and in Kent. He considered the former infinitely more pressing: on 7 May he set off for Worcester, while Anthony Woodville, Sir John Scott and the Earls of Arundel and Essex were sent south to deal with the problems there. Between 11 and 14 April, Edward was in Coventry, awaiting fresh troops, and he received a visit from Henry Percy, who wanted to convince him of his undying loyalty, face-to-face, and to further convince him that the northern rebellion had collapsed. On 12 May, Edward received a more important though less humble 'visitor'. Margaret of Anjou had been left utterly devastated by her son's death, for now all hope of a Lancastrian revival lay interred within the confines of Tewkesbury Abbey. Margaret had been apprehended on 7 May, probably at Malvern Priory: with her were fourteen-year old Anne Neville, the Countess of Devon, and her French lady-in-waiting Catherine Vaux—all three widowed at Tewkesbury. This was probably Edward's first meeting with Margaret, and sadly nothing was recorded of their conversation. Edward gave orders for her to be kept under close guard, and turned his attention towards the troubles in the south: London was being besieged by the Bastard of Fauconberg, reputedly with a 17,000-strong force. Edward sent off an advance guard, and soon afterwards himself set off for the capital.

Fauconberg's army comprised the men of Kent, always ready to throw themselves into any riot, and additional forces from Essex, Surrey and the Cinque Ports. The governors of Calais were Sir Geoffrey Gate and Sir Walter Wrottesley, former Warwick supporters. They had sent out a force of 300 men under the command of Sir George Broke: the Mayor of Canterbury, Nicholas Faunt, had loaned a helping hand. Much of the fighting did not centre around Edward's alleged unpopularity—on the contrary, there were many local grievances, and fighting for fighting's sake. The men of Essex put on their wives' skirts and donned cheese-cloths to protest against the low prices they were getting for their dairy produce. But Fauconberg was intent on destroying the king, and knew that Elizabeth Woodville and her children were installed within the Tower. On 12 May his fleet appeared in the Thames, and he demanded entry into London. This was refused, and undeterred he assailed the city again two days later, firing his guns at London Bridge, setting it on fire and razing most of the houses south of the drawbridge. An attack on the eastern gates was beaten off by the Recorder of London, Thomas Urswick, backed by Essex, Anthony Woodville, and Lord Dudley, the seventy-one-year old Lieutenant of the Tower. Anthony eventually routed the rebels, who were driven over the fields to Stepney and Poplar, where some were captured but most of them butchered. Even so, Fauconberg had no intention of abandoning his mission: he withdrew to Blackheath where he lingered from 16 to 18 May. He was however severely disheartened when Edward's 1,500-strong advance guard appeared on the scene: he and his men retreated to Sandwich, via Rochester, leaving Nicholas Faunt and the Kentishmen to their fate. The Calicians hastened to the garrison, but Fauconberg stayed put, hoping to be granted a pardon by the king, who was now said to have 30,000 men. [2]

On Tuesday 21 May, Edward and his massive army reached the outskirts of London. Riding behind, in an open-topped cart, was Margaret of Anjou, now an object of ridicule and scorn. The Mayor, John Stockton, and the aldermen met Edward in the fields between Islington and Shoreditch. Thenon the party made a spectacular entry into London: with Edward were his brothers, Hastings, the Dukes of Suffolk, Norfolk and Buckingham, and Lord Dynham, who had somehow managed to get out of Devon during the Courtenay's absence.

Behind the king's glamorous smile, however, there lurked a very serious intent. Fauconberg's rebellion had been the last straw, for Edward knew that the longer Henry VI lived, the more insurrections there would be. He therefore made the ultimate but very necessary decision of ordering Henry's death:

> And that same night that King Edward came to London, King Henry, being inward in prison in the Tower of London, was put to death, the 21st day of May, on a Tuesday night, betwixt eleven and twelve of the clock, being then at the Tower the Duke of Gloucester, brother to King Edward, and many other; and on the morrow he was chested and brought to St Paul's, and his face open that every man might see him; and in his lying he bled on the pament there; and afterward at the Blackfriars was brought, and there he bled new and fresh... [3]

The Arrivall states that Henry 'died of shock' on 23 May, after hearing of the Lancastrians' trouncing at Tewkesbury, but here the chronicler is narrating second-hand gossip, and may not be believed. From St Paul's, Henry's corpse was conveyed by boat Chertsey Abbey, where it is said to have bled intermittently en route, a theory probably invented by the monks, who made a profit from the pilgrims who visited the shrine here until Richard III had Henry's remains transferred to St George's Chapel, Windsor, in 1484. The exact manner of his death, and the name of his executioner, has never been revealed. Richard, as Constable, doubtless would have been responsible for making the arrangements, but there is no evidence to suggest that he was present at the murder—equally that he was not—but in any case, overall responsibility rested with the King. [4]

In 1910, George V gave permission for Henry's remains to be examined, and it was suggested he could have been clubbed over the head. This seems unlikely, for who would murder a king in such a way, put him on public display, and expect all who saw him to believe he had died of natural causes? In all probability the skull could have been damaged while Henry's bones were being transferred to Windsor: alternatively, those viewing his corpse could have been told that he had died as the result of a fall, for his skull was also said to have been unusually thin, which may also have accounted for his lunacy. [5]

NOTES

1. Richard Beauchamp, son and heir of Lord Beauchamp.
2. Thomas Neville, the illegitimate son of William Fauconberg.
3. Warkworth's *Chronicle*, p 21.
4. If the murder *did* take place on 23 May, which is extremely unlikely, Richard may be fully exonerated because he was not in London.
5. The remains were crammed into a wooden box measuring 39.5 x 10 inches, and 9 inches deep. Not all of Henry's bones were there: the right arm was missing, and there was the additional left humerous of a small pig. The fragment of jaw had lost most of its teeth before death. The anatomist, Dr Mcalister, suggested the bones belonged to a strong man aged between 45 and 55, who measured 5 feet 10 inches. The bones of the head were very damaged, and brown hair was attached to a piece of the skull, stained with what was thought to be blood, but this does not necessarily mean that he was clubbed over the head. Henry may have been poisoned, or stabbed (i.e., anally) where it would not show, as had almost certainly happened with Edward II.

Margaret of Anjou

19

The Second Reign: Rewards, Pardons & Punishments
1471-1474

It is unlikely that Margaret of Anjou mourned her husband: dim-witted and over-pious towards the point of absurdity, even by 15th century standards, Henry had never been king in any accepted sense. Because of his physical and mental shortcomings, his wife had commanded armies, destroyed magnates, toppled governments, and had sexual relationships with some of the handsomest men in the realm. Now, her power-and-sex-fuelled reign of terror was over, and she had nowhere to go. She could not return home to her father: René had wanted little to do with her during her exile, and how he had a young wife of his own whom he adored, and a bevy of much-loved illegitimate daughters. Margaret was transferred from the Tower to Windsor: eventually she would be moved to Wallingford, in Berkshire, a castle noted for housing royal ladies. Edward allowed her every luxury: she was permitted to keep her ladies-in-waiting, and Catherine de Vaux stayed with her for the rest of her life. Old, 'safe' friends paid courtesy calls. But despite her opulent surroundings, there can be little doubt that Margaret ended her days a bitter, lonely and miserable woman.

The day after his entry into London, Edward knighted a large number of men. These included the Recorder of London, Thomas Urswick, and John Stokker, Ralph Verney, Thomas Stalbroke, John Crosby, Richard Lee, John Stockton, John Yonge, George Ireland, William Hampton and Matthew Philip, all aldermen of the City. [1] On 26 May, he left for Canterbury, intent on settling his dispute with the Bastard of Fauconberg by granting him a pardon: the rebel leader submitted in Sandwich to Richard of Gloucester, who gained custody of his fleet. Two of his captains—Quint and Spicing, who had attacked London's eastern gates—were beheaded. Fauconberg's ally, Nicholas Faunt, was hanged, drawn and quartered in the Buttermarket on 29 May. Fauconberg joined forces with Richard in mid-June and they travelled north. The alliance did not work: Edward should never have pardoned him in the first place, particularly as he had not shown leniency towards the other rebels after Tewkesbury. Fauconberg was subsequently condemned of an undisclosed charge and executed: on 27 September, his head was set upon London Bridge, 'looking Kent-ward', as John Paston put it.

Edward's authority over Warwick's former men of Kent was enforced on 15-16 July when two powerful commisions were appointed under Lord Dynham, Sir Thomas Bourchier, William Nottingham, Nicholas Stathum, Sir John Fogge and the Earl of Arundel 'to enquire into the rebellions in Kent, Essex and Surrey and to make fine and ransom of all offences committed before 7 July.' As was to be expected of Dynham, there were few if any executions, though his fines were heavy—one aspect of

Dynham's character which adhered him to Henry VII, fifteen years later when appointed Treasurer, an office he kept until the end of his life. According to *The Great Chronicle of London*, 'such as were rich were hanged by the purse, and the other that were needy were hanged by the necks.' In all, £1,700 in fines were collected in Kent, and £250 in Essex. One of the men so punished was Sir John Arundel, a Cornish adherent of Margaret of Anjou—not only did Dynham get this difficult man on side, he arranged a marriage alliance between Arundel's only surviving son, Thomas, and his own sister. [2]

Edward made little effort to punish those who had supported Margaret. After the troubles of 1469-71 there were just seven outstanding sentences of attainder—the most dangerous rebels were all dead, and many formerly die-hard Lancastrians had entered the king's service. In October 1471, Edward issued several hundred pardons to men implicated of treason during the previous two years. Six of the eight bishops who had supported Henry VI's Re-Adeption were pardoned before the end of the year: Bishops Hunden of Llandaff and Tully of St David's, both Welsh Sees, were pardoned in February and September 1472. Sir Richard Tunstall, King Henry's Master of The Mint, became a royal councillor. Doctor Morton, Henry Lowys and Sir John Fortescue were also pardoned—the latter was far too old to offer Edward active service and retired to his manor at Ebrington, in the Cotswolds, where he devoted his twilight years to writing and upgrading his constitutional masterpiece, *The Governance of England*, the first work of its kind to be written in the English language. An earlier work, *De Laudibus Legum Angliae*, had been written for Edward of Lancaster, though its subtle philosophies could equally have applied to Edward IV, especially concerning his policies over the next few years:

> For the king of England cannot alter nor change the lawes of his Realme at his pleasure, for he can neither change Lawes without the consent of his subjects, nor change them with strange impositions against their wils…that it may not bee in the kings power to oppresse his people with tyrannie which thing is performed onely, while the power Royall is restrained by power politique. Rejoice, therefore, O severaigne Prince, and been glad, that the Lawe of your Realme, wherein you shall succeed, is such, for it shall exhibit and minister to you and your people no small securities and comfort. [3]

Doctor Morton became Master of the Rolls in 1473, and in 1479 would be ordained Bishop of Ely. Louis de Gruthuyse would be created Earl of Winchester, with an annuity of £200. Mark Symondson and Robert Michelson, the master and helmsman of the *Antony*, which had conveyed Edward back to England after his exile, received annuities. Thomas Milling, Abbot of Westminster, who had looked after Edward's queen and their children during the Re-Adeption, was appointed the Prince of Wales' Chancellor on 8 July.

William Dudley was created Dean and Windsor and Chancellor to the queen. Richard Beauchamp, the Governor of Gloucester who had aided Edward on the eve of Tewkesbury, was granted an annuity of just forty marks. William Hastings, Edward's faithful friend, was especially rewarded. On 17 July he became Lieutenant of Calais after Anthony Woodville relinquished the post to go abroad on a crusade to fight the Saracens. Hastings and his deputy, Lord Howard, left for the garrison with 1,500 men: Sir Richard Whetehill and John Blount were re-appointed as captains of Hammes and Guines. [4] Hastings was further granted the stewardship of Sherwood Forest: he became Constable of Nottingham Castle and was given custody of the majority of the Devon estates of Cecily Bonvile. [5] Lastly, on 22 April the Earl of Essex was re-appointed Treasurer, an office he kept until the end of the reign.

The young man who undoubtedly gained the most from Edward's restoration was his brother, Richard of Gloucester, whose loyalty, courage and support during and immediately after his exile was boundless. In addition to his offices as Constable and Admiral of England, Richard took Warwick's former office of Great Chamberlain on 18 May, and at the same time took over the Kingmaker's all-powerful role in the north of England which he had come to know and love, and which he always preferred to London, even while king: on 29 June he was granted Warwick's lordships of Sheriff Hutton and Middleham, and many of the earl's estates in Yorkshire—the others of course still belonged to Warwick's widow. On 4 December, Richard was granted the Earl of Oxford's forfeited estates, together with those of the attainted Lincolnshire rebels in Essex and the eastern counties. In comparison, Clarence was offered little, probably because he had so much already and deserved nothing more. Edward allowed him to retain his lieutenancy of Ireland, and on 28 August he was compensated for the loss of his Percy estates by being granted the forfeited Devonshire and Cornish estates of the Courtenays, which must have angered his West Country rival, Lord Dynham, from whom Clarence was still extracting money by threatening his family.

If Edward had forgiven Clarence, he had no intention of forgiving Henry Holland, Duke of Exeter: he was taken from Westminster sanctuary and locked up in the Tower. His wife—Edward's sister, Anne—was granted permission to divorce him and later married her young lover, Thomas St Leger. Another man who ultimately fell foul of the king was Robert Stillington, Bishop of Bath and Wells. Initially Edward appointed him Chancellor: he was responsible for the Parliamentary prorogue of April 1473, and two months later was stripped of his office. In 1475 he would be summoned to Rome on an undisclosed charge, and considering the trouble he caused later, this could only have had something to do with Edward's private life.

There were severe problems in Wales, and soon after Tewkesbury, Sir Roger Vaughan of Tretower Court, in Breconshire, was sent out after Jasper Tudor. This was an injurious insult towards the Welshman, for Vaughan is said to have been the one who had led Jasper's father, Owen, to the block after Mortimer's Cross. Needless to say, Jasper had his revenge: Vaughan was captured and executed at Chepstow, after which Jasper retreated to Pembroke Castle with his nephew, Henry Tudor, now a considerable threat to Edward as a claimant to the throne. The pair embarked for France in the middle of September: while at sea they encountered bad weather and were blown off course. They landed at Le Conquet, in Brittany, where they were apprehended and held semi-prisoner by Duke Francis, who nevertheless treated them kindly and allowed them to wander freely throughout his dominions. They moved from Nantes to Vanves, where they were welcomed at the ducal palace, the Chateau de l'Hermine. From here Jasper set about moulding Henry for the throne which would one day be his.

For a number of years the Tudors were treated as pawns by the French and English kings, but under Duke Francis' protection they could come to no harm. England's relations with Brittany were affable enough: in April 1472, Anthony Woodville, having returned from his crusade, arrived at the Breton court with a detachment of soldiers for the duke's service. Anthony was instrumental in beating back a French invasion and on 11 September, at Chateaugiron, he negotiated a treaty with Francis, a prelude to an Anglo-French invasion of French territories. Reinforcements sent over to him fared badly, however, when many of these were taken ill. Even so, Francis refused to hand the Tudors back to the English, though he did promise to keep them under stricter surveillance.

Louis XI of France was equally anxious to get his hands on these valuable pawns. In 1474 he sent an envoy, Guillaume de Compaing, to Duke Francis' court, and there was no mincing of words. Compaing *ordered* that the Tudors should be released at once—his argument was that they had intended to sail to France after the battle of Tewkesbury, not Brittany, and it was only by accident that they were there. It was further stressed that Jasper and Henry were blood-relations of the French king. Francis reciprocated by saying that the Tudors were arch enemies of his friend, Edward IV, and the French envoy argued that by holding the prisoners against their will, Francis was ostensibly declaring war on France.

A compromise was reached wherein Francis reiterated what had been said before—the Tudors would be guarded more closely, in the event that Edward should try to kidnap them. In October they were taken to the Chateau de Suscinio, at Sarzeau, the property of Jean de Quelenhec, Admiral of Brittany. Here they stayed for about a year, when they were removed to Nantes. Early in 1474, after numerous alleged threats on Henry's life, they were separated: Henry was transferred to the Chateau de Largoet, still under construction, while Jasper was installed in the great fortress at Josselin, twenty-five miles from Vannes.

Edward's major problem during the first years of his second reign was the emnity between his brothers. George grabbed, while initially at least, Richard gratefully accepted whatever

Edward gave him, and demanded nothing. One grant which tormented Clarence was Edward's gift to Richard of Richmond, in North Yorkshire—he made such a fuss that Edward took it off Richard and gave it to him. Many of the king's advisers and lords believed of course that Clarence should have received nothing, and that he was lucky to be alive considering he had always been infinitely more troublesome than many of those who had paid for their treason with their heads, perhaps with the exception of the hated Butcher Tiptoft. Indeed, Edward cannot be credited with having much sense where Clarence was concerned, otherwise he would have rid himself of his most embarrassing problem long before he did. Much has been said about alleged brotherly love, yet Edward must have been very foolish or extremely short-sighted not to have realised how shallow Clarence truly was—or that even now he was plotting behind his back and menacing his friends. Richard on the other hand was far from gullible, and offered Clarence the supreme insult by announcing that he wanted to marry Anne Neville—Warwick's daughter and Edward of Lancaster's politically-abused daughter.

Clarence had anticipated keeping the vast Beauchamp inheritance for himself, by way of his own wife, Isabel, and Richard was of course the only husband capable of enforcing Anne's rights against his brother. How she felt about the prospective match is not known: she had practically grown up with Richard at Middleham, and is more likely to have regarded him as a step-brother rather than a prospective groom, and they are not likely to have started out as lovers, as romantic novelists would like us to believe. In time, however, the couple would apparently become devoted to each other. For now, Anne Neville was an extremely wealthy and powerful pawn, nothing more, and the fact that she allegedly attempted to conceal herself in the guise of a kitchen-maid in London meant one of two things: either Clarence forced her to do so, or she was acutely against the marriage. Her last few years had been miserable, and she is hardly likely to have welcomed another husband so soon, particularly one who was reputed to have been as keen on blood-letting as the last one. Richard is said to have been so intent on getting one over on Clarence that he went looking for her, and once he found her was reluctant to let her out of his sight. He installed her within St Martin's Sanctuary, and seems to have been too impatient to wait for the papal dispensation required to allow cousins to wed: they were probably married between 12 February and 18 March 1472, when Richard was nineteen and Anne fifteen, though the date of the ceremony is generally given as 12 July. [6]

Clarence violently opposed the union, and there was a nasty exchange between him and the king at Sheen: one week later, Edward tried to console him by creating him Earl of Warwick and Shrewsbury. He was granted some of Warwick's manors in Essex and the Midlands, together with The Erber, Salisbury's house in London. Additionally, Richard resigned his Chamberlainship of England in Clarence's favour.

There were further problems when, during the winter of 1472, the Countess of Warwick petitioned Parliament from her sanctuary at Beaulieu over her rights. Many of her husband's estates had been held by him in tail-male, and his legal heir was Montagu's son, George Neville, recently returned to London from Calais. For Richard and Clarence to be secure in their grants, it was essential that George Neville's claims be extinguished, and this caused a further rift between the king's brothers. In June 1473, the Countess of Warwick left Beaulieu and was conveyed north by Sir James Tyrell, one of Richard's retainers, and it was rumoured that her estates would be given back to her, so that she might bestow them—of her own free will—on Richard. [7] At just nineteen, largely due to Clarence's greed, Richard was beginning to acquire a taste for property and power at the expense of others. The matter was settled during the Parliament of May 1474, when Warwick's widow was treated as if "naturally dead"—and her daughter Anne's marriage was yet to be confirmed by papal dispensation. Richard was allowed control of his wife's lands, even in the event of a future divorce, so long as he himself did not re-marry. The couple retreated to Middleham, where their only son was born, most likely in December 1473. The child was baptised Edward—one presumes in honour of the king, and not in memory of Anne's slain first husband. [8] Some time later, on 23 February 1475, Parliament passed an act barring Montagu's son from any part of Warwick's legacy. This was a crafty but legal move on Edward's part to allow his brothers to take up the vast Neville inheritance of their respective wives, and not by royal grant. As such, it serves Edward's reputation little good and proves that, with determination, even his own laws could be bent to suit the occasion.

The exact machinations between Clarence, Oxford, Archbishop Neville and Louis XI during the early years of Edward's second reign are not known. After Barnet, Oxford had fled to Scotland, then to France, where he was welcomed by Louis, always ready to do Edward a dis-service. Almost certainly, throughout his exile Oxford kept in touch with Clarence and the Archbishop, and Edward must have had at least a slight suspicion of what was going on. On 25 April 1472, Edward was expected at The Moor, ostensibly for a hunting party, and there are numerous accounts as to exactly what happened here. The gist of the matter is: Neville was apprehended and conveyed across the Channel to Hammes, where he was imprisoned. Two officers of the royal household, Sir Thomas Vaughan and Sir William Parr, confiscated the cleric's jewels and plate, and his sumptuous jeweled mitre was later broken up and made into a new crown for the king, who appears to have also made an attempt to deprive him of his See. [9]

Since Barnet, Oxford had nurtured the idea of an invasion of England from Scotland, and aided by Louis XI and the Hansards had recently taken to raiding the Calais marches. On 28 May 1473, he attempted to land at St Osyth's, in Essex, but was routed by a force led by Lords Dynham and Duras, and the Earl of Essex. [10] Throughout the summer, Oxford plundered the Channel, and on 30 September he, and Lord Beaumont made an unexpected attack on St Michael's Mount, a remote fortress off the tip of Cornwall. Initially his threat was not taken seriously: the only preventative measures taken were to stop the Mount's supplies. According to John Paston, Oxford hoped to mount an insurrection by securing the support of twenty-four knights and a duke. And of course, the duke could only be Clarence. **[11]** Bodrugan, the Cornish Sheriff, was instructed to besiege the Mount, but instead offered supplies to the rebels. A squire named Richard Fortescue intervened, and this resulted in the fortress being besieged on 23 December: there was a skirmish, with casualties on both sides, and Oxford was left with but a handful of men to protect him. Finally, four ships were brought in by Sir Edward Brampton and William Fetherston. Oxford was granted pardon on 1 February, and on 17 February capitulated. He was taken to Hammes, and incarcerated. For some reason, Richard of Gloucester then pressed for the release of Archbishop Neville: Edward bided his time, and the scurrilous cleric was not released until November 1474. He died on 8 June 1476, by which time the Neville-Lancastrian faction was no more. Only Clarence would still conspire to cause trouble for his elder brother.

NOTES

1. Matthew Philip had sold the king a cup and basin for £108 5s 6d for Elizabeth Woodville's coronation in 1465. John Crosby, Sheriff of London, 1471.
2. Sir Thomas Arundel (1450-85) was Lord Dynham's paramour who also married his sister, Katherine. After the Buckingham rebellion he was attainted by Richard III, and like Dynham's first wife died mysteriously soon after Bosworth, almost certainly murdered.
3. The extract is taken from the edition of 1616, Ch9, 25b.
4. Soon afterwards Whetehill's sister Anne married Sir John Radcliffe, Lord Dynham's step-son, executed 1496.
5. Cecily Bonvile (c1460-1530) married Sir Thomas Grey, Marquess of Dorset. After his death in 1501 she married Henry Stafford, Earl of Wiltshire (s 1523).
6. Pugh: *15th Century England, 1399-1509*, pp 200 and 613.
7. Sir James Tyrell (d 1502) had married Sir Thomas Arundel's sister Anne in 1469.
8. This is the generally accepted date, but which according to Ross, "lacks authority. In fact, he was probably not born until 1476." Ross: *Richard III*, p 29, n.22, citing Hammond: *Edward of Middleham*, pp 12, 35-6 (1973).
9. For more than two years, Edward retained all revenues from the See of York.

10. It is interesting to note that Dynham, Clarence and Gloucester had served on a commission together, dated 7 March 1472, to defend the king against the French and the Easterlings (*Patent Roll, 12, Edward IV*, p.i., m.25d. In the same year Dynham had also been appointed to serve the king in his fleet at sea with 3,580 soldiers and mariners. Prince: *Worthies of Devon*; Dugdale, 1, 514.
11. *Paston Letters, V,* pp 184-6,195.

Anne Neville and her husbands:
Edward of Lancaster and Richard of Gloucester

Louis XI of France

20

The French Invasion
1474-1475

Edward's son and heir had formerly been declared Prince of Wales and Earl of Chester on 26 June 1471, and Duke of Cornwall on 17 July, when a body of fifteen councilors had been appointed to run his household and affairs until he reached the age of fourteen. Young Edward and his advisers moved to Ludlow in November 1473.

During the rout of Ludlow in October 1459, the victorious Lancastrians had pillaged the castle, inflicting much structural damage. Edward had affected repairs, and the luxury previously enjoyed by the Duke of York was passed on to his posthumous grandson. The queen must have thought it a wrench, having to give up her infant son, though she was probably compensated by her second son, Richard, who had been born at Shrewsbury on 17 August.

The prince's Council was hand-picked, and the queen must have had a say in this. The Bishop of Rochester was its President and the prince's tutor. [1] The Chamberlain was still Sir Thomas Vaughan—the rest of the Council was made up of Woodvilles or their relations. Sir Richard and Sir Edward Woodville were given important positions, and Lionel was chaplain until becoming Bishop of Exeter in 1478. Lords Lisle and Grey—the queen's brother-in-law and son—were Master of the Horse and Comptroller of the

Household, the latter engaging Sir Richard Haute as his deputy. The recently-widowed Anthony Woodville was appointed Prince Edward's guardian.

Edward set out the somewhat severe rules for his son's upbringing:

> He shall arise every morning at a convenient time, and till he be made ready non but Earl Rivers, his chamberlain and chaplain to enter his chamber: no man shall sit at his board but as Earl Rivers shall allow; noble stories shall be read to him as behoveth a Prince to understand; that he be in his chamber and for all night, and the traverse be drawn by eight of the clock… [2]

In July 1473, shortly before taking up his new office, Anthony and a group of friends had travelled on a pilgrimage to the shrine of St James of Compostella. They had embarked from Southampton, and while at sea, Louis de Bretailles had loaned Anthony a book, a French translation by Jean de Tenoville of a Latin work. Anthony had asked if he might himself translate this into English: *The Dictes And Sayengs of The Philosphres*, dated 1477, would be the first book printed in England, by William Caxton on his new press at Westminster. [3]

After the Earl of Oxford's failed insurrection, Edward saw fit to establish lasting peace between England and Scotland:

a marriage alliance was suggested between his third daughter, Cecily, and James, the eldest son of James III. **[4]** The marriage treaty was signed on 8 October 1474 by the Bishop of Durham, and on 26 October a treaty signed between the two kings. The couple would marry within six months of reaching marriageable age, which would not be for years—Cecily was five, James nineteen months—and in the event of the death of either party, suitable substitutes would be found. Edward agreed to provide a dowry of 20,000 crowns, to be paid in installments over a period of seventeen years. Cecily would be granted a jointure of land during the lifetime of the Scots king, and a truce would be signed to last until October 1519.

In May 1475, Edward renewed his treaty with Ferdinand and Isabella of Castile—her half-brother, Henry the Impotent, had died on 11 December 1474. Edward was also on good terms with the merchants from the Hanseatic League, and a treaty had been secured at Utrecht on 28 February: the signatories were his secretary William Hatteclyffe, John Russell, and William Rosse. **[5]**

Now that these and his domestic disputes had been settled, more or less, Edward turned towards making good his relations with the foreign super-powers. Louis XI was of course "the principal ground, root and provoker of the King's let and trouble," and at the end of 1471 both Brittany and Burgundy had attempted to include him in their anti-French intrigues. **[6]** Charles, after refusing to even acknowledge the English king during the early months of Edward's exile, was not to be trusted: in September 1471 Edward had drawn up a truce with Louis—to last until May

1472. In March of this year, however, Duke Francis of Brittany had appealed to Edward for 6,000 archers to help defend his dominions against the encroaching French, hence the previously mentioned aid from Anthony Woodville. At around the same time, Francis had begun discussing an alliance with Charles of Burgundy, wherein it had been hoped that an anti-French coalition would take place. Louis had retaliated by attacking Brittany, the weakest by far of the Continental powers: in September 1472, Anthony had been given 1,000 more archers, and Lord Dynham had put his fleet on standby. The conditions laid down by Anthony's embassy prior to this had been accepted by Francis: the aforementioned treaty had been signed at Chateaugiron wherein the English would invade France by 1 April 1473, assisted by the Bretons. Edward had agreed to finance the enterprise on the understanding that any territory gained from France should become his unless he deemed otherwise.

Similar overtures were discussed with Burgundy. Eager to promote the invasion, Charles dispatched Louis de Gruthuyse to England: his conditions were that, should Edward's mission prove successful, Charles should be given full hereditary rights to the counties of Nevers, Eu, Champagne, Guise, Rethel, and the Duchy of Bar. The question of raising finances was brought up in the Parliament of 6 October 1472, and a lengthy speech delivered by the Speaker, Sir Robert Stillington: the king was asserting his claim for his legal inheritance of France, but it was also stressed that if the people of the realm became involved in such an invasion, their minds would be taken off internal problems and the usual family squabbles, and that this in itself would be for the good of the realm. Also, once Normandy and Gascony had been conquered, much expense of patrolling the Channel would be lifted.

For the time being, there would *be* no invasion. On 15 October, five weeks after the Treaty of Chateaugiron, the weak-willed Francis of Brittany signed a brief truce with France which was later extended to a year, and Breton envoys visited London in the hope of persuading Edward to defer the invasion until November 1473. Burgundy signed a subsequent truce with France to last until 1 April 1473, and on 22 March of this year, Edward signed a truce with Louis XI to last until 1 April 1474. The February-April 1473 Parliament was told nothing of this: Edward was still intent on the invasion taking place.

As his Parliament was reluctant to give him money for his enterprise, between November 1474 and March 1475 Edward toured England gathering subscriptions, and as usual exercised his red-blooded charm. *The Great Chronicle* records a wealthy widow who, having offered £10, doubled this in exchange for a kiss. Edward's loquaciousness worked. Not only was he a great king, he was an accomplished actor who knew when and how to put on a show. He raised more than £20,000: most of this was already owed to his men, whose first quarter's wages were due 31 January 1475. The Parliament of July 1474 had promised him £51,000, but when it convened again on 23 January, the money still had not been found. There were also problems relating to the king's new "income-tax", first discussed in the Parliament of October 1472, wherein the lords had voted a special tax of ten per cent of their incomes, and the Commons had agreed to pay the wages of 13,000 archers for a period of one year: initially this had been due on 2 February 1473, but payment had been deferred until 24 June, and again until Michaelmas. Finally, it was scheduled to be handed over on 4 May 1475, but when this happened, there was a shortfall. Other grants were agreed upon, subsequently so long as Edward set sail for France "before St John's Day" 1476. He now had, or had been promised, a staggering £180,000 with which to finance his expedition, the preparation of which was in its final stages.

The dockyards of England became hives of activity. Back in December 1474 a squire of the body, Avery Cornburgh, had requisitioned all ships of sixteen tons or more within the ports of the south-west, and Bristol in particular. [7] Similar commissions were issued along the south and east coasts. Several old flagships were repaired, including royal "good-luck" favourites such as the *Antony* and *Grace Dieu*. In March 1475, a commission was issued to Lord Arundel, the Warden of the Cinque Ports, to fit out the fifty-seven vessels the Ports were obliged to supply at their own expense, furthermore to have them ready in Sandwich and Dover by no later than 26 May.

On 15 April, Lord Dynham was appointed Admiral of the Fleet: he was given eight ships and 3,000 men, and personal command of the *Grace Dieu*. On 30 May, Edward travelled by barge from London to Greenwich. He arrived in Canterbury on 7 June to find most of his army waiting—the first contingencies had already left for Calais, and now the others followed. There were so many ships that it took them three weeks to get across to the garrison. The French, expecting them to land in Normandy, were patrolling this part of the coast, and apparently Louis XI knew nothing of Edward's route until mid-June, when an English herald was arrested. By then it was too late to do anything. Dynham was manning the Straits: he was a military genius on land and sea, and had there been a sea-battle with the French he almost certainly would have been victorious.

The Prince of Wales had been brought from Ludlow on 12 May, and on 20 June, the day the king signed and sealed his will, the boy was appointed Keeper of the Realm, though during Edward's absence the actual management of the realm was passed to four bishops (including those of Canterbury and Rochester) and five peers—Dynham, Arundel, Essex, Dacre and Dudley. Edward had hoped to land in Calais by 22 June: this proved impossible when he suddenly ran short of finances. Money was not forthcoming from London, so he borrowed 1,000 marks from Gerard Caniziani, and a further £5,000 from the de Medici bankers. Charles of Burgundy sent a fleet of 500 flat-bottomed scutes for transporting the horses: amongst the agents sent to collect these was Margaret of Burgundy's financial adviser, the printer William Caxton. Charles himself had purposely ignored the conditions of his peace treaty by continuing his siege of the Swiss township of Neuss, which had begun in July 1474. Anthony Woodville had tried to talk him out of it in April 1475, to no avail.

Edward finally sailed to Calais on 4 July. In his memoirs, Philip de Commines describes the crossing and the ensuing "invasion" in great detail, though as usual his tone is severe and occasionally offensive. Before leaving England, Edward sent a herald to the French king with a letter of defiance "in fine language and elegant style (I believe no Englishman could have had a hand in composing it!)," wherein he required Louis to deliver unto him his rightful kingdom of France, "so that he could restore the Church, the nobles and the people to their ancient liberties and remove the great taxes and burdens which the King had imposed upon them." The herald was given 300 crowns and sent back to Edward, with the promise of another thousand if peace was agreed upon. **[8]**

Edward was warmly received by the people of Calais, and renewed acquaintances with many people who, in 1459, had succumbed to the charms of the slender, golden-haired youth. He was now portly, but according to Commines no less endearing and handsome than he had been then. On 6 July he received a visit from his sister Margaret; this lasted but a few days before the Duchess left Calais, escorted by Richard of Gloucester and Clarence. Her husband arrived on 14 July, accompanied only by bodyguards, which put the whole question of Edward's campaign into some doubt—he had been banking on Burgundian support, though according to the Croyland Continuator Charles publicly declared that Edward's army was big enough to take care of itself without needing his men.

Edward knew that he could not turn back now, even though many of his lords wanted to: financing his adventure had almost bled England dry, and the last thing he wanted was more civil unrest. Duke Charles suggested that the English army should march through Burgundian territory to Péronne, then to the French towns of St Quentin, Laon and Reims, the traditional crowning place of the French kings. The Constable of France was Jacquetta of Luxembourg's brother, Jacques, Count of St Pol, who held lands between France and Burgundy, and was allegedly a friend of Charles. St Pol offered to hand over St Quentin to Edward, and on 18 July Edward and Charles marched to St Omer, via Guisnes and Ardres. On 23 July they reached Fauquembergues. The nights of 25 and 26 July were spent on the site of Agincourt, and by 29 July the army had reached Doullens. By now it is said to have numbered around 13,000, and for once the chroniclers may not be exaggerating. In all there were some 11,000 archers and 1,200 men-at-arms: Clarence had brought over a hundred mounted lancers, Richard considerably more. These were just the royal men. The Dukes of Norfolk and Suffolk provided 300 men-at-arms and 1,000 archers each: Henry Percy brought a force of around 400. The French king, leading a force of no more than 6,000, had reached Beauvais on 27 July, and was heading towards Compiegne.

By 5 August, Edward was at Éclusier, near Péronne, when a message arrived from St Pol, claiming that he still wished to give up St Quentin. There was treason afoot: an English detachment, while approaching the town, was greeted by cannon-fire. A handful of English soldiers were slain, and the detachment retreated through a sheet of rain to the main camp, now south of Péronne at St Christ-sur-Somme: Charles of Burgundy himself had entered Péronne, and had persuaded the guardians to close the gates against the English.

Edward was faced with a most vulnerable predicament but cannot have been too surprised by St Pol's and Charles' actions, especially since the former had failed to keep up his promise of turning up at Calais with an army, and on time. Behind him, the French were plundering Artois and Picardy, and Edward realised that his massive army would soon run out of provisions: it was almost autumn, and the prospect of a winter in France appealed to few. Ahead of him, Reims was fortified ready for the attack, and it would have been madness to advance further into France without Burgundy's aid. Moreover, Francis of Brittany had offered no assistance whatsoever. The final straw came on 12 August, when Charles left for the Duchy of Bar. Edward at once entered into negotiations with Louis XI.

These opened with a great deal of flanneling on Edward's part. Prior to Charles' departure, the English had captured the valet of Jacques de Grassay, an important member of Louis' household. He was released when Lords Stanley and Howard, who spoke French, each gave him a gold noble and instructed him to put in a good word with the French king. The valet managed to get an audience with Louis, only to be accused of espionage and clapped in irons for the night—his master's brother, Gilbert de Grassay, Lord of Chapéroux, was in Brittany with Duke Francis. Louis' advisers—including Commines—persuaded him to release the man and listen to him: as a result, another valet—a servant of Olivier Merchon, Lord of Halles—was sent to Edward, after being briefed by Commines. On behalf of Louis, he told Edward that any wrongs committed by the French against the English, including their support of Warwick, had in reality only been directed at Charles of Burgundy. He added that Louis was well aware of the expense Edward had gone to, financing his expedition, and that he also understood how many Englishmen wanted a war with France. He concluded that, should Edward agree to a treaty, terms would be offered which would benefit himself and his people. The valet suggested a meeting of the two great powers: either the French would send their envoys into the English camp, or the two kings would meet on neutral territory, with representatives from both sides. Edward discussed the proposition with his advisers, and on 13 August appointed his delegates. These were Doctor Morton, Lord Howard, Thomas St Leger, and Sir William Dudley. Clarence and Gloucester were witnesses. Louis' representatives included Lord Saint-Pierre, the Bishop of Evreux, and the Bastard of Bourbon. The next day, the delegates met at Lihons-en-Santerre, a village near Amiens. Louis promised to pay Edward 75,000 crowns within fifteen days, and 50,000 crowns a year for as long as they both lived. It was further agreed that the Dauphin should marry Edward's eldest or second daughter and provide her with an annual income of 50,000 crowns for nine years, or "for her maintenance the Duchy of Guyenne," after which time the couple would be entitled to the revenues of Guyenne, whence the payments would cease. Louis further agreed to ransom Margaret of Anjou and secure for himself whatever she inherited from her father. Once Edward had agreed to these proposals, it was agreed that he should take his army home—Sir John Cheyne (the Master of the King's Horse) and Lord Howard would be left in France as hostages until this had been achieved. Edward then requested a "private amity" wherein the two powers would come to each other's aid in the event of an emergency, and he further proffered a truce and an "intercourse of merchandise" for seven years, and agreed "to name certain persons who he said were traitors to the King and his crown, and to give written proof of this."

Louis discussed the matter with his Council, many of whom thought it was a trick on Edward's part: the French king convinced them that he had a good understanding of Edward's character—and in any case, the summer was almost over and the English had nowhere to spend the winter. Philip de Commines ends by saying that Louis had vowed to find the money as quickly as possible, "for there was nothing in the world that he would not do to boot the English out of France, save that he would never consent to giving them any land. Before doing this he would rather hazard all."

The terms for the truce had been decided by 18 August, and a meeting was arranged to take place on the Somme, near Amiens. Upon hearing this the Count of St Pol wrote to Edward, begging him to change his mind, and the next day an irate Charles of Burgundy returned to the English camp, now at Valenciennes, to be told he would only be included in the truce with France providing he gave three months' notice. Charles refused, and retreated to Namur, where he at once set about concocting some other devilish scheme.

The English and French armies drew up near Amiens on 25 August and Louis, benevolent for once, provided as much free food as the English could eat, and ordered local innkeepers to give free drink to any English soldier who demanded it. The result was to be expected: for several days the town was overrun with drunken rowdies, and Edward was forced to bar them from the town and post sentries at the gates.

The famous meeting between Edward and Louis XI took place at Picquigny, three miles down the Somme from Amiens, on 29 August 1475. Very elaborate preparations ensured that there would be safeguards against treason from both sides. The river was narrow, but fordable, as Commines explains:

> Close to the river there was a causeway, two good bow-shots long with a marsh on either side, which might have produced very dangerous consequences for the English had our intentions not been honourable. A bridge was ordered to be built, large and strong, for which purpose we furnished our carpenters with materials. In the midst of the bridge there was contrived a strong wooden lattice, such as the lions' cages are made with, the hole being no wider than to thrust in a man's arm: the top was covered with boards to keep off only the rain, and the body of it was big enough to contain ten or

twelve men of a side, with the bars running across both sides of the bridge to hinder any person from passing over it, either to the one side or the other…

Commines describes how *two* Louis initially appeared, wearing identical clothes to confuse would-be assassins. Then the decoy retreated and the real Louis stepped forwards, with 600 men behind him and canons aimed at the ready. Edward brought his entire army, which must have been an impressive sight, and worrying for the French should anything go wrong. Each king was personally accompanied by twelve lords, four of which took up position on the enemy side of the barrier. With Edward were Clarence, Henry Percy, Hastings and Chancellor Rotherham. Edward wore satin-lined cloth of gold, and a black velvet cap ornamented with a huge jeweled brooch fashioned in the shape of a fleur-de-lys. Commines observed once more that he had grown fat, and contradicts his earlier comment, saying that he *had* seen him looking better. Approaching the trellis, he says, the two kings bowed to within six inches of the ground (an impossible gesture, certainly, for Edward to perform if he was as obese as reported) before embracing through the grill. The most solemn of oaths was taken to observe the treaty, and Louis told Edward "in a jocular way he should be glad to see his majesty at Paris and divert himself with the ladies." Louis further assured him that if he did this, the Cardinal of Bourbon would be appointed as his confessor and absolve him of his licentious activities. Clearly, the Cardinal was a man of Edward's heart. Later, Louis changed his mind, and announced that he would have to leave at once to wage war on Burgundy.

The treaty was complex, but may be defined as follows:

> 1: Edward's claim to the French throne was to be referred for settlement to four arbitrators: the Archbishops of Canterbury and Lyons, the Count of Dunois, and Clarence. The first meeting would be held in England before Easter; the second to take place in France before Michaelmas.
>
> 2: Edward was to take his army home, upon receiving 75,000 crowns from the French king, leaving behind the prescribed hostages until the army had reached England.
>
> 3: There would be a seven years' truce between England and France. Englishmen would be able to visit and travel through France without the usual safe-conducts. Charges paid by English merchants in France and vice versa should be dispensed with. The truce would last until 29 August 1482.
>
> 4: The Treaty of Amity would prevent either king from entering into any agreement with any ally of the other without that party's knowledge. The marriage alliance would be arranged within a year: the Dauphin of France would wed Elizabeth of York at the prescribed time: should she die, her sister Mary would take her place. The jointure of £60,000 per annum would apply to either, and would be paid by Louis.

> 5: For as long as both kings lived, Louis would pay 25,000 crowns twice-yearly, promptly at Easter and Michaelmas to the English king, and guarantee for the payments would take the form of a bond from the de Medici bank, or a papal bull in the event of default.

The next day, English sailors were selling their spare horses to the citizens of Amiens, and were boasting of a "sign from above": at the time of the meeting on the bridge, a white dove had perched on top of Edward's tent. The men had tried to frighten it away, but since it had not budged, they were convinced it had been a messenger from the Holy Ghost. At once they knew that Edward had done the just thing by not waging war on the French.

Louis may have changed his mind about inviting Edward to stay with him in Paris, but he was generous towards his supporters. Sir Thomas Montgomery and Lord Howard were each given pensions of 1,200 crowns, Chancellor Neville was given 1,000, and Doctor Morton 600. Thomas St Leger, the Marquess of Dorset and Sir John Cheyne were also suitably rewarded. Lord Hastings was awarded 2,000 crowns, and though he would not sign the customary receipt because Charles of Burgundy was already paying him 1,000 crowns a year, Louis kept up the payments. Such extravagance, however, left Louis short of money: Edward was only given 55,000 crowns, and a bond for the shortfall.

Not everyone agreed with the conditions of the truce, or even with the truce itself. According to Commines, Louis de Bretailles declared Edward had scored eight victories in the past and lost just one battle—this one—and he exploded the myth about the "dove of peace" seen on Edward's tent: this had been but a common pigeon, drying itself out after a shower, having chosen the king's tent only because it was the highest. A noticeable absentee from Picquigny Bridge had been Richard of Gloucester, the first time he had ever gone against his brother's wishes—though willing to witness and sign the initial agreement, it appears that Richard had wanted to fight the French rather than parley with them. According to Commines, Richard soon changed his mind once Louis XI began doling out gifts and he had been given "some very fine presents such as plate and horses splendidly caparisoned."

Edward's great enterprise was over. His army reached Calais on 4 September and began crossing the Channel. Some 2,000 men stayed behind to join the Burgundian army. During the journey there was a minor calamity when the Duke of Exeter fell overboard and drowned. Edward himself remained in Calais until 18 September, and even then took his time getting back to London, wary of what public opinion would be like after a "war" without fighting. He was worrying over nothing: met at Blackheath, he made a triumphant entry into the city. To celebrate his "victory" over the French, a misericord was placed under one of the stalls of his new Garter Chapel, in Windsor. Edward is not represented here as the typical warrior king, but is depicted standing on Picquigny Bridge with Louis XI. It is ironic that, while the carving retains most of its intricately carved features, the head of the French king has been lopped off.

NOTES

1. John Alcock had been Dean of St Stephens, Dean of St Paul's, Master of the Rolls, and Privy Councillor, later Bishop of Worcester.
2. J.O.Halliwell: *Letters of The Kings of England, I,* pp136-44.
3. William Caxton (c1422-91) was over fifty when he began printing, encouraged to do so by Margaret of Burgundy. *The Recuyell of The Histoyes of Troye* (1474) and *The Game And Playe of Chesse* (1475) were translated and were the first books printed in English on his press in Bruges: the former was dedicated to Margaret. His English press was set up in the Westminster precincts: at the time of his death he had printed 99 books, including the works of Chaucer and Thomas Malory.
4. James III (1451-88), murdered after the battle of Sauchie Burn. James IV (1473-1513) features in Scott's *Lady of The Lake*. He was killed at the battle of Flodden.
5. John Russell, Bishop of Lincoln, Chancellor to Richard III. He is thought responsible for the sections of the *Croyland Chronicle* covering the reigns of Edward IV and Richard III.
6. *Literae Cantuarienses: Sheppard* (Rolls Series 1889), III, 277-9.
7. Avery Cornburgh, squire of the body 1474-85, and JP of Essex.
8. For the French Invasion: *Commines*, 237-62.

21

Edward's Lifestyle & Character/ The Death of Charles of Burgundy
1475-1477

Margaret of Anjou had been moved from Wallingford Castle back to the Tower of London. Louis XI's ransom amounted to 50,000 crowns: the first 10,000 to be paid once she had been handed over. On 13 November 1475 she was escorted across the Channel: on 29 January, at Rouen, Sir Thomas Montgomery gave her back to the French. England had suffered this despotic woman for over thirty years. On 7 March, Margaret renounced all her hereditary rights in favour of Louis: as such, these were few. Her father was still alive, and her late mother's lands were occupied by Charles of Burgundy. When René of Anjou did in 1480, all Margaret had left was Louis' pension of 6,000 livres. She retired to the Chateau de Dampierre, in Anjou, where she died on 25 August 1482, aged fifty-two, mourned by few.

Edward IV will be remembered for two traits in particular: winning battles, and the pursuit of sexual pleasure. The first half of his reign finds within him an astute military technician, almost in the same calibre as Henry V, with more than his share of good fortune, and less than his share of ready money with which to finance his enterprises. That he was courageous, level-headed, but at times lazy goes without saying. Yet more than any other medieval king, Edward was a personal sovereign, a man much loved and respected by his subjects. The second half of his reign finds him entirely different. Of his relatively short life, only seven years remained. Had he been more cautious, there could have been many more. As a young man he had reached unprecedented heights, and during his last years he would maintain a civil peace marred only by his brother Clarence's murky intrigues. If some of his adherents were disappointed at his unwillingness to fight the French, many were content that, for the first time in his reign, Edward was solvent and free of having to borrow from his Parliament. Louis XI paid his dues promptly, albeit that he encountered mighty problems raising the money. For the first time ever, Edward's Exchequer showed a surfeit. He was therefore at liberty to indulge in his fancies.

Commines' intention while writing his memoirs had been to set the French king on a higher pedestal than he merited by belittling his contemporaries: this would in turn lead to the scathing, erroneous and frequently exaggerated accounts of Edward's character by prudish 18th century historians. There is no reason not to believe Commines, however, when he discusses Edward's gluttony and fondness for swallowing emetics in order to gorge himself some more. Sir John Fortescue, in his *Governance of England*, though not specifically writing for Edward, readily urged the king to accumulate wealth in order to spend freely on expensive clothes and ornaments, and other trappings of state which he believed essential to command and maintain the respect of his subjects. Henry VI, during his Re-Adeption, was publicly seen as a shabbily-dressed, dirty figure, a puppet king who no one had taken seriously. Edward had to keep up appearances so far as foreign visitors to his court were concerned, and his *personal* appearance had always proved a winning factor. He had come to the throne young, handsome, determined, loquacious, but above all courageous and oozing with a charm which even his enemies found irresistible. During his early years, money had always been a major problem, yet he had put on spectacular displays and pageantries—for his and his queen's coronations, and especially for the Great Smithfield Tournament. His expenditure on himself and his household had been inordinately high: between April 1461 and September 1462 a staggering £4,784 had been spent on clothes, furs and fabrics alone—even more between then and April 1465. [1] He spent vast amounts on plate, jewels, tapestries and books—as the first English monarch to establish a library collection, his taste for great literary works developed during his second exile, while staying with Louis de Gruthuyse in Bruges. Most were historical tomes, such as de Beauvais' *Speculum Historiae*, the anonymous *La Grante Hystoire de Cesar*, Waurin's *Anchiennes et Nouvelles Chronicques Dangleterre*, and Mansel's *Fleurs des Hystoires*. Some of these beautiful works depict Edward in miniature, wearing the Order of the Golden Fleece, and are bound in silk and velvet, with gold clasps. Some were so beloved by their owner that they followed him around the country. Many have survived.

Edward was a keen builder, plowing huge sums of money into secular ventures. A new barbican was added to the Tower of London: there were additions to the Calais defences, and the Castle at Guisnes was restored. A polygonal tower was added to Nottingham Castle at a cost of £3,000, and work had been going on for some time at Fotheringay and Dartmouth. Most of his time during his later years was spent at the royal palaces of Westminster, Eltham, Greenwich, Sheen, and Eltham where the great hall was begun soon after his return from France, and completed shortly before his death. His proudest project was St George's Chapel, Windsor. On 19 February 1473, Richard Beauchamp, Bishop of Salisbury was appointed royal surveyor, and requisitions for materials sent out at once, though until 1477 much of Beauchamp's work involved demolishing the great hall and the Vicar's Choral lodgings. Edward's dream was that he should be buried here: this happened, despite the work being far from finished when he died. The Croyland Chronicler was justified in praising Edward's legacy:

> For collecting vessels of gold and silver, tapestries and decorations of the most precious nature for his palaces and various churches; for building castles and colleges not one of his predecessors was able to equal his achievements… [2]

After his French expedition, Edward's charm and good looks did not diminish, though his girth increased the more insular he became, and his tours of the country became less frequent now that law and order was restored. His so-called debaucheries and loose-living have been discussed by Commines and his genre. The Italian, Dominic Mancini, writing soon after the reign, observed:

> He was licentious in the extreme: moreover it was said that he had been most insolent to numerous women after he had seduced them, for as soon as he grew weary of dalliance, he gave up the ladies much against their will to the other courtiers. He pursued with no discrimination the married and the unmarried, noble and lowly, but took none by force. [3]

Sir Thomas More, utterly scathing towards Richard III, managed to get Edward's age and the date of his death wrong, and thus cannot be taken seriously as an accurate biographer. He was nevertheless not unkind to Edward when he wrote:

> He was a goodly personage and very princely to behold, of heart courageous, in peace just and merciful, in war fierce and sharp. He was of visage lovely, of body mighty, strong and clean made. In his later days he was somewhat corpulent and burly, nonetheless not uncomely, a youth greatly given to wantonness. This fault not greatly grieved the people, for neither could any one man's pleasure stretch and extend to the displeasure of very many…
> [4]

The most vituperative account of Edward's character comes from Bishop William Stubbs, and is included here only because it typifies the nasty, condescending, and frequently bigoted attitude of Victorian historians:

> Edward IV was not perhaps quite so bad a man or king as his enemies have represented: but even those writers who have laboured hardest to rehabilitate him have failed to discover any conspicuous merits. He was a man vicious far beyond anything that England had seen since the days of John, and more cruel and bloodthirsty than any king she had ever known. The death of Clarence was but the summing up and crowning act of an unparalleled list of judicial and extra-judicial cruelties which those of the next reign supplement but do not surpass. [5]

To a certain extent, More's appraisal was accurate, for there is no evidence to suggest that Edward was any different from many of his contemporaries. Between February 1466 and November 1480 he sired ten legitimate children, and no doubt many bastards. This was considered neither unusual nor immoral: few of Edward's lords did not acknowledge bastards and even staunch moralists such as Jasper Tudor, Anthony Woodville, and Richard III had at least one child born on the wrong side of the blanket. Homosexuality was frowned upon by the church, but not uncommon. Charles of Burgundy, the Dukes of Somerset and Buckingham, and Lord Dynham were all thus. Though Edward is recorded as only having one definite homosexual relationship—the one with Somerset—given his love of adventure there may well have been more, by choice or way of experimentation, and despite his serial infidelity he is believed to have genuinely loved his wife throughout the entirety of the marriage which *he* chose for himself. It was not an over-surfeit of sex, but gluttony and lack of exercise which contributed to his premature demise. [6]

Edward's most cherished mistress was Jane Shore, whose real name was in fact Elizabeth. She was the daughter of the goldsmith, John Lambert, and the wife of another mercer, William Shore. [7] Exactly when and where she met Edward is not known: a clue may lay in the Parliament Rolls entry of 4 December 1476, when Edward "bestowed protection" upon William Shore, his servants and possessions. Jane obviously was not happily married: she had petitioned for an annulment on the grounds of William's impotence, and the case was sufficiently strong enough for the Pope to appoint three bishops to make a decision in March 1476. The result was not made public, but towards the end of his reign Edward openly supported her, and the queen seems to have condoned the match, aware that if Edward was "cuckolding" Jane Shore, then at least she knew where he was. She also appears to have been much more than a lover, as Sir Thomas More observes:

> Proper she was and fair; nothing in her body that you would have changed. Yet delighted men not so much in her beauty, as in her pleasant behaviour. A proper wit had she, and could both read well and write, merry in company, ready and quick of answer,

neither mute nor full of babble, sometime taunting without displeasure and not without disport. Where the King took displeasure she would mitigate and appease his mind…where men were out of favour, she would bring them in his grace. For many that had highly offended she obtained pardon. Her doings…be less remembered because they were not so evil. For men use if they have an evil turn, to write it in marble: and whoso doth us a good turn, we write it in dust, which is not worst proved by her… [9]

Edward loved her: the queen tolerated her presence at court, while Richard of Gloucester appears to have despised her for her lack of morals—for flaunting herself in front of Edward's family. After Edward's death, he would present her to the world as *the* supreme example of human degradation.

On 6 October 1476 at Tewkesbury infirmary, Clarence's wife, Isabel, gave birth to her fourth child, a son which was baptised Richard. Mother and child were chronically ill, and on 12 November were conveyed to Warwick Castle, where Isabel died on 21/22 December, aged twenty-five, most likely of tuberculosis. Her baby died on 1 January 1477. Isabel's body was embalmed and returned to Tewkesbury on 4 January: after lying in state for thirty-five days, Warwick's daughter was buried behind the high altar. [9]

It is not known how Clarence was affected by his wife's death, or indeed if he was affected at all. The fact that he was free to marry again, still young, and almost as handsome as his elder brother would cause innumerable problems for Edward—Clarence would now use Isabel's death as an excuse for getting at him, and in doing so attempt to destroy anyone who crossed his path.

After the Treaty of Picquigny, Charles of Burgundy continued wreaking havoc: having plundered Lorraine and captured its capital, Nancy, on 9 February 1476, he reported to the Milanese ambassador that he had a better claim to the English throne than Edward IV, but that he was going to allow the dust to settle before doing anything about it. He then focused his attention on the Swiss: at the end of February he attacked Granson, on the shores of Lake Neuchatel, and gave orders for the defenders to be hanged and drowned. The Swiss retaliated by attacking the Burgundian army, and Charles was lucky to escape with his life. He at once set about raising an army at Lausanne: in April there were scuffles amongst his own ranks which had to be dealt with by the Bastard of Burgundy. During the first week of June, he set out for Berne, in Switzerland, and his army encamped on the shores of Lake Morat. On 22 June, the Swiss attacked: Charles suffered a second humiliating defeat, and again set about collecting an army. By now he was clutching at straws. On 7 July, Anthony Woodville arrived on the scene. While on a pilgrimage, he and his baggage-train had been robbed of their valuables: he had written to his sister the queen and had been sent a letter-of-exchange for 1,000 ducats. But this was only a courtesy call on the Burgundian court, and the moment Charles tried to persuade him to join in with the fighting, Anthony left.

By October, the Duke of Lorraine had recaptured Nancy. On 5 January 1477, Charles was attacked by the Swiss for the third time. His men fled, his camp was pillaged, and in the midst of the confusion, he disappeared. His corpse was later found in the snow:

> Amongst those who died on the field of battle was the Duke of Burgundy. I was not there but I was told about his death by those who saw him struck to the ground; in their view he was not killed then: later a crowd of people killed and stripped him without recognising him. [10]

Charles had no legitimate son, and there was a sudden rush for the hand of his heiress, Mary, who at nineteen was at a convenient age for marriage. Louis XI proposed the Dauphin, who was only five-years old and in any case nominally engaged to Elizabeth of York—not that Louis would have thought twice about revoking the terms of his treaty with England if it meant getting his hands on Burgundy. Margaret, the Dowager Duchess, suggested her brother Clarence, but if King Edward had once thought this a good idea, he did not think so now—besides being the Duchess of Burgundy, Mary had inherited Charles' claim to the English throne, and with Clarence as her husband there was no telling what might happen. Edward might have considered the widowed Anthony Woodville as a prospective bridegroom, but as Commines rightly points out, Anthony was only an earl, and Mary was aiming much higher. In fact, she was in the enviable position of being able to choose her own husband, and on 19 August she married Maximilian of Hapsburg, reputed to have been one of the handsomest men in Europe. [11]

NOTES

1. Scofield, I, 283.
2. *Croyland Chronicle*: 559-63.
3. Mancini's *The Usurpation of Richard III* was written in 1483, but not discovered until 1934, in the Lille City Archives. It was translated and published by C.A.J. Armstrong two years later. Mancini, of whom little is known, appears to have been a spy of sorts. His missive was addressed to fellow Italian Angelo Cato, confidant-physician to Charles of Burgundy, then Louis XI who appointed him Archbishop of Vienne in 1482. Cato (d 1496), who persuaded Commines to write his memoir, commissioned Mancini's work so that Louis XI might be kept up to date with the intrigues of the English court. He sent him to England in the summer of 1482, but was recalled on 6 July 1483 while he was in the middle of his work—Louis was dying—and *The Usurpation* was finished and edited at Beaugency some time between Louis' death on 30 August and the end of the year. Latter-day Richard III supporters denounce Mancini because he makes no pretence of Richard's ruthlessness in clearing the pathway to the throne. Yet as an outsider, Mancini had absolutely no prejudices one way or the other, and reported events as he saw them with no exterior influence or personal axe to grind.
4. Sir Thomas More: *The Historie of Kyng Rycharde The Thirde*, English translation, Cambridge University Press, 1883, pp 2,15-32.

5. William Stubbs (1825-1901) Bishop of Oxford 1889. His *Constitutional History of England* was published 1878. Extract: III, pp 219-20.
6. The Channel 4 drama, *The Princes In The Tower* may be criticised for its albeit feasible conclusions regarding the fate of Edward's sons. It is however spot on of its analysis of Edward when Perkin Warbeck, aka the alleged Richard of York, is asked by his inquisitor what he remembers of normal family life and scoffs, "*There was no normal. Across the corridor in his bedroom the King is throwing a private party. There might be any one of his three regular mistresses and any number of passing fancies of either sex. He'd try anything at least once. He had an adventurous palate and a huge appetite. If it was alive, he'd fuck it, and if it was dead he'd eat it.*"
7. John Lambert (d 1487); William Shore (d 1494). Jane Shore (c 1455-c 1527)
8. More: as above, 54-5.
9. Scofield, II, 184. Also *Tewkesbury Chronicle*.
10. Commines, 306-7.
11. Maximilian I (1459-1519), Emperor of Austria 1493, and Holy Roman Emperor. By marrying Mary he inherited Burgundy and the Netherlands.

22

The Downfall of Clarence
1477-1478

The Twynhos lived at Cayford, in Somerset. They were neighbours of the Zouches, relatives of Lord Dynham. Ankarette, the matriarch of the family, was born about 1405, and was a dependent of the queen who had also attended upon Clarence's wife, Isabel, during her last confinement.

On 20 February 1478, two days after Clarence's death, Ankarette's grandson, Roger, submitted a petition to the king, primarily for the restoration of her lands, of which he was the sole heir. Roger claimed that at two in the afternoon of Saturday 12 April 1477, eighty armed men wearing the Black Bull livery of the Duke of Clarence had burst into Ankarette's home and arrested her on summary charges. They had taken her to Bath, and on the Sunday had halted at Cirencester before conveying her to Warwick prison, which they had reached on the Monday evening—a distance of about a hundred miles. The widow's daughter and son-in-law had pursued the party, but had been prevented from entering Warwick by Clarence's men, and had subsequently spent the night eight miles away at Stratford-upon-Avon. The next morning, at 9 am, Ankarette had been unceremoniously stripped of her valuables and dragged to the Guildhall, and brought before the Justices of the Peace and a jury of twenty-four. The charge was that on 10 October 1476, at Warwick Castle, she had given her mistress the Duchess of Clarence "a venemous drink of ale mixed with poison", after which Isabel had sickened until her death on the Sunday before Christmas. The jury, threatened by Clarence "for fear and great menaces and doubt of loss of their lives and goods," had found her guilty, and on 15 April she had been taken to the gallows at Myton Hill, on the outskirts of Warwick, and hanged. The trial and execution had taken place in just three hours, and several members of the jury had come before Ankarette and craved her forgiveness. [1] According to the entry in the Rolls of Parliament, John Thursby of Warwick had been accused of poisoning Isobel's baby, and hanged at the same time: Sir Roger Tucotes was also accused, but had escaped. [2]

In arresting Ankarette Twynho, Clarence had broken the law. Though it would have been necessary to take his charge to Warwick for trial because the alleged offence had been committed there, Clarence had used the arbitrary power of arrest exclusive to the king—and by not having the relevant warrants to convey Ankarette through not one but three counties, he had flagrantly flouted Edward's authority.

The reason for Clarence's despicable behaviour was only too obvious: if Edward saw that his brother suspected Elizabeth Woodville and her relatives of paying Ankarette to poison his wife and son, then he might force a wedge between the king and queen and get Edward on his side. He was particularly aggrieved because Anthony Woodville had been put forward as a match for Mary of Burgundy while he

—Edward's own brother—had not. To get his point across, on the rare occasions that he visited court, Clarence refused to eat or drink while in the Woodvilles' company, hinting that they might try and poison him next. The fact that Ankarette had been a dependent of the queen was not, however, Clarence's only reason for selecting her as his scapegoat: as previously mentioned she was a relative of Lord Dynham, from whom he was still exacting money. [3]

The Twynho affair must have been discussed at some length by Edward and his Council, particularly since Roger Tucotes had got away. Nothing was made public, however, and for the time being Edward appears to have officially ignored Tucote's plea, though he obviously believed that Clarence was far too dangerous to be left at liberty for much longer, especially after what happened next.

In May 1477 an Oxford astronomer, Doctor John Stacey, was arrested on suspicion that he had used his "magical arts" to forecast the deaths of the king and the Prince of Wales. It was illegal to set up royal horoscopes without the sovereign's permission, and under torture Stacey confessed the names of his accomplices: Thomas Blake, an astrologer and chaplain at Stacey's college of Merton, Oxford—and Thomas Burdett, a member of Clarence's household who lived at Arrowe Park, in Warwickshire. As a firm believer in the precognitive dream, Edward was genuinely frightened. He also thought that Clarence should be taught a lesson, and decided to play him at his own game—but at someone else's expense. On 12 May he appointed an unusually powerful commission of oyer and terminer comprising five earls, twelve barons, six justices, and Thomas Grey, Marquess of Dorset—the queen's son and Clarence's mortal enemy. Needless to say, on 19 May, Stacey, Burdett and Blake were sentenced to death. The latter was given a last-minute reprieve following the intervention of the Bishop of Norwich, but the other two were hanged at Tyburn the next morning—on the very day that Roger Tucotes came out of hiding and the Twynho enquiry was re-opened by the king himself.

The trial of the "necromancers" was politically inspired, and clearly aimed at Clarence, who was either incredibly thick-skinned, or just too sure of himself to heed the warning. Once the proceedings were concluded, Edward went to Windsor: Clarence then made matters infinitely worse by turning up at the Council chamber at Westminster with his spokesman, Dr John Goddard, the Franciscan preacher who had read out Henry VI's claim to the throne at St Paul's in September 1470.

Goddard read aloud Burdett and Stacey's declarations of innocence, while at the same time insurrections occurred in Huntingdonshire and Cambridgeshire, instigated by a rebel-leader said to have been the Earl of Oxford. Edward had had enough: he summoned Clarence to Westminster and before the Mayor and alderman accused him of going over his head by threatening judges and illegally executing Ankarette Twynho. Few documents of this mysterious year have survived, and the chronicles are scanty, so there may well have been other accusations as well. Clarence was sent to the Tower, but actually lodged within the Bowyer Tower, not because of its inordinate luxury, but because it was between the Brick and Flint Towers, and hidden from the windows of the royal apartments by the bulky mass of the White Tower. No one, least of all Edward, wanted to see Clarence once he had been taken away.

Edward now had to decide what to do with his brother. Banishment was out of the question, for no prison in England would prevent Clarence from plotting in the future. Edward may already have been in poor health, though nothing is recorded to this effect, and he was sensible to realise that, should he die while his sons were minors, Clarence would make another bid for the throne and almost twenty years of hard work, tough diplomacy, military strategies and sacrifice would have been in vain. Ultimately, he decided that death would be the only solution. No doubt it was the most crucial decision he had ever made in his life, and the matter would have been discussed amongst his family, which meant that his brother Richard and the queen must have had their say. Parliament was therefore summoned to meet at Westminster on 15 January 1478.

As if to take everyone's minds off these nasty goings-on, the most ridiculous marriage of the 15th century took place on the very day that Edward's Parliament convened. It was uncommon for very young children to be *formerly* married: usually they were betrothed—and many such alliances were subsequently changed or cancelled. This one was an exception. The bride was the late Duke of Norfolk's five-year old daughter and sole heiress, Anne Mowbray, and the bridegroom Edward's youngest son, Richard Duke of York, aged four. [4] Ann was extremely wealthy, having inherited not just her father's title but that of hereditary Earl Marshall. Edward naturally wanted to ensure that in the event of her death, her estates would revert to his son—as had happened with the Countess of Warwick's estates, Edward proved that there was always a way, and an act of Parliament was passed to this effect. Later, young Richard was formerly created Duke of Norfolk, Earl of Nottingham and Earl of Warenne. This must have been very disappointing for Anne's all-powerful relatives, particularly Lord Howard, who had hoped to marry her to his grandson and keep her estates within the immediate family.

The ceremony took place in the richly-decorated St Stephen's Chapel, Westminster, and was officiated by the Bishop of Norwich. Anyone who was anyone was invited: the bride was escorted by Anthony Woodville and the Earl of Lincoln, and given away by Edward himself, who was standing under a canopy of gold. [5] Afterwards, Richard of Gloucester and the Duke of Buckingham escorted her to a sumptuous banquet laid on in the Painted Chamber. On 20 January, as part of the wedding celebrations, a tournament was organised by Anthony Woodville and the Marquess of Dorset which almost rivaled the Great Smithfield Tournament of 1467, save that many participants complained about the exhorbitant entry charges: these ranged from 28s 6d, for esquires and the lower ranks of the nobility, to ten marks for Earls. The prizes were a gold badge shaped like an "E" and set with a diamond, presented by twelve-year old Elizabeth of York—and two badges shaped like an "A" and an "M", set with a diamond and a ruby, presented by the bride. Anthony, ever the show-off, entered the lists wearing a hermit's costume: his horse was dressed in a "hermitage" of black velvet, with glass windows, and surmounted by St Anthony's Cross, a bell and a rosary. His servants wore liveries of tawny and blue, decorated with flames and columbines. Lord Robert was awarded the "M", Sir Richard Haute the "E", and the "A" was won by Sir Thomas Lymes. It is interesting to note that one of Anthony's opponents was Sir Thomas de Vere, the Earl of Oxford's brother, one of those who had occupied St Michael's Mount in 1473. Obviously, Edward had too much on his his mind to worry over this.

The Speaker for the Parliament of January 1478 was Sir William Allington. The opening address was read by Chancellor Rotherham, whose theme was the opening line of the Psalm 23, "The Lord is my ruler, therefore I shall not want." [6] He then pronounced St Paul's portentous words, "For He beareth not the sword in vain." After this, Edward's bill of attainder against Clarence was read out, with the brothers standing face to face. The murder of Ankarette Twynho, strangely, was not mentioned. Clarence was found guilty of high treason, in that he had been about to incite a rebellion, and Edward indicted him thus:

1. Clarence had paid men to say that his servant, Thomas Burdett, had been wrongly executed.
2. He had accused his brother, the king, of necromancy, and of poisoning the minds of his subjects.
3. He had accused Edward of being a bastard, and their mother the Duchess of York of adultery by saying that the king had been conceived during an extra-marital affair.
4. Clarence had threatened judges, and forced others to swear fealty to him by claiming that Edward had disinherited him.
5. Edward had witnessed a document, drawn up between Clarence and Margaret of Anjou in 1470, and bearing Henry VI's seal, wherein Henry, in the event of his son the Prince of Wales' death, had named Clarence as his heir.
6. Clarence had entered into an agreement with the Abbot of Tewkesbury, subsequently rejected, wherein a "strange child" would be sent into Warwick Castle to double for Clarence's son, whom he intended smuggling out of the country for his safety, to Flanders or Ireland, with the hope of invoking an invasion from these parts.

"Witnesses" substantiated these indictments, though the Croyland Chronicler dismisses these as "accusers", and recent research suggests that the document of 1470 may have been invented by the king himself. [7] Clarence fervently denied each of the charges and demanded to prove his innocence by way of the ancient wager of battle, which naturally was ignored.

Even so, Edward was reluctant to sentence his own brother to death, and feared the consequences of a public execution on Tower Green, which suggests that there was considerably more to the Clarence case than meets the eye. Subsequently, on 7 February, the young Duke of Buckingham—himself little better than Clarence—was appointed Seneschal of England so that Richard of Gloucester, as Constable, would not have to pass sentence. It was all very convenient, and on 18 February the dreaded words were pronounced by Sir William Allington.

Clarence was put to death within the privacy of the Tower that same night, and there seems no reason not to believe that he was drowned in his bathtub. Most of the chroniclers, including Dominic Mancini and Olivier de la Marche, state this as does the *Chronicle of London*. [8] The *Croyland Chronicle* merely refers to the event as "the execution, whatever its manner may have been." [9] The infamous butt of malmsey wine incident first occurs many years later, in the works More and Polydore Vergil, and one modern historian writes of "some punnish connection between the Frankish castle of Clarence, in Greece, and malmsey, a Greek wine." [10]

Clarence appears to have been told beforehand of his approaching death: the *Calendar of Patent Rolls* records that he granted some of the incomes from his manors and estates to Anthony Woodville, "in consideration of the injuries perpetrated on him and his parents by George, late Duke of Clarence," a statement which can only refer to Clarence's part in the murders of Anthony's father and brother, in the summer of 1469. Thomas Grey, Marquess of

Dorset was granted the wardships of other Clarence manors and estates, from which he would be allowed to draw revenues until Warwick's heirs came of age. [11]

It is a great pity, for Edward's subsequent reputation at least, that Clarence was *not* afforded a proper trial and public execution, though this can only mean one thing: not everything reached the chronicles, and many of Clarence's "other crimes", which would have no doubt been embarrassing to the House of York, were conveniently hushed up. Edward is supposed to have been weighted down with remorse, once the deed had been done—Richard of Gloucester likewise, if one heeds Mancini and Kendall, which is unlikely considering their violent quarrel over the Countess of Warwick's estates—one point which makes Kendall's theory that Richard pleaded with Edward to spare his brother's life absurd. It must also be remembered that by now, in this respect, Richard was as greedy for power and possessions as anyone.

Other points must be considered. In 1471, Edward had granted Richard the forfeited estates of the Earl of Oxford, in which Elizabeth Howard, the Dowager Countess, had a one-third share. By 1473, Richard had "by heinous menace of loss and life and imprisonment" acquired her entire estate. [12] On 15 January 1478, three days *before* Clarence's death, Richard's son, Edward, had been made Earl of Salisbury, one of Clarence's titles, only offers more proof of him supporting Edward's decision to put Clarence to death. Three days *after* Clarence's death, Richard was re-appointed Great Chamberlain of England, the office he had surrendered to Clarence. In March he would receive the fee-farm and castle of Richmond which had precipitated the hostilities with Clarence in the first place.

Pressed by his brother, advised by his queen as may have been the case, the fact remains that Edward and Edward alone was responsible for what happened in the Tower that night. It is also an undisputed fact that Clarence had tried everyone's patience for far too long, and been forgiven too many times. Edward's only honest regret may well have been not getting rid of this nuisance sooner.

Clarence's body "lay in state" for several days, not because anyone wanted to mourn him, but because the world needed to see that he was finally dead. It was then taken to Tewkesbury and buried next to that of his wife: Edward of Lancaster was interred nearby. Clarence was just twenty-eight. Edward did not consider his children much of a threat, and after selling their wardships, reserved the earldom of Warwick for Clarence's son and heir, while retaining the majority of his estates for himself. One week after the murder, Parliament was wound up—it would not sit again until 1483.

NOTES

1. *Parliament Rolls, VI*, pp 173-4. *Patent Rolls, 1476-85*, pp 72-3.
2. Sir Roger Tucotes (1430-92), created a Knight of the Banneret after Tewkesbury.
3. *Calendar of Patent Rolls*, 1476-85, p 137.
4. Anne Mowbray (10 December 1472-19 November 1481). Norfolk had died in January 1476: his wife was pregnant, but her baby died. Anne was buried in St Erasmus' Chapel, Westminster. On 11 December 1964, her lead coffin was accidentally unearthed during a road-widening scheme in Stepney, found in a sealed vault eleven feet underground, which suggests she may have died of the plague. It had ended up there because the chapel had been demolished during the reign of Henry VII and several of the coffins moved to the Abbey of the Minoresses. The skeleton, particularly the hair, was extremely well-preserved, and was displayed in the London Museum before being reburied close to its original resting place in Westminster during the evening of 31 May 1965.
5. John de la Pole (c 1462-87) was the eldest of the seven sons of the Duke of Suffolk who had married Edward IV's sister, Elizabeth. He was an adherent of Richard III, subsequently supported the Lambert Simnel rebellion, and was killed at the battle of Stoke.
6. i.e., as in the Latin Vulgate, *Dominus regit me*.
7. Lander: *The Treason & Death of The Duke of Clarence*, pp 27-8.
8. Vitellius A XVI, *f*. 136 ro.
9. *Croyland Chronicle*, 562.

10. Mary Clive: *This Sun of York*, 219: "Clarencia (now Glarentza) is a long way from Monevasia which gave its name to malmsey, but close enough to get a laugh."
11. Ross: *Edward IV*, 381, especially Note 2.
12. *Parliament Rolls, VI*, 282, 473-4. See also Ross: *Richard III*, 31.

23

The Scottish Invasion & The Fading Sun of York
April 1478-April 1483

Much of Edward's time and flagging energy during the next few years was spent arranging marriages for his children, none of which would take place, thus helping to pave the way for the anarchy of the next reign. Edward had passed the peak of his magnificent career, and it is quite likely that he knew his days were numbered. Perhaps had there been another war, civil or otherwise, his energies might have been channeled away from his ever-rounded platter. As things stood, he was slowly eating himself to death: medieval food was notoriously rich and spicy, and in Edward's case there was little to do *but* eat.

Edward began searching overseas for a suitable bride for the Prince of Wales. The Infanta Isabella, the daughter and heiress apparent of Ferdinand of Aragon and Isabella of Castile, had been a clear favourite since the winter of 1476, but in 1478 Edward was put off when Queen Isabella gave birth to a son. Towards the end of 1478, Maximilian of Hapsburg proposed a marriage alliance between his younger sister (their father was Frederick III of Austria) and the Prince of Wales. Edward preferred the daughter of the recently assassinated Duke of Milan. This presented a problem: the girl's mother was Bona of Savoy, who many years before had been considered as a bride for Edward himself, and Bona would hear nothing of such a match, even when advised to accept the offer by her brother-in-law, Louis XI of France. Edward was undeterred: he entered negotiations with Duke Francis of Brittany, and Francis proposed Anne, his four-year old heiress daughter. An agreement would eventually be ratified in May 1481, even though Edward's terms were over-demanding. When she reached the age of twelve, Anne would marry the Prince of Wales: should she die before then, she would be replaced by her sister, Isabella. Similarly, should Prince Edward die, his replacement would be Richard of York. Anne's dowry was set at 100,000 crowns, providing Francis' wife did not produce a son before the marriage took place, otherwise it would be doubled. The Breton chronicler, Pocquet du Haut-Jussé, quite rightly branded Edward a miser, though it must not be forgotten that in allying himself with Brittany in such a way, Edward would have been taking a calculated risk—he knew that Louis of France would not sit back and watch his long-hungered-for Brittany being handed over to the English, especially since the Dauphin was nominally engaged to Edward's daughter. War would have been inevitable.

Edward re-entered negotiations with Maximilian and Mary of Burgundy, and no doubt a good word was put in by his influential and much-respected sister, Dowager Duchess Margaret. Edward's second daughter, Mary, was held in reserve for the Dauphin. When she died on 23 May 1482, Edward proposed his next available daughter, Anne, as a bride for Maximilian's son Philip, born in June 1478. When

Maximilian demanded a dowry of 200,000 crowns, he must have been exasperated when Edward announced that he intended paying no dowry whatsoever—he thought it enough that he was offering an alliance with Burgundy in the first place, The marriage treaty was signed on 5 August 1480, and amended slightly on 14 and 21 August: the dowry was wavered in exchange for the first installment of an annual pension of 50,000 crowns which Edward promised to pay Maximilian. Philip de Commines, discussing the young duke, is disapproving:

> Maximilian understood nothing…besides, he had been brought up badly for the understanding of important affairs: nor did he have sufficient men to make any great show. For this reason the country has been in great trouble up to the present and looks likely to be for some time to come. There is great invonvenience for a country when it is forced to seek a lord from abroad. God has greatly blessed the kingdom of France with the law, that daughters should not inherit. Nobody supported Maximilian. [1]

In Lille, on 12 July 1478, an English embassy signed a commercial treaty between England and France, and the next day Edward met the Bishop of Elne, Louis XI's resident ambassador in England, and persuaded him that the Treaty of Amity and the pension agreed upon at Picquigny should be extended to at least a hundred years after the date of the death of whichever king died first. In August, further demands were made on Louis: Elizabeth of York was now thirteen, and Edward wanted no delay in her betrothal to the Dauphin—he was eager to get his hands on the promised jointure of 60,000 crowns. Louis was a wily old fox: in December he sent an envoy to England, and Edward was told that the jointure would only be forthcoming once the *marriage* had taken place and been consummated, and added blithely that this would not be for some time because the Dauphin was only eight years old. The truce was discussed amicably in February 1479, when the Bishop of Elne met with Anthony Woodville, the Earl of Essex, and Bishops Morton and Stillington. Edward's terms were accepted, and on his behalf it was agreed that the English king would enter into a formal alliance with Maximilian of Burgundy, and the appropriate documents were signed.

It would appear that Louis XI had suffered a slight stroke at Chinon, in March 1479: his speech was badly affected for two weeks, and if anyone brought him an important document he only pretended to read it. Commines became his interpreter, and several of his most intimate courtiers were banished—the reason being that, during his illness, they had confined him to his chamber and prevented him from seeing his beloved dogs, or which he had dozens from all over Europe.

Louis' aggression intensified as his health deteriorated, as did his hatred of England and Burgundy: when his truce with the latter expired in July 1479, he refused to extend it, and set about securing Burgundy for himself. Maximilian advanced his army into Artois, and on 7 August, Lord d'Esquerdes attacked the Burgundians near the village of Guinegatte, only to suffer a humiliating defeat. [2]

Even so, Maximilian knew that he would never feel fully secure against France without England's aid, and with this in mind, in the summer of 1480, the Dowager Duchess set off to visit her brother. She was escorted from Calais by Edward's fleet, and attended by a retinue of servants clad in royal blue and purple velvet. Edward lodged her at Cold Harbour, a large house not far from the Tower and their mother's residence at Baynard's Castle. Here, Margaret met her two young nephews for the first time.

Delighted as Edward must have been to see his sister, he refused to be drawn into the struggle, and again his reasons were pecuniary—he knew that if he took up arms against Louis he would have to forfeit his annual 50,000 crowns, and the chance of having the Dauphin as a son-in-law.

Louis was distressed over Margaret's visit to London: his was a warped mind which only saw the worst in people. Also, he had never ceased working behind the scenes with the Scots, who after a brief respite were about to go on the rampage. On 12 May 1480, Richard of Gloucester, who had been in the north at Middleham since the month after Clarence's death, was appointed King's Lieutenant General and on 20 June commissions of array to protect the northern borders were sent out to Yorkshire, Northumberland and Cumberland. [3] The king then issued a threat to James III: return Berwick to the English, or suffer the consequences of a full-scale war. His daughter Cecily was engaged to the Scottish heir, and in December 1478 a marriage alliance had been agreed between James' sister Margaret and Anthony Woodville—with the wedding scheduled to take place at Nottingham in October 1479. Edward therefore demanded that James' son, the Duke of Rothsay, be sent to England as security. James reciprocated by getting the Earl of Angus to execute a number of border raids, and Berwick was attacked and burned in September. Gloucester and his second-in-command, Henry Percy—who seemed to be getting along with each other despite the fact that Richard and not Percy was now Lord of the North—in turn laid waste the Scottish countryside as far as Dumfries, while from his London base Edward set about making preparations for an invasion. A Council meeting to this aim was held in Westminster in November 1480.

One may not be certain how Edward meant to go about his invasion of Scotland. A repeat performance of his French campaign of 1475 would have been out of the question: if Edward raised all the available fighting men and set off for the north, he would be leaving London, the southern ports and Calais open to an attack from the French. Also, there were the two marriage alliances to consider.

In December 1480, Lord Howard, almost sixty, was given command of 3,000 men and appointed Captain of the Fleet. The Clerk of the King's Ships was a strange choice in that Edward appointed Thomas Rogers—one of Warwick's former captains. Equally surprising, Thomas Fulford, one of the most dangerous of his former enemies in the West Country, was given three-hundred troops and command of a naval operation which began patrolling off the western coast of Scotland. **[4]** Calais provided artillery and two-hundred handguns and Edward, still keen, travelled to Sandwich—taking the Prince of Wales with him—to formerly inspect his fleet.

The enterprise looked like being a costly one. At the same time preparations were made for a land-invasion, and between February and April 1481 commands were sent out to victual the royal army. A now solvent Edward did not ask Parliament for money, and there was no pressuring of adherents. Lord Stanley and Anthony Woodville promised 3,000 men each, and the Marquess of Dorset 600. Edward requisitioned 80 butts of expensive malmsey wine for himself and his personal army, and the exiled Earl of Douglas was sent ahead as an agent-provocateur. Richard of Gloucester, now the most powerful man in England after the king, demanded £10,000 for his men's wages and got it. Lord Howard received £5,000 and a further £5,000 was spent on commissioning ships. These included the *Antony*, *Falcon*, and *Carvel of Portugal*, and the *Mary Howard*, Howard's flagship which would be captained by Robert Michelson—the man who had conveyed Edward home to England after his second exile. The City of London, paid Edward 500 marks, while a staggering £23,000 came from the war-taxation subsidy voted in 1475.

At the end of May, Lord Howard attacked the Firth of Forth and burned the town of Blackness, but achieved little else, and was back in Sandwich by 18 August. Lapsing into what may have been another period of lethargy, or failing health, Edward opted against marching north, and the Scottish campaign was left in the capable but ruthless hands of Gloucester and Percy. Edward spent two weeks at Woodstock, and at the end of November travelled to Nottingham, where he lingered for three weeks before returning to London.

In January 1482 Maximilian's agent, the Comte de Chimay, arrived to pressure Edward into invading France. Louis XI was desperately ill, having suffered another stroke in September 1481. Edward declared that he was too busy waging war against the Scots to bother with the French: he could not afford to spare the 5,000 soldiers he had promised earlier, and advised Maximilian to be patient. Louis would be unlikely to invade Burgundy now, but if he did, Edward would send in the troops, but not before. In March another agent, Piers Puissant, came to see Edward and received the same response, though by now negotiations were under way for a peace conference to be held at Arras, in December.

On 27 March 1482, Burgundy was plunged into a period of intense mourning:

> The King received letters saying that the Duchess of Austria had died as the result of a fall, for she used to ride a fiery little horse. He had thrown her and she had fallen on a large log. Some said it was not the fall but a fever. But whatever it may have been, she

died a few days after the fall and it was a bitter blow to her subjects and friends because never since then have they enjoyed good fortune or peace. For the people respected her more than her husband... [5]

Edward is said to have been devastated by the news of Mary's death, and may have suffered a mild heart-attack or a stroke on account of this early in April. [6] Certainly he was too ill to travel far, and though his invasion of Scotland was not put off, overall command was given to Richard of Gloucester, who attacked and burned Dumfries and even had the nerve to ask his brother for a share of the plunder.

James III of Scotland had two brothers: Alexander, Duke of Albany—and John, Earl of Mar. These had been imprisoned by the young king in 1479 because they had threatened the throne. Soon afterwards, Mar had died mysteriously in his bath: Albany had killed his guards, escaped from his cell down a rope, and had subsequently fled to France—leaving one wife in Scotland, and marrying another, Anne de la Tour, while in exile. In France, he had styled himself King of the Scots, and for more than two years had planned his brother's deposition. In April 1482, Albany landed at Southampton, and the following month turned up at Fotheringay. Here, he signed an agreement with Edward and Richard of Gloucester, lately returned after his border adventure: Albany swore that as soon as he legally became King of Scotland—he would return Berwick to the English and dissolve the Scottish alliance with Louis XI. He further promised that he himself would marry Edward's daughter Cecily—as soon as he had rid himself of his two unwanted wives.

On 12 June, Edward left for London, while Richard and Albany headed north. On 17 June, they made a triumphant entry into York, Richard's favourite city. An affinity had developed between him and its people which continues more than five-hundred years after his death. Soon afterwards they were joined by Lord Stanley and Henry Percy, and marched towards Scotland. Berwick capitulated, though not the castle, and Stanley was left behind while the other three resumed their campaign, leading around 20,000 men, which only proves Richard's popularity in this part of the country.

On 22 July, James III was seized at the Bridge of Lauder: many of his supporters were summarily hanged, and the king was taken back to Edinburgh and incarcerated in the castle. Richard and his party entered the city with little resistance on 1 August. Albany then did an about-turn, renouncing his claim on the Scottish throne in lieu of the restoration of his property and position. Richard seems to have agreed to this. He may well have wanted to besiege Edinburgh Castle and seize James III himself, but he was in a hostile country and desperately short of funds. At the eleventh hour, Albany defected and joined his brother, leaving Richard with no alternative but to make a hasty retreat. He rejoined Lord Stanley in Berwick, and the town which Margaret of Anjou had sold to the Scots surrendered to him on 24 August.

England's first courier system was in operation between 4 July and 12 October 1482. Effectively this meant that with men stationed at twenty-mile intervals a message could travel a hundred miles in a single day, therefore Edward was aware of his brother's movements throughout the entire Scottish campaign. Probably suspecting that public opinion might not be entirely on his side after his failed invasion, Richard relayed the false news that he had sacked Edinburgh, though he told the truth about Berwick. The news travelled as far as the Calais garrison, where there were celebrations and bonfires.

Meanwhile, the political situation between France and Burgundy was undergoing a drastic change. Brabant and Flanders, previously loyal to Mary and her predecessors, wanted nothing to do with the unpopular Maximilian: they formed a protectorship around Mary's children, Philip and Margaret, and began peace negotiations with Louis XI. In September 1482, Louis made public knowledge the truce he had signed with England the previous year and duly refused to send Edward the next payment on his pension, which fell due on 29 September. As allies of Burgundy, England and Brittany were excluded from the Treaty of Arras on 23 December, wherein a marriage alliance between the Dauphin and Maximilian's daughter was arranged, with Artois and Burgundy comprising part of her dowry. For Edward, this was a bitter blow. He had lost not just his valuable pension, but the French marriage deal as well.

Edward's sixth and final Parliament opened on 20 January 1483, when the Speaker was John Wode, an adherent of Richard of Gloucester. The king's state of health at this precise time is not known, though he was still intent on a summer invasion of Scotland, and asked for funds to be voted. The marriage alliances between his daughter Cecily, Anthony Woodville and their prospective partners had all been called off, and Anthony had married Mary, the daughter of Sir Henry Fitzlewis, though they were not living under the same roof. Richard of Gloucester was suitably rewarded for his services of the previous year: he was given the extremely lucrative office of Warden of the West Marches, and to this was added Carlisle and its castle, estates in Cumberland formerly held by the king, and whichever others he chose to claim by conquest on the other side of the border. A number of petty issues were also discussed, including a protest against the use of machinery in the hat-making trade, and a complaint against the Jews threatening the livelihood of the London by importing silk into the country. The selling-price of long-bows made from yew was not allowed to exceed three-shillings and fourpence, etc. An interesting edict concerned the strict code of dress reserved for the upper classes: only members of the royal family would be allowed to wear purple; cloth-of-gold tissue could only be worn by those above and including the rank of duke, and plain cloth-of-gold was prohibited for anyone less than a lord; only knights and above could wear velvet; very short, buttock-revealing tunics could only be worn by those ranking above a lord. [7]

Edward had spent the festive season of 1482/3 at Windsor where, though "tired", he had put on a great show:

> ….frequently appearing clad in a variety of most costly garments, of quite a different cut to those which had been usually seen hitherto in our kingdom. The sleeves of the robes were very full and hanging, greatly ressembling a monk's frock, and so lined with most costly furs, and rolled over the shoulders as to give that Prince a new and distinguished air to beholers…remarkable beyond all others for the attractions of his person. [8]

At Eastertide, towards the end of March, Edward was taken ill at Windsor and conveyed to Westminster. Here, on Wednesday 9 April, he died—nineteen days before what would have been his forty-first birthday.

Sadly, most of those who mattered to Edward were not with him at the end. Anthony Woodville and the Prince of Wales were at Ludlow. Lord Howard was en route for London. Richard of Gloucester, at home in Yorkshire, was not officially told of his brother's death and received the news second-hand from Lord Hastings—who on 10 April sent the *Little Jesus* across to the Calais garrison to inform Lord Dynham. Buckingham was at Brecon Castle. [9]

Details of Edward's final illness are not known, though someone must have been aware that he was dying: in York, his death was reported three days before it actually happened, and a mass for his soul sung in the Minster on 7 April. The chroniclers do not agree on the symptoms. The Croyland Chronicler wrote that the king was "neither worn out by old age nor yet seized with any known kind of malady." Three months later, Bishop Russell fancifully stated in a public address that Edward had died of melancholy after the Treaty of Arras. Russell's speech may of course have been prompted by Richard of Gloucester, who by this time had usurped the throne. It may also have fueled the imagination of Philip de Commines, who had always been biased against everyone but the French—for what a boon this would have been, as Louis XI's most trusted friend and adviser, for Commines to convince the ailing king that, in robbing Edward of his marriage alliance and pension, *Louis* could have contributed to the English king's early demise. Nonsense, of course. [10]

Edward Hall, equally prejudiced, recorded that Edward had contracted malaria during his French expedition, which *might* have been credible, save for the fact that it had taken eight years to surface, and which in any case would have been recognised by Edward's physicians. [11] Polydore Vergil, writing at the beginning of the 16th century, agrees with the Croyland Chronicler, but also hints at poison, which of course would fit in with the Tudor propagandists' character assassination of Richard III. [12]

Of the modern historians, Sir Winston Churchill wrote that Edward had died of appendicitis, which again is not out of the question. [13] The likeliest theory comes from Dominic Mancini, who arrived in England soon after Edward's death. Mancini avows that Edward caught a cold during a fishing trip while at Windsor—a claim enlarged upon by Dr John Rae, who proposed pneumonia because "the King laid him down on his side,"—which would suggest discomfort or pain in the left lung. [14]

To a degree, most of the chroniclers may have been right. On the face of it, it would seem ludicrous that Edward had died of melancholy after the Treaty of Arras. During his younger days he had been immensely strong, physically and mentally, and had emerged emotionally unscathed from two exiles and one apprehension. Throughout his reign he had been extremely promiscuous, and this obvious priapism does not appear to have diminished in his last years, when he had grown immensely fat by way of gluttony. Common sense tells us that an obese, inactive man who over-indulges in food and sex may be prone to any number of ailments, not least of all heart trouble, and it is entirely credible that a common cold developed into pneumonia, and that Edward's immune system failed and he succumbed to heart-failure.

There is therefore little doubt that Edward's death was self-inflicted. Had he seen sense and taken better care of himself, he would have lived longer—enabling his son to inherit the throne and rule without the Protectorship. The terrible events of the next two years would have been avoided, and the future of the English monarchy changed very much for the better, certainly from a religious stance.

Edward's funeral was as colourful and extravagant as his life had been. It cost a staggering £1,496 17s 2d, much of which came from the sale of his jewels. **[15]**

The king's body was stripped and washed, and clad only in a loin-cloth laid upon a wooden board to be viewed by the Mayor and aldermen, and whoever else happened to be there. Masses and prayers were endless: it was as if Edward's subjects refused to believe that this great, energy-charged soldier was dead, and many knew that the future would be black indeed. The body was embalmed, swaddled in waxed linen, and dressed in Edward's robes of state and cap of maintenance. His feet were shod in red leather. For eight days, he lay in state within St Stephen's Chapel, Westminster, while his lords held the wake.

On 17 April, Edward was placed upon a bier draped with cloth-of-gold, and surmounted by a canopy fringed with blue and gold silk and banners depicting St George, Our Lady, and the Blessed Trinity. In a solemn procession led by Lord Howard bearing the banner displaying his Sun in Splendour device, fifteen knights and squires of the body carried him into Westminster Abbey. Behind the bier were Chancellor Rotherham in his capacity of Archbishop of York, Lords Hastings and Ferrers of Chartley, nine bishops, two abbots, and most of Edward's family and friends. On top of the bier was a life-sized image of the dead king, wearing his crown and clutching the orb and sceptre.

On the morning of 18 April, the cortege set out for Windsor, halting at Charing Cross and Sion Nunnery, where it spent the night. The next morning it made its way to Eton, where Edward's body was blessed by the Bishops of Ely and Lincoln. Finally it arrived at Windsor, where during the night it was guarded by nine knights, and various members of the household and pursuivants of arms. On 20 April the final masses were celebrated by Archbishop Rotherham, assisted by the Bishops of Durham and Lincoln, and the customary offerings were made. The Comptroller of the Household, Sir William Parr, wore full armour and presented the inverted battle-axe: the lords wore cloth-of-gold. Edward's body was placed inside the grave, according to his wishes—"buried low in the ground, upon the same a stone to be laid and wrought with the figure of death and a scutcheon of armour and writings convenient about the borders of the same, remembering the day and year of our decease." On top of this were placed Edward's great surcoat of gilt mail and crimson velvet, and his royal arms embroidered with rubies, pearls and gold. Finally, the members of the household place their staves of office within the void, and the grave was sealed.

Edward had arranged for a vault to be built over his grave, surmounted by a chantry chapel, and a tomb housing his effigy. Sadly, the effigy was never completed, and the tomb was destroyed by Oliver Cromwell's men in 1642 when most of the accoutrements, including the surcoat and royal arms, were removed. The grave was opened in 1739, and resealed with the present, ugly touchstone slab. Thus St George's Chapel bears precious little evidence of its illustrious founder. [16]

NOTES

1. Commines, 368
2. Philippe de Crevecoeur, known to the English as Lord Cordes.
3. He had in fact visited London once to see Margaret of Burgundy.
4. Thomas Fulford of Dunsford (c 1440-90), the eldest son of Baldwin, executed in 1461.
5. Commines, 386.
6. Ross, 287-8: in the Canterbury records is an entry wherein Lord Hastings told the Mayor that the king's health was not good, and the Mayor feared another revolution.
7. Notable exceptions were Sir Thomas Vaughan, Sir John Donne, Sir Thomas Bourchier, the Marquess of Dorset, Sir Thomas Montgomery, Sir Thomas St Leger, Sir Thomas Burgh, Sir William Parr, the Treasurer Sir John Elrington, Edward's secretary Doctor Oliver King, and the Dean of his Chapel, Oliver Gunthorpe.
8. *Croyland Chronicle*, 562-4.
9. Dynham was Hastings' deputy at Calais. The message was conveyed by John Grene. *Devon: Issues of The Exchequer*, 505.
10. Commines: 303-4; *Croyland Chronicle*, 563.
11. *Hall's Chronicle*, 338.
12. Vergil: *English History*, 171-2.
13. Sir Winston Churchill: *History of The English-Speaking People*.
14. Mancini, 59.
15. *Registrum Thome Bourgchier: II*, 54.

16. The records for the financial year 1482-3 state that 33 casks of touchstone or black marble had been delivered from the Low Countries for the construction of the tomb. The wrought-iron gates, meant to be suspended before the tomb, separating the chapel from the aisle, are currently flat against the presbytery wall. They are thought to be the work of John Tresilian, hired to execute the ironwork in 1477.

Select Bibliography

ANDRÉ, BERNARD: *Historia Regis Henrici Septimi*, ed Gairdner, 1858.

ARMSTRONG, C.A.J.: 'England & Burgundy', in *500me Anniversaire de la Bataille de Nancy*, 1979.

The Inauguration Ceremonies of the Yorkist Kings & Their Title To The Throne, TRHS, 1948.

Politics & The Battle of St Albans, 1455: BIHR, xxxiii, 1960.

Distribution & Speed of News In England At The Time of The Wars of The Roses, Oxford, 1948.

BALDWIN: J.F.: *The King's Council In England During The Middle Ages*, Oxford, 1913.

BARKER & BIRLEY: *Jane Shore*, Etonia 125, 1972.

BARNARD: F. P.: *Edward IV's French Expedition of 1475*, 1925.

BARTIER, J: *Charles le Téméraire*, Brussels, 1972.

BEAN: J.M.W.: *Estates of The Percy Family 1416-1537*, 1958.

BENNETT, M: *Lambert Simnel & The Battle of Stoke*, Sutton, 1987.

'Brief Latin Chronicle', in *Three 15th Century Chronicles*, edited by Gairdner, Camden Society, 1880.

BLYTH, J. D.: 'The Battle of Tewkesbury', *Transactions of The Bristol & Gloucs. Archeological Society, lxx,* 1961.

BROOKS, F. W.:'The Council of The North', Historical Association, 1966.

BROWN & WEBSTER: 'The Movements of The Earl of Warwick In The Summer of 1464', EHR, lxxxi, 1966.

BUCK: Sir George: *The History of King Richard III*, ed Kinkaid, 1979.

BURNE, A.H.: *Battlefields of England*, 1950. *More Battlefields of England*, 1952.

BERNARD, J.: 'A Contested Parliamentary Election of 1461', *The Ricardian,* 63, 1978.

Calendar of Patent Rolls, VI, 1427-1516 (1927).

Calendar of Close Rolls Henry VI: VI, 1454-61 (1967); *Edward IV, I-II, 1461-8, 1468-76* (1949 & 1953); *Edward IV, Edward V, Richard III, 1476-85* (1954).

Calendar of Fine Rolls, XIX, Henry VI, 1452-61 (1940); *XX, Edward IV, 1461-71* (1949); *Edward IV-Richard III, 1471-85* (1961).

Calendar of Documents Relating To Scotland, IV, 1357-1509 (Bain, 1888).

Calendar of Patent Rolls: Henry VI, VI, 1452-61 (1911); *Edward IV, I-II, 1461-7, 1467-77* (1897 & 1899); *Edward IV-Edward V-Richard III, 1476-85* (1901).

Calendar of State Papers & Manuscripts In The Archives & Collections of Milan: I, 1385-1618 (edited Hinds, 1913).

CALMETTE, J.: 'Le mariage de Charles le Téméraire et de Marguerite d'York', *Annales de Bourgogne, I*, 1929.

CALMETTE & PERINELLE: *Louis XI et l'Angleterre,* Paris, 1930.

The Cely Papers, ed H.E. Malden, Camden Society, 1930.

CARUS-WILSON, E.M.: *The Expansion of Exeter At The Close of The Middle Ages* (Exeter, 1961).

CHANDLER, R.: *The Life of William Waynflete, Bishop of Winchester*, 1811.

CHASTELAIN, Georges: *Le Temple de Bocace: Remonstrances Par Maniere de Consolation a Une Desolée Reyne d'Angleterre: Ouevres, Vol 4*, 1863.

CHOPE, R.P.: 'The Last of The Dynhams', *Transactions of The Devonshire Association, I*, 1918.

'The Early History of The Manor of Hartland, 1902.

CHRIMES, S.B.: *English Constitutional Ideas of the 15th Century*, Cambridge, 1936.

'The 15th Century', *History, xlviii*, 1963.

'The Landing Place of Henry of Richmond', *Welsh History Review*, 1964.

Lancastrians, Yorkists & Henry VII, MacMillan, 1964.

Henry VII, Methuen, 1988.

'Sir John Fortescue's *De Laudibus Legum Angliae*', a translation.

Chronicles of London, edited by C. Kingsford, 1905.

Chronicles of The Lincolnshire Rebellion, ed Nichols, Camden Society, 1847.

Chronicles of The White Rose of York, ed Giles, 1845.

CHURCHILL, G.B.: *Richard III Up To Shakespeare*, Gloucester, 1976.

CHURCHILL, Sir Winston: *A History of The English Speaking Peoples, I*, 1956.

COLES, C.H.D.: 'The Lordship of Middleham', Liverpool University, 1961.

COMMYNES, Philip de: *Memoirs*, Penguin Classics, 1972.

Complete Peerage of England, Scotland, Ireland & The United Kingdom, 13 volumes, Doubleday, 1910-59.

'Confession of Sir Robert Welles', *Excerpta Historica*, pp 282-4, Bentley.

CONWAY, A.E.: 'The Maidstone Sector of Buckingham's Rebellion, Oct 18th,' *Archeologia Cantiana, xxxvii*, 1925.

CRAWFORD, A.: 'The Career of John Howard, Duke of Norfolk, 1420-85,' University of London, 1975. 'John Howard, Duke of Norfolk: A Possible Murderer of The Princes?' *The Ricardian*, v, 1980.

Croyland Chronicle: *Historieae Croylaandensis Continuatio*, in *Rerum Anglicarum Scriptores Veterum*, ed Fulman, Oxford, 1684.

CURTIS, E.: 'Richard Duke of York As Viceroy of Ireland 1447-1460, in *Journal of The Royal Society of Antiquaries of Ireland'*, lxii, 1932.

COULTON, G.G.: *Social Life In Britain*, Cambridge, 1956.

DAVIES, R.: *Municipal Records of The City of York During The Reigns of Edward IV, Edward V & Richard III*, 1843.

DRAKE, Francis: *Eboracum*, 1736.

DUGDALE, W.: *The Baronage of England I & II*, 1675.

EDWARDS, J.G.: 'The Second Continuation of The Croyland Chronicle: Was It Written in Ten Days?', BIHR, xxxix, 1966.

ELTON, G.R.: *England Under The Tudors*, 1962.

EMDEN, A.B.: 'English Chronicle of The Reigns of Richard II, Henry IV, Henry V & Henry VI, Written Before The Year 1470'. Ed J.S. Davies, Camden Society, 1856.

Excerpta Historica, ed Bentley, 1831.

EVANS, H.T.: *Wales In The Wars of The Roses*, Cambridge, 1915.

FABYAN, Robert: *New Chronicles of England & France,* ed Ellis, 1812.

FAHY, C.: 'The Marriage of Edward IV & Elizabeth Woodville: A New Italian Source', EHR, lxxvi, 1961.

Fifteenth Century England, 1399-1509, ed Chrimes, Ross & Griffiths, Manchester, 1972.

FONBLANQUE, E.B. de: *Annals of The House of Percy,* 2 Volumes, 1887.

FORTESCUE, J.: *The Governance of England,*ed Plummer, Oxford, 1885.

GAIRDNER, James: *Letters & Papers Illustrative of The Reigns of Richard III & Henry VII,* two volumes, Rolls Series, 1861 & 1863.

The Battle of Bosworth: Arcaeologia, lv, 1896. *History of The Life & Reign of Richard III,* Cambridge, 1898.

Grants From The Crown During The Reign of Richard III, Ed Nichols, 1854.

The Great Chronicle of London, ed Thomas & Thornley, 1938.

GOODMAN & MACKAY: 'A Castilian Report of English Affairs, 1486', *English Historical Review, lxxxviii,* 1973.

GREEN, V.H.R.: *The Later Plantagenets,* Arnold, 1955.

Gregory's Chronicle, in *The Historical Collections of A Citizen of London,* ed Gairdner, Camden Society, 1876.

GRIFFITHS & THOMAS: *The Making of The Tudor Dynasty,* Sutton, 1985.

GRIFFITHS, R.A.: 'The Principality of Wales In The Later Middle Ages: South Wales, 1277-1536,' Cardiff, 1972.

'Local Rivalries/National Politics: The Percies, The Nevilles/The Duke of Exeter, 1452-5.'*Speculum xliii,* 1968.

HALL, Edward: *Union of The Two Illustre Families of Lancaster & York*, ed Ellis, 1809.

HALLAM, H,: *A View of The State of Europe During The Middle Ages*, 3 volumnes, 1860.

HALSTED, Caroline: *Richard II As Duke of Gloucester & King of England*, 2 volumes, 1844.

HAMMOND, F.W.: *Edward of Middleham, Prince of Wales*, 1973.

HAMPTON, W.E.: 'Sir James Tyrell', *The Ricardian*, 63, 1978.

HANHAM. A.: 'Richard III, Lord Hastings & The Historians,' EHR, 1972; 'The Cely Letters, 1472-88*, EETS,* 1975.

HARRISS, G.L.: *The Struggle For Calais: An Aspect of The Rivalry of Lancaster & York, lxxv*, 1960.

HARVEY, N.L.: *Elizabeth of York*, MacMillan, 1973.

HASSALL, W.O.: *They Saw It Happen, 55BC-1485*, Blackwell, 1957.

HICKS, M.A.: *The Career of George Plantagenet, Duke of Clarence, 1449-78*, Oxford, 1974.

'Dynastic Change & Northern Society: The Career of The Fourth Earl Of Northumberland, 1470-89,' *Northern History, xiv*, 1978.

Historiae Croylandensis Continuato, ed Riley, 1893.

Historie of The Arrivall of Edward IV In England, ed Bruce, Camden Society, 1838.

HOLMES, G.A.: *The Later Middle Ages, 1272-1485*, 1962.

Household Books of John, Duke of Norfolk & Thomas, Earl Of Surrey, 1481-90, ed Collier, Roxburghe Club, 1844.

HUTTON, W.: *The Battle of Bosworth Field*, 1788.

INNES, I.D.: *England Under The Tudors*, Methuen, 1905.
Inquisitions Post Morton, Henry IV & Henry V, ed Baildon & Clay, *Yorkshire Archaeological Socoety lix,* 1918.
JACK, R.I.: 'A Quincentenary: The Battle of Northampton, July 10th 1460,' *Northamptonshire Past & Present, Iii, I,* 1960.
JACOB, E.F.: *The Fifteenth Century*, Oxford, 1961.
JENKINS, E.: *The Princes In The Tower*,Hamish Hamilton, 1978.
KEEN, M.M.: *England In The Later Middle Ages*, 1973.
KENDALL, Paul Murray: *Richard III*, 1955.
Warwick The Kingmaker, 1957.
Louis XI, 1971.
KNAPP, J.L.: 'The Lincolnshire Rising & Its Part In The Downfall of The Earl of Warwick, *Ricardiaan*, 62, 1978.
KINGSFORD, C.L.: *Chronicles of London* (1905); *English Historical Literature In The 15th Century,* 1913.
KIRBY, J.L.: *Henry IV of England*, 1970.
LA MARCHE, Olivier de: *Memoires*, 4 volumes, edited by Beaune & d'Arbaumont, Sociéte de l'Histoire de France, 1883-8.
LANDER, J.R.: *The Administration of the Yorkist Kings*, 1949, Cambridge.
'Attainder & Forfeture, 1453-9, *Historical Journal*, IV, 1961.
'Bonds, Coercion & Fear: Henry VII & The Peerage, *Florilegium Historiale: Essays Presented To Wallace K. Ferguson,* Toronto, 1971.
Conflict & Stability In 15th Century England, 1969. Henry VI & The Duke of York's 2nd Protectorate, 1455-6, (1960).

'Edward IV: The Modern Legend', *History, xli*, 1956.
The Wars of The Roses, 1965.
'The Treason & Death of the Duke Of Clarence: A Re-interpretation, *Canadia Journal Of History, ii*, 1967.
'Marriage & Politics In The 15th Century: The Nevill & The Wydevills, BIHR, xxxvi, 1963. 'Council, Administration & Councillors, 1461-85, BIHR, xxxiii, 1959.
'The Hundred Years War & Edward IV's 1475 Campaign in France, *Tudor Men & Institutions: Studies In English Law & Government,* ed Slavin, Louisiana, 1972.
'The Yorkist Council & Administration, EHR, lxxxiii, 1958.
LESLAU, J.: 'Did The Sons of Edward IV Outlive Henry VII?' *Ricardian*, 62, 1978.
LEADAM & BALDWIN: 'Select Cases Before The King's Council 1243-1482,' Seldon Society, 1918.
LESLEY, J.: *History of Scotland From The Death of King James I In The Year 1436 To The Year 1561*, Bannatyne Club, 1830.
Letters & Papers Illustrative of The Wars of The English In France During the Reign of Henry VI, 2 volumes, ed Stevenson, 1861-4.
Literae Cantuarienses, ed Sheppard (Rolls Series III, 1889)
LOCKYER, R.W.: *Henry VI*, 1968.
LINDSAY, Sir Philip: *King Richard III*, Westminster Press, 1933.
MaCGIBBON, D.: *Elizabeth Woodville*, 1938.
McKISACK, M.: *The Fourteenth Century*, Oxford, 1959.
MAKINSON, A.: 'The Road To Bosworth Field, August 1485, *History Today,* xiii, 1963.

MALDEN, H.E.: 'An Unedited Cely Letter of 1482,' TRHS, x, 1916.

McFARLANE, K.B.: *Lancastrian Kings & Lollard Knights* 1972.

The Lancastrian Kings: 1399-1461, Cambridge, 1936.

Parliament & Bastard Feudalism,' TRHS, xvvi, 1944.

MANCINI, Dominic: *The Usurpation of Richard III*, ed & translated by Armstrong, Oxford, 1936.

MARKHAM, C.R.: *Richard III: His Life & Character,* 1906.

METCALFE, W.C.: *A Book of Knights Banneret, Knights Of The Bath & Knights Bachelor*, 1885.

MILLES, Jeremiah: 'Observations On The Wardrobe Accounts For The Year 1483, *Archaeologia I*, 1779.

MITCHELL, R.J.: *John Tiptoft*, 1938.

MORE, Sir Thomas: *The History of Richard III*, Pitt, 1883.

MORGAN, D.A.L.: 'The King's Affinity In The Polity of Yorkist England,' TRHS, xxiii, 1973.

MORRAT, A.J.: 'Robert Stillington,' *Ricardian*, 53, 1976.

MOLINET, Jean: *Chroniques*, ed Buchon, 1828.

MORICE, H.: *Memoires Pour Servir De Preuves A L'Histoire de Bretagne*, 3 vols. (Paris, 1742-6).

MYERS, A.R.: *The Household of Edward IV*, Manchester, 1959.

'Richard III & Historical Tradition,' *History Today*, Iv, 1954.

'The Household of Queen Elizabeth Woodville, 1466-7,' *Bulletin of The John Rylands Library,* 1967-8.

NOKES & WHEELER: 'A Spanish Account of The Battle Of Bosworth,' *Ricardian*, 36, 1972.

OMAN, C.W.C.: *Warwick The Kingmaker*, 1891.

O'REGAN, M: 'Richard III & The Monks of Durham,'*Ricardian*, 1978.

Paston Letters, 1422-1509, 6 vols, ed Gairdner, 1904.

Paston Letters & Papers of The Fifteenth Century, ed Davies, 1971.

PEAKE, M.I.: 'London & The Wars of The Roses', BIHR, iv, 1926-7.

Plumpton Correspondence, ed Stapleton, Camden Society, 1839.

POQUET DU HAUT-JUSSÉ, B.A.: *Francois II, Duc de Bretagne*, 1929, Paris.

POLLARD, A. F.: *Parliament In The Wars of The Roses*, Glasgow, 1936.

POLLARD, A.J.: *The Family of Talbot, Lords Talbot & Earls of Shrewsbury In The 15th Century*, 1968.

'The Northern Retainers of Richard Neville, Earl Of Salisbury,' *Northern History*, xi, 1976.

'The Tyranny of Richard III,' *Journal of Medieval History*, 1977.

'The Richmondshire Community of Gentry During The Wars of The Roses,' in *Patronage, Pedigree & Power In Late Medieval England*, ed Ross, 1979.

OLIVER, Dr.: *The Royal Visits To Exeter*, 1863.

POWELL & WALLIS: *The House of Lords In The Middle Ages*, 1968.

POWICKE, M.: *Military Obligation In Medieval England*, Oxford, 1962.

Privy Purse Expenses of Elizabeth of York: Wardrobe Accounts of Edward IV, ed Nicholas, 1830.
Proceedings Before The Justices of The Peace in The 14th & 15th Centuries, ed Putnam, 1938.
PUGH, T.B.: *The Marcher Lordships of South Wales, 1416-1536*, 1963.
RAMSAY, J.H.: *Lancaster & York*, 2 vols, Oxford, 1892.
RAWCLIFFE, C.: *The Staffords, Earls of Stafford & Dukes of Buckingham, 1394-1521*, Cambridge, 1978.
Records of the Borough of Nottingham, 9 volss, 1882-1956.
Registrum Thome Bourgchier, 1454-86, ed Boulay, 1955-6.
REID, R.R.: *The King's Council In The North*, 1921.
RHODES, P.: 'The Physical Deformity of Richard III, BMJ, 1977.
RICHMOND, C.F.: 'Fauconberg's Kentish Rising of May 1471', EHR, lxxxv, 1970.
'English Naval Power in The Fifteenth Century, *History*, lii, 1967.
ROSKELL, J.S.: 'The Office & Dignity of Protector of England With Special Reference To Its Origins,' EHR, lxviii, 1953.
'The Commons & Their Speakers In English Parliaments, 1376-1523,' Manchester, 1965.
'John, Lord Wenlock of Someries,' *Bedfordshire Historical Records Society Pub*, xxxviii, 1956.
'Sir Thomas Tresham, Knight, Speaker For The Commons Under Henry VI,' *Northamptonshire Past & Present*, 11, 1959.
'William Catesby, Councillor To Richard III,' *Bulletin of the John Rylands Library*, xliii, 1959.

ROSS, Charles D.: *Edward IV*, 1974.
Richard III, Methuen, 1988.
'Rumour, Propaganda & Popular Opinion During The Wars of the Roses,' *The Crown, Patronage & The Provinces*, ed Griffiths, 1981.
'Some Servants & Lovers of Richard III In His Youth,': *Ricardian*, 55, 1976.
The Wars of The Roses, 1976.
'The Estates & Finances of Richard Beauchamp, Earl of Warwick,'*Dugdale Society Papers*, 1956.
'The Estates & Finances of Richard Duke of York,' *Welsh Historical Review*, iii, 1967.
Rotuli Parliamentorium, ed Strachey, 6 vols, 1767-76.
ROUS, John: *Antiquarii Warwickensis Historia Regum Angliae*, ed Hearne, Oxford, 1745.
ROWSE, A.L.: *Bosworth Field & The Wars of The Roses*, 1966.
RYMER, T.: *Foedera, Conventiones, Literae…Et Acta Publica, Etc*, 20 vols, 1704-35.
SALISBURY, G.T.: *Street Life In Medieval England*, Oxford, 1939.
SCOFIELD, Cora: 'The Early Life of John de Vere, Earl of Oxford, EHR, xxxiv, 1914.
The Life & Reign of King Edward The Fourth, 2 vols, 1923.
'Select Cases Before The Exchequer Chamber, ed Hemnant, in Vols 38-50, *The Selden Society*, 1948.
SHAW, W.A.: *Knights of England*, 2 vols, 1906.
SIMONS, E.N.: *The Reign of Edward IV*, 1966.
SMITH, G.: *The Coronation of Elizabeth Woodville*, 1935.
SHORTO, A.M.: *The Story of Exeter*, 1906.

SOMERVILLE, R.: *History of The Duchy of Lancaster, 1265-1603*, 1953.
Statutes of The Realm, 11 vols, ed Luthers, RC 1810-28.
The Stonor Letters & Papers, 1290-1483, 2 vols, ed Kingsford, *Camden Society, xxix-xx,* 1919.
STOREY, R.L.: *The End of The House of Lancaster*, 1966.
'Lincolnshire & The Wars of The Roses', *Nottingham Medieval Studies, xiv*, 1970
The Reign of Henry VII, 1968.
'The Wardens of The Marches of England Towards Scotland, 1377-1489,' EHR, lxxii, 1957.
STOW, John: *Annales, Or A Generall Chronicle of England*, 1615.
STUBBS, W.: *Constitutional History of England*, 3 vols, 1878.
TAYLOR, J.: *The Plumpton Letters, 1416-1553,* in *Northern History,* 1975.
THIELMANS, M.R.: *Bourgogne Et Angleterre: Relations Politiques et Economiques Entres Les Pays-Bas Et L'Angleterre, 1435-67*, Brussels, 1966.
THOMAS, D.H.: *The Herberts of Raglan As Supporters of The House of York In The Second Half of The Fifteenth Century*, 1968.
THOMSON, J.A.F.: 'The Courtenay Family In The Yorkist Period,' BIHR, xiv, 1972.
'Richard III & Lord Hastings,' BIHR, xiviii, 1975.
The Arrivall of Edward IV: Development of The Text, printed in *Speculum*, xlvi, 1971.
Three Fifteenth Century Chronicles, ed Gairdner, Camden Society, 1880.

THRUPP, S.: *The Merchant Class of Medieval London, 1300-1500*, 1948.

TOUCHARD, H.: *Le Commerce Maritime Au Fin Du Moyen Ages*, 1967.

THORPE, L.: 'Philippe de Crevecoeur, Seigneur D'Esquerdes: To epitaphs by Jean Molinet & Nicholas Ladam,' *Bulletin de La Commission Royale d'Histoire*, ccix, Brussels, 1954.

Travels of Leo of Rozmital, ed/translated by Letts, Hakluyt Society, cviii, Cambridge, 1957.

TUCKER, M.J.: *The Life of Thomas Howard, Earl of Surrey & Second Duke of Norfolk*, The Hague, 1964.

VAUGHAN, R.: *Philip The Good*, 1970.

Charles The Bold, 1973.

VERGIL, Polydore.: *Three Books of Polydore Vergil's English History*, ed Ellis, Camden Society, 1844.

The Anglica Historia of Polydore Vergil, AD 1485-1537, ed/translated Hay (RHS, Camden Society, lxxiv, 1950.

Victoria History of The Counties of England: Durham, 1907; *Yorkshire*, 1913; *Oxfordshire*, 1954; *Leicestershire*, 1955; *Cambridgeshire*, 1959;

City of York, 1976.

WALPOLE, Horace: *Historic Doubts On The Life & Reign of Richard III*, reprint, 1965.

WARKWORTH, John: *A Chronicle of The First Thirteen Years of The Reign of King Edward The Fourth*, ed Halliwell, Camden Society, 1839.

WAURIN, Jean de: *Anchiennes Croniques d'Engleterre*, 3 vols, ed Dupont, Société de l'Histoire de France, 1858-63.

WEBSTER, W.: 'An Unknown Treaty Between Edward IV & Louis XI,' EHR xii, 1897.

WEDGWOOD, J.H.: *History of Parliament, 1439-1509: Biographies*, 1936.

WEINBAUM, N.: *British Borough Charters, 1307-1660*, Cambridge, 1943.

WEISS, M.: *A Power In The North? The Percies In The Fifteenth Century*, Oxford, 1967.

WEISS, R.: *Humanism In England During The 15th Century*, Oxford, 1967.

WIGRAM, I.: 'The Death of Hastings', *Ricardian*, 50, 1975.

WILKINSON, B.: *Constitutional History of England In The 15th Century, 1399-1485*, 1464.

WILLIAMS, D.T.: *The Battle of Bosworth*, Leicester, 1973.

WILLIAMS, C.H.: *England: The Yorkist Kings, 1461-85*, in *Cambridge Medieval History*, viii, 1936.

WOLFFE, B.P.: 'Hastings Reinterred', EHR, xci, 1976.

York Civic Records, ed Raine, YAS Record Series, XCVIII-CIII, 1939-41.

York Records: Extracts From The Municipal Records of The City of York, ed Davies, 1843.

Index

Albany, Alexander, Duke of 302-4

Allington, Sir William 287, 289

Angus, George Douglas, 1st Earl of 114, 118, 299

Anjou, Margaret of 25-9, 34-7, 40-1, 47, 49, 52-3, 60-3, 65-72, 77-86, 91-6, 100, 103-4, 109, 112-14, 116-17, 119, 121, 128-31, 142, 157, 164, 170-1, 195-7, 204-5, 207, 209-10, 213, 215, 221-4, 227-9, 234, 236, 261, 268, 288, 304

Anjou, René of 15, 112, 130, 196, 234, 268

Antoine, Bastard of Burgundy 14, 157-61, 166-7, 276

Antwerp, Lionel of 9-10

Arundel, Sir Thomas 236, 247

Arundel, William Fitzalan, Earl of 77, 82, 87, 184, 187, 227, 235, 255-6

Atkyn, Sir Philip 57

Audley, James Tuchet 5th Lord 38-40, 44

Beauchamp, Sir Richard 223, 232

Beaufort, Lady Margaret 44, 101, 108, 118, 180

Beaumont, John, Viscount 60, 62, 218

Beaumont, William, Viscount 211, 220, 245, 248

Blake, Thomas 283-4

Blount, Sir John 42, 238

Bona of Savoy 132, 135, 137, 294-5

Bonvile, Cecily 238, 247

Bonvile, William, Lord 30-2, 77, 82

Booth, Lawrence 103, 118

Booth, William, Archbishop of York 140, 149

328

Bourchier, Archbishop Thomas 35, 44, 105, 144, 202
Brampton, Sir Edward 174-5, 181, 246
Brezé, Piers de 35-6, 112-16, 129
Brittany, Anne of 295
Brittany, Francis, Duke of 112, 122, 147, 163, 206, 240-1, 253-4, 259, 295
Buckingham, Henry Stafford 2nd Duke of 141, 144, 149, 184, 229, 246, 273, 286, 289, 307
Buckingham, Humphrey Stafford 1st Duke of 13, 28, 34-5, 60-2, 66, 91
Burdett, Thomas 283-4
Burgh, Sir Thomas 186, 193, 312
Burgundy, Charles, Duke of 16, 67-8, 73, 79, 121-2, 128-9, 145-7, 156-7, 160, 162-7, 183, 186, 191, 195, 205-6, 252-4, 256, 258-62, 265, 268, 273, 276-9
Burgundy, Philip, Duke of 36, 44, 49, 55, 68, 103, 112, 128-30, 135, 145-6, 156-7, 160-1
Cade, Jack 19-20, 91
Caniziani, Gerard 163, 169, 256
Carew, Nicholas, Baron 44, 189-90, 192-3, 210
Caxton, Thomas 251, 256, 267
Cecily of York 252, 299, 303, 305
Charles VII of France 36, 131
Chastelain, Georges 128-31, 137
Clarence, George, Duke of 10, 17, 42, 68-9, 78, 102, 105, 136, 146, 154-5, 158-9, 161, 165, 176-8, 182-92, 196-8, 203, 206, 210, 212-16, 220, 224, 226, 229, 239, 241-8, 257-8, 250, 263-4, 269, 273, 275-8, 281-5, 288-91, 298
Clifford, John, 9th Lord 29, 32, 66, 71, 79, 95
Clifford, Thomas, 8th Lord 25, 28

Clinton, John, Lord 37, 41, 96
Cluny, Guillaume de 146, 150
Cobham, Edward Brook, Lord 59, 64
Commines, Philip de 202, 207, 214, 220, 257, 259-63, 269, 272, 280, 296-7
Compaing, Guillaume de 241
Conyers, Sir John 173-4
Conyers, Sir William 173-4, 181
Cook, Sir Thomas 171-2, 203, 209
Coppini, Francesco 54-5, 57, 59-61, 67, 77-8
Cornburgh, Avery 255, 267
Crosby, John 235, 247
Courtenay, Sir Hugh of Boconnoc 189-90
Courtenay, Sir John 42, 53
Courtenay, Thomas, Earl of Devon 30-2
Croft, Sir Richard 81
Dacre, William, Lord 71, 79, 99
Donne, Sir John 188, 193
Dorset, Thomas Grey, Marquess of 14, 141, 149, 247, 250-1, 265, 287, 290, 300
Dudley, John Sutton, Lord 40, 44
Dudley, Sir William 211, 220, 229, 238, 256, 260
Dymoke, Sir Thomas 186, 188, 193
Dynham, Lady Joan 43-4, 47
Dynham, Sir John IV 31-2, 41
Dynham, John, Lord 31-2, 41-4, 47, 50-4, 57, 77, 98-9, 101-2, 105, 130, 132, 134, 158, 168, 184-6, 189-90, 192-3, 198, 203, 213, 229-30, 235-6, 239, 245, 247-8, 253, 255-6, 273, 281, 283, 307, 312
Edward II 120, 177

Edward III 8, 9, 14
Edward of Lancaster, Prince of Wales 21, 34, 40, 47, 61, 65, 69-70, 78-9, 85, 131-2, 195-7, 204-5, 207, 209, 211, 215, 221-2, 224-6, 228, 237, 242, 291
Edward of Middleham (Richard III's son) 244, 247, 297
Edward, Prince of Wales (Edward IV's son) 204, 250-1, 256, 283, 288, 294-5, 300, 309
Egremont, Thomas Percy, Lord 60, 62
Elizabeth of York 185-6, 264, 277, 287, 297
Esquerdes, Philippe d' 298, 312
Exeter, Henry Holland, Duke of 14, 24, 52, 66, 71, 108, 239, 266
Fastolff, Sir John 110, 174-5
Fauconberg, Thomas Neville, Bastard of 191, 195, 209, 222, 228-9, 230, 235
Fauconberg, William Neville, Lord 39, 43-4, 53, 55, 61, 64, 94-6, 105, 113-4
Faunt, Nicholas 228-9, 235
Ferdinand of Aragon 137, 252, 294
Ferdinand of Naples 162, 168
Ferrers of Chartley, Walter Devereux, Lord 78, 87, 93, 105, 183, 310
Fitzhugh, Henry, 6th Lord 79, 87
Fitzwalter, John Radcliffe, Lord 93, 95, 101
Fitzwarin, Fulk Bourchier, Lord 190-2
Fogge, Sir John 58, 64, 171, 177, 235
Fortescue, Sir John 100-1, 130, 196, 221, 226, 236, 269
Fulford, Sir Baldwin 52, 57, 107
Fulford, Sir Thomas 300, 312
Gate, Sir Geoffrey 200-1, 228

Gaunt, John of 10, 12, 14, 207
Gloucester, Humphrey, Duke of 13, 15
Gloucester, Richard, Duke of (later RICHARD III) 10, 37, 42, 48, 68-9, 70, 78, 140, 152-6, 212, 216-7, 219, 224-5, 229-31, 235, 242-4, 246, 248, 257-8, 260, 266, 272-3, 375, 279, 285-6, 292, 298-308
Grey, Sir John 86, 88, 132-3
Grey de Ruthyn, Edmund, Lord 60-2, 65, 96, 102, 105, 116, 141, 144, 174, 184-5, 189, 199-200, 204
Gruthuyse, Louis de 157, 161, 168, 201-2, 237, 253, 270
Hastings, William, Lord 37, 44, 105-6, 115, 120, 134, 136, 146, 182, 184, 187, 193, 199-200, 216, 224, 229, 238, 263, 307, 310
Henry IV 9, 69
Henry V 9, 10, 51, 268
HENRY VI: 9-10, 13-17, 19-22, 25-31, 34, 38, 41, 47, 50, 52, 56-63, 65, 69-70, 76-7, 82, 85, 91-3, 100, 103-4, 107, 109, 113, 116-17, 121-2, 128, 157, 177, 183, 191, 195-6, 199, 201-2, 207, 230-1, 234, 236, 270, 286
Herbert, William, Lord 78, 87, 105-6, 158, 165, 170, 173, 177-80, 182, 185, 203
Holderness, Robin of 173-4
Horne, Robert 95, 99
Howard, John, Lord 110-11, 159, 165, 184-5, 191, 199, 215, 226, 238, 259-61, 268, 300-1, 307, 309
Hungerford, Robert, Lord 52, 58, 66, 115, 122-4
Isabella of Castille 132, 137, 252, 294
Jacquetta of Luxembourg 50, 56, 91, 133-4, 145, 171-2, 204, 258
James II of Scotland 103

James III of Scotland 103, 116, 252, 267, 299, 302-4
James IV of Scotland 252, 267
Kynaston, Sir Roger 40
Kyriell, Sir Thomas 77, 82, 85
Langley, Edmund of 9-10, 14
Lannoy, Jean de 116, 122, 131
Lincoln, John de la Pole, Earl of 15, 286, 292
Louis XI of France 95, 112-3, 122, 136, 147-8, 156, 160-5, 170, 191, 195-6, 201, 205-6, 209, 241, 245, 252-66, 268-9, 277, 279, 295, 297-8, 301, 303-4, 307
Lovelace, Captain 82-3, 85
Maltravers, Thomas, Lord 141, 144, 149
Mancini, Dominic 143-4, 150, 272, 279, 289-90, 308
Marche, Olivier de la 158-9, 168, 289
Margaret of York, Duchess of Burgundy 146-8, 156, 162-3, 165-7, 169-70, 256, 277, 295, 298
Mary of Burgundy 146, 150, 155, 166, 277-8, 280, 282, 295, 302, 304
Mary of Guelders 78, 87, 103, 116, 199, 131
Maximilian I 278, 280, 294-6, 298, 301, 304-5
Montagu, John Neville, Lord 38, 44, 82, 84-5, 100, 104, 106, 115, 122-5, 134, 155, 162, 173-4, 184-5, 189, 199, 202-3, 206, 210-9
Montgomery, Sir Thomas 111, 118, 265, 268, 312
More, Sir Thomas 153, 272-5, 279, 289
Morton, Dr John 103, 112, 130, 221, 236-7, 260, 265
Mountjoy, Osbert 54, 164, 184, 202
Mowbray, Anne 286-7
Neville, Anne 140, 155, 190, 195-7, 207, 228, 242, 244
Neville, Catherine, Duchess of Norfolk 141, 149, 165

333

Neville, Cecily, Duchess of York 12, 14, 17, 24, 42, 68, 78, 145, 176, 187, 205, 288
Neville, George, Archbishop of York 66, 73, 93, 115, 157, 176, 179, 184-5, 198, 201, 203, 214, 245-6
Neville, George, Duke of Bedford 141, 149
Neville, George (Montagu's son) 185-6, 193, 244
Neville, Humphrey of Brancepeth 121, 124, 126, 183
Neville, Isabel 140, 146, 149, 154-5, 190-2, 196, 242, 275-6, 281-2, 291
Neville, Sir Thomas 38, 44, 71-2
Norfolk, John Mowbray, 3rd Duke of 20, 24, 73-4, 82-3, 92-5, 98, 102, 114
Norfolk, John Mowbray 4th Duke of 159, 168, 174-5, 183, 202, 210, 229, 258
Northumberland, Henry Percy, 2nd Earl of 22, 25, 28
Northumberland, Henry Percy, 3rd Earl of 29, 32, 70-1, 73, 79, 99, 174, 185, 187, 199, 206, 211-12, 227, 258, 263, 299, 301, 303
Ogle, Sir Robert 27-8
Oxford, Thomas, Earl of 111, 118
Paston family 109-11, 166-7, 174-5, 183-4, 193, 204, 218, 235, 245-6, 248
Philip, Matthew 235, 247
Popincourt, Jehan de 161
Radford, Nicholas 30-1
Redesdale, Robin of 173, 177-9, 189
Richard, Duke of York (Edward's son) 250, 286-7, 295
Richard II 9, 109, 120, 177

Rivers, Anthony Woodville, 2nd Earl 50-1, 56, 104, 114, 132, 143-4, 156-7, 159-61, 164-7, 174-5, 191, 210, 219, 227, 229, 238, 240, 251, 257, 273, 276-8, 282, 286-7, 290, 297

Rivers, Richard Woodville, 1st Earl 50-1, 54, 56, 104, 132, 134, 143, 156, 171-2, 177, 180, 199-200, 206

Rochester, John Alcock, Bishop of Rochester 250, 267

Rotherham, Thomas, Archbishop of York 158, 168, 263, 287-8, 310

Russell, John, Bishop of Lincoln 252, 267, 307

Rutland, Edmund of 37, 41, 44, 71-2, 76, 95, 99

Salisbury, Richard Neville, Earl of 20, 22, 25, 29, 34, 38-43, 46, 50-1, 53, 59, 66-7, 71-2, 76-7, 94, 99

Scales, Thomas, Lord 52, 56, 58, 66, 91

Scott, John 58, 64

Scrope of Bolton, John, Lord 96, 114, 121, 189, 210

Sforza, Francesco, Duke of Milan 54, 57, 87, 294

Shore, Jane 274-5, 280

Shore, William 274, 280

Shrewsbury, John Talbot, 2nd Earl of 60, 62, 66, 79

Somerset, Edmund Beaufort, 4th Duke of 86, 88, 210, 215, 221-7, 243

Somerset, Henry Beaufort, 3rd Duke of 29, 36, 48-9, 51, 53, 60, 67-8, 70-1, 78-9, 82, 86, 94-6, 100, 102, 106, 115, 119-25, 128, 133-4, 137, 142, 147, 197, 219, 221, 273-4

Stacey, Dr John 283-4

Stafford, Humphrey of Southwick 49, 56, 78, 105, 172, 177-9, 185-6, 189

Stanley, Thomas, Lord 96, 101, 116, 144, 189, 198-9, 211, 259, 300, 303

Stillington, Robert, Bishop of Bath & Wells 67, 73, 156-8, 163, 203, 222, 239, 253, 297

St Pol, Jacques, Count of 258-9, 261

Strangeways, Sir James 109

Stubbs, William, Bishop of Oxford 273, 280

Suffolk, John de la Pole, Duke of 15-16, 19, 82, 174-5, 184, 210, 229, 258

Tetzel, Gabriel 145, 150

Tiptoft, John "Butcher", Earl of Worcester 111, 114, 116, 118, 124, 143, 159, 191, 199, 203-4, 242

Trollope, Andrew 41, 43, 48-9, 54, 71, 79, 85, 94, 97, 99

Tucotes, Sir Roger 281-4, 292

Tudor, Edmund 34, 44, 108

Tudor, Henry, later HENRY VII 108, 180, 203, 236, 240-1

Tudor, Jasper, Earl of Pembroke 34, 44, 65, 78, 81, 107-8, 122-13, 170, 180, 198, 203, 210, 222, 239, 273

Tudor, Owen 81-2, 87, 239

Tunstall, Sir Richard 203, 207, 236

Twynho, Ankarette 281-5, 288

Tyrell, Sir James 244, 247

Vaughan, Sir Roger 239-40, 245, 247

Vaughan, Sir Thomas 250

Vere, Aubrey de 111, 118

Warwick, Richard Neville, Earl of 18-23, 25, 28-30, 34-43, 46-55, 60-1, 66-71, 76-7, 82-7, 91-8, 100, 102-4, 113-16, 121-2, 131-2, 135-6, 140-2, 145-8, 154-62, 165, 170-80, 182-91, 195-205, 209-19, 221, 227, 235, 238, 244

Waynfleet, William, Bishop of Winchester 106, 118

Welles, Lionel, Lord 99, 101

Welles, Richard, Lord 186-8, 193
Wenlock, John Lord 29, 36-7, 42, 50, 54, 59, 66, 99, 105, 131, 135-6, 146, 156, 165, 171, 190-1, 221, 225
Westmoreland, Earl of 12, 24
Whetehill, Sir Richard 238, 247
Wiltshire, James Butler, 1st Earl of 21, 24, 25, 28, 47-8, 52-3, 60, 78-81, 94, 100, 103, 197, 221
Wiltshire, John, 2nd Earl of 130-1, 137, 202
Woodville, Elizabeth 10, 132-6, 140-4, 155, 158, 160, 175, 180, 185, 199-200, 204, 228
Woodville, Sir Edward 141, 149, 250
Woodville, Sir John 141, 144, 149, 161, 165, 174, 180
Woodville, Lionel, Bishop of Salisbury 142, 149, 157, 161, 166, 250
Woodville, Sir Richard 141, 144, 149, 250
York, Richard, Duke of 9-13, 17-20, 22, 25-30, 34-8, 41-2, 46-8, 51-3, 68-72, 76, 92, 153, 176, 250
Zouche, John, Lord 213, 220

Printed in Great Britain
by Amazon